365
dish a day

365
dish a day

A RECIPE FOR EACH OF THE 365 DAYS IN A YEAR

+ ONE FOR A LEAP YEAR

p

This is a Parragon Book
First published in 2006

Parragon
Queen Street House
4 Queen Street
Bath BA1 1HE, UK

Copyright © Parragon Books Ltd 2006

ISBN: 1-40547-922-1

Printed in China

Produced by terryjeavons&company

Notes for the Reader
This book uses imperial, metric, or US cup measurements. Follow the same
units of measurement throughout; do not mix imperial and metric. All spoon
measurements are level: teaspoons are assumed to be 5 ml, and tablespoons
are assumed to be 15 ml. Unless otherwise stated, milk is assumed to be
whole, eggs and individual vegetables such as potatoes are medium, and
pepper is freshly ground black pepper. Recipes using raw or very lightly
cooked eggs should be avoided by infants, the elderly, pregnant women,
convalescents, and anyone suffering from an illness.

contents

introduction

Cooking should be one of life's great joys, but when you're preparing meals day in, day out, just for yourself or for a hungry family, it can be hard to stay inspired or try something new. Whether you love food or have to drag yourself into the kitchen, Dish a Day gives a little daily inspiration to put delicious homemade food on your table. From revisiting well-loved classics to ideas for including today's new ingredients and tastes in your day-to-day cooking, this is a book that will ensure your dish of the day is a treat to both cook and eat.

The book is divided into twelve monthly chapters with a recipe for every day of the year. How you use the book is up to you. You might want to flick through the whole year first and get stuck into the most appealing recipes straight away, or perhaps turn over a page a day, using the book like a real-life food calendar. Dish a Day has also been organized in a way that makes a bit of forward planning easy. Simply scan a month ahead for seasonal ideas and put together a shopping list straight from the pages. However you like to do things, you'll find a whole year's worth of great food ideas in one place.

Set up like a calendar, this is a book that follows the cook's year, guiding you through the freshest ingredients available each month. Every recipe has been specially selected to make the best use of our seasonal produce and to guarantee that you don't miss out on the month's best buys. Keep an eye out for wonderful ideas for using asparagus in May, blueberries in July and wild mushrooms in October. By following the year's natural rhythms and using its seasonal produce, you'll find you get the finest flavours when they're at their most inexpensive. You'll also get a chance to enjoy cooking in the way our mothers and grandmothers did, using a glut of summer tomatoes for little tomato and courgette tartlets or turning an autumn harvest of pumpkins into delicious pumpkin chestnut risotto. Bring your cooking into line with the seasons and you will no longer find that the recipe you're shopping for in December requires the fruits of a hot Italian summer or that you're a month too early for that fresh rhubarb or crop of new potatoes.

Ingredients aren't the only things that change for the cook as the year passes

by. The way we want to eat and prepare food varies too. To reflect this, these recipes run from the warm, hearty comfort food of autumn and winter to the light and refreshing dishes of spring and summer. So chilly January hots up with hot & spicy beef with toasted pine nuts, while easy-to-prepare dishes using the new season's vegetables, fresh fish and eggs dominate our healthy springtime menus. Summer takes us outside to enjoy main-course salads and some inspiration for weekend barbecuing, while winter reintroduces the joys of afternoon baking and the slow cooking of comfort food.

As befits an everyday cookery book, we've tried to keep things simple and most of the recipes make an ideal after work supper or no-fuss pudding or teatime treat. However, with every day of the year covered, there's room for those special food days too, so if you fancy making apricot-stuffed roast duck for New Year's Eve; eating the ultimate cheeseburger on July the fourth; or welcoming in the Chinese New Year with a dish of ginger chicken with toasted sesame seeds, you'll find these here too. Let Dish a Day breathe new life into your everyday cooking and start enjoying the best our seasons have to offer.

CHAPTER

1

January

ingredients

5 tbsp fresh brown breadcrumbs

200 g/7 oz low-fat fromage frais

5 tbsp chopped fresh parsley

5 tbsp snipped fresh chives

salt and pepper

4 poussins

1 tbsp sunflower oil

675 g/1 lb 8 oz young spring
    vegetables, such as carrots,
    courgettes, sugar snap peas,
    baby sweetcorn and turnips,
    cut into small chunks

125 ml/4 fl oz boiling chicken stock

2 tsp cornflour

150 ml/5 fl oz dry white wine

poussins with herbs & wine

Preheat the oven to 220°C/425°F/Gas Mark 7.

Mix the breadcrumbs, one-third of the fromage frais and 2 tablespoons each of the parsley and chives together in a bowl. Season well with salt and pepper. Spoon into the neck ends of the poussins. Place on a rack in a roasting tin, brush with the oil and season with salt and pepper.

Roast in the oven for 30–35 minutes, or until the juices run clear when the thickest part of the meat is pierced with a skewer.

Place the vegetables in a shallow ovenproof dish in a single layer and add half the remaining herbs with the stock.

Cover and bake in the oven for 25–30 minutes until tender. Lift the poussins onto a warmed serving plate and skim any fat from the juices in the tin. Add the vegetable juices and place the tin over a medium heat.

Blend the cornflour with the wine and whisk into the sauce with the remaining fromage frais. Whisk until boiling, then add the remaining herbs. Season to taste with salt and pepper. Spoon the sauce over the poussins and serve with the vegetables.

cabbage soup with sausage

Put the sausages in water to cover generously and bring to the boil. Reduce the heat and simmer until firm. Drain and, when cool enough to handle, remove the skin and slice thinly. Heat the oil in a saucepan over a medium heat, add the onion, leek and carrots and cook for 3–4 minutes until the onion starts to soften.

Add the tomatoes, cabbage, garlic, thyme, stock and sausages. Bring to the boil, reduce the heat to low and cook, partially covered, for 40 minutes until the vegetables are tender. Taste and adjust the seasoning, if necessary. Ladle into warm bowls and serve with Parmesan.

ingredients

350 g/12 oz lean sausages,
    preferably highly seasoned
2 tsp oil
1 onion, finely chopped
1 leek, halved lengthways and
    thinly sliced
2 carrots, halved and thinly sliced
400 g/14 oz canned chopped
    tomatoes
350 g/12 oz young green cabbage,
    cored and coarsely shredded
1–2 garlic cloves, finely chopped
pinch dried thyme
1.5 litres/2¾ pints chicken
    or meat stock
salt and pepper
freshly grated Parmesan cheese,
    to serve

pasta with prosciutto

Trim off the fat from the prosciutto, then finely chop both the fat and the lean meat, keeping them separate. Melt the butter in a heavy-based frying pan. Add the prosciutto fat and onion and cook over a low heat, stirring occasionally, for 10 minutes.

Meanwhile, bring a large heavy-based saucepan of lightly salted water to the boil. Add the pasta, return to the boil and cook for 8–10 minutes, or until tender but still firm to the bite.

Add the lean prosciutto to the frying pan and cook for about 2 minutes. Stir in the cream, then season to taste with pepper and gently heat. Drain the pasta, add the prosciutto mixture and toss well, then stir in the Parmesan. Serve immediately.

ingredients

115 g/4 oz prosciutto
55 g/2 oz unsalted butter
1 small onion, finely chopped
salt and pepper
350 g/12 oz dried green and white
    tagliatelle
150 ml/5 fl oz double cream or
    panna da cucina
55 g/2 oz freshly grated Parmesan
    cheese

fillet steak with blue cheese sauce

Preheat the grill or barbecue. Tie the steak widthways at regular intervals with string to form a neat shape. Put the butter into a small bowl and beat with a wooden spoon until softened. Spread 2 tablespoons of the softened butter evenly all over the steak. Season to taste with pepper.

Put the steak onto an oiled grill or barbecue rack and cook under or over high heat, turning frequently, until browned on all sides, then cook over a medium heat for 18–25 minutes, according to your taste, turning frequently.

Meanwhile, add the blue cheese to the remaining softened butter and blend together until the mixture is smooth.

Put the shallot and Madeira into a pan, bring to the boil and boil until reduced to about 2 tablespoons. Stir in the cream, then simmer for 3 minutes. Add the cheese mixture, a little at a time, whisking after each addition until the sauce is smooth. Remove from the heat and season with salt and pepper.

Transfer the steak to a warmed serving dish and let rest for 5 minutes. Slice into steaks and serve with green beans and the blue cheese sauce drizzled over, garnishing with the parsley. Serve any remaining sauce in a jug.

ingredients

1.3 kg/3 lb fillet steak

75 g/2½ oz butter, softened

salt and pepper

135 g/5 oz blue cheese, crumbled

1 shallot, finely chopped

80 ml/2½ fl oz Madeira or dry sherry

175 ml/6 fl oz double cream

chopped fresh parsley, to garnish

freshly cooked green beans,
   to serve

peach & pecan empanadas

Preheat the oven to 200°C/400°F/Gas Mark 6. Roll out the pastry on a lightly floured surface. Using a 15 cm/6-inch saucer as a guide, cut out 8 circles.

Cut a small cross in the stem end of each peach. Lower them into a pan of boiling water and let stand for 10–30 seconds, depending on ripeness. Drain and cool under cold running water to prevent further cooking. Peel using a small knife.

Place a spoonful of sour cream on the centre of each pastry circle and top with a few peach slices. Sprinkle over a little brown sugar and nuts. Brush each edge with a little beaten egg, fold the pastry over the filling, and press the edges together to seal. Crimp the edges and prick the tops.

Place on a baking tray, brush with egg, and sprinkle with the sugar. Bake for 20 minutes, or until golden. Serve warm.

ingredients

plain flour, for dusting

350 g/12 oz ready-made puff pastry, thawed if frozen

3 fresh peaches

150 ml/5 fl oz sour cream

4 tbsp brown sugar

4 tbsp pecan halves, toasted and finely chopped

beaten egg, to glaze

icing sugar, for sprinkling

sweet potato & cheese soup

Melt the butter in a large pan over medium heat. Add the onion and leeks and cook, stirring, for about 3 minutes, until slightly softened. Add the sweet potatoes and cook for another 5 minutes, stirring, then pour in the stock, add the parsley and the bay leaf and season with pepper. Bring to the boil, then lower the heat, cover the pan and simmer for about 30 minutes.

Remove from the heat and let cool for 10 minutes. Remove and discard the bay leaf. Transfer half of the soup into a food processor and blend until smooth. Return to the pan with the rest of the soup, stir in the cream, and cook for another 5 minutes.

Gradually stir in the crumbled cheese until melted (do not let the soup boil). Remove from the heat and ladle into serving bowls. Garnish with finely crumbled blue cheese and serve with slices of fresh bread.

ingredients

55 g/2 oz butter

1 large onion, chopped

2 leeks, trimmed and sliced

175 g/6 oz sweet potatoes, peeled and diced

800 ml/1⅓ pints vegetable stock

1 tbsp chopped fresh parsley

1 bay leaf

pepper

150 ml/5 fl oz double cream

150 g/5½ oz blue cheese, crumbled

2 tbsp finely crumbled blue cheese, to serve

thick slices of fresh bread, to serve

SERVES 4

lone star chilli

Dry-fry the cumin seeds in a heavy-based frying pan over medium heat, shaking the pan, for 3–4 minutes until lightly toasted. Let cool, then crush in a mortar with a pestle. Alternatively, use a coffee grinder.

Toss the beef in the seasoned flour to coat. Melt the fat in a large, heavy-bottomed pan. Add the beef, in batches, and cook until browned on all sides. Remove the beef with a slotted spoon and set aside.

Add the onion and garlic to the pan and cook gently for 5 minutes, or until softened. Add the cumin, oregano, paprika and chillies and cook, stirring, for 2 minutes. Return the beef to the pan, pour over the lager, then add the chocolate. Bring to the boil, stirring, then reduce the heat, cover, and let simmer for 2–3 hours until the beef is very tender, adding more lager if necessary.

Serve with warmed flour tortillas and some sour cream to douse the flames. Wash it down with some additional ice-cold beer of your choice.

ingredients

1 tbsp cumin seeds

650 g/1 lb 7 oz rump steak, cut into
   2.5 cm/1 inch cubes

plain flour, well seasoned with salt
   and pepper, for coating

3 tbsp beef dripping, bacon fat
   or vegetable oil

2 onions, finely chopped

4 garlic cloves, finely chopped

1 tbsp dried oregano

2 tsp paprika

4 dried red chillies, such as ancho
   or pasilla, crushed, or to taste

1 large bottle of lager (preferably
   South American)

4 squares plain chocolate

TO SERVE

warmed flour tortillas

sour cream

steak waldorf salad

Heat a griddle pan or heavy-based frying pan over medium heat. Brush each steak with oil and season to taste with pepper. When the pan is hot, add the steaks and cook for 6–7 minutes for rare or 8–10 minutes for medium, turning the steaks frequently and brushing once or twice with oil. Remove from the pan and set aside.

Meanwhile, stir the mustard into the mayonnaise. Put the lemon juice into a large bowl. Peel and core the apples, then cut them into small chunks and immediately toss them in the lemon juice. Stir in the mustard mayonnaise. Add the celery and walnuts to the apples and toss together.

Arrange the salad leaves on 4 plates, then divide the apple mixture among them. Very thinly slice the steaks, arrange on top of the salad and serve immediately.

ingredients

2 fillet steaks, about 175 g/6 oz each
   and 2.5 cm/1 inch thick
olive or sunflower oil,
   for brushing
pepper
1 tbsp wholegrain mustard
150 ml/5 fl oz mayonnaise
1 tbsp lemon juice
500 g/1 lb 2 oz eating apples
4 celery sticks, thinly sliced
50 g/1¾ oz walnut halves, broken
   into pieces
100 g/3½ oz mixed salad leaves

SERVES 4

breadcrumbed chicken morsels

Preheat the oven to 200°C/400°F/Gas Mark 6. Put the breadcrumbs into a large, shallow bowl. Add the pecorino cheese and mixed herbs and season well with salt and pepper. Mix together well. Beat the egg in a separate bowl. Dip the chicken strips into the beaten egg, then coat them in the breadcrumb mixture. Arrange on a baking sheet, then transfer to the preheated oven. Bake for 30 minutes until golden brown.

Meanwhile, to make the tartare sauce, put the mayonnaise into a bowl and stir in the lemon juice and chives. Add the garlic, capers, shallots, gherkins and olives and mix together.

Remove the chicken from the oven and arrange on a large serving platter. Garnish with lemon wedges and serve with the tartare sauce and salad leaves.

ingredients

85 g/3 oz fresh white or wholemeal
   breadcrumbs

3 tbsp grated pecorino cheese

1 tbsp dried mixed herbs

salt and pepper

1 egg

4 skinless chicken breasts, cut into
   thick strips

TARTARE SAUCE

200 ml/7fl oz mayonnaise

1 tbsp lemon juice

2 tbsp chopped fresh chives

1 garlic clove, finely chopped

1 tbsp capers, chopped

2 shallots, finely chopped

50 g/1¾ oz gherkins, chopped

6 black olives, stoned and finely
   chopped

wedges of lemon, to garnish

mixed salad leaves, to serve

ginger pears with chocolate sauce

Peel the pears, leaving the stalks intact. Cut the base of each pear so that it sits upright. Carefully remove as much of the core as possible with a small spoon.

Place the water, sugar, ginger, cinnamon stick and lemon juice in a small, heavy-based saucepan. Bring to the boil and boil for 5 minutes. Stand the pears upright in the saucepan and cook, turning occasionally, for 15–20 minutes, or until softened. Place each pear on a serving plate.

To make the chocolate sauce, place the cream and chocolate in a heatproof bowl and set over a saucepan of gently simmering water until the chocolate has melted. Stir until smooth. Transfer to a jug and serve immediately with the warm pears.

ingredients

4 dessert pears
450 ml/16 fl oz water
150 g/5½ oz golden caster sugar
10-cm/4-inch piece fresh root
    ginger, peeled and sliced
½ cinnamon stick
dash of lemon juice

CHOCOLATE SAUCE
4 tbsp single cream
200 g/7 oz plain chocolate, broken
    into pieces

carrots à la grecque

Cut the carrots in half and then into quarters to form fingers of equal thickness. Put the carrots and all the remaining ingredients in a large saucepan and bring to the boil then simmer, uncovered, for about 20 minutes until the carrots are tender.

Using a slotted spoon, transfer the carrots to a serving dish. Return the cooking liquid to the boil and boil until reduced by about half.

Strain the cooking liquid over the carrots and leave to cool. When cool, chill in the fridge for 3–4 hours or overnight. Serve at room temperature, garnished with chopped fresh herbs.

ingredients

700 g/1 lb 9 oz young carrots
50 ml/2 fl oz olive oil
425 ml/¾ pint dry white wine
1 tbsp Greek honey
2 sprigs fresh thyme
6 sprigs fresh parsley
1 bay leaf
2 garlic cloves, chopped finely
1 tbsp coriander seeds, crushed
    lightly
salt and pepper
chopped fresh herbs, to garnish

12

SERVES 4

hot & spicy beef with toasted pine nuts

To make the marinade, mix the soy sauce with the cornflour and water. Add the beef and stir until well coated. Cover with clingfilm and chill in the refrigerator for 1 hour. Spread the pine nuts on a baking sheet and toast under a grill.

Mix the lime juice, soy sauce, vinegar, cornflour and half the groundnut oil in a small bowl and set aside. Heat the remaining groundnut oil in a large frying pan or wok. Stir-fry the ginger, chilli peppers and leek for 2 minutes. Add the beef and the marinade and stir-fry for a further minute.

Stir in the carrot, asparagus and shallots and fry for 7 minutes or until the beef is cooked through. Add the lime mixture, reduce the heat and simmer until the liquid thickens. Remove from the heat, sprinkle with the pine nuts and serve with cooked noodles.

ingredients

MARINADE

2 tbsp soy sauce

1 tbsp cornflour

1 tbsp water

STIR-FRY

450 g/1 lb rump steak,
    cut into thin strips

55 g/2 oz pine nuts

1 lime, juiced

1 tbsp soy sauce

2 tbsp white wine vinegar

1 tsp cornflour

2 tbsp groundnut oil

3 tsp grated fresh root ginger

2 hot red chillis, chopped finely

1 leek, sliced thinly

2 carrots, sliced thinly

100 g/3½ oz fine tip asparagus

3 shallots, sliced thinly

freshly cooked noodles, to serve

ingredients

5 tbsp oil

2 onions, sliced

450 g/1 lb minced lamb

2 tbsp yogurt

1 tsp chilli powder

1 tsp finely chopped fresh
   root ginger

1 tsp crushed garlic

1 tsp salt

1½ tsp garam masala

½ tsp ground allspice

2 fresh green chillies

4 tbsp fresh coriander leaves, plus
   extra to garnish

wedges of lemon, to garnish

salad leaves and naan bread,
   to serve

grilled minced lamb

Heat the oil in a pan. Add the sliced onions and cook over a low heat until golden brown.

Place the minced lamb in a large bowl. Add the yogurt, chilli powder, ginger, garlic, salt, garam masala and ground allspice and mix to combine. Add the lamb mixture to the fried onions and stir-fry for 10–15 minutes. Remove the mixture from the heat and set aside.

Meanwhile, place the chillies and coriander leaves in a food processor and process. Alternatively, finely chop the chillies and coriander with a sharp knife. Set aside until required.

Put the minced lamb mixture in a food processor and process. Alternatively, place in a large bowl and mash with a fork. Mix the lamb mixture with the chillies and coriander and blend well.

Transfer the mixture to a shallow heatproof dish. Cook under a preheated medium-hot grill for 10–15 minutes, moving the mixture about with a fork. Watch it carefully to prevent it from burning. Garnish with coriander leaves and lemon wedges and serve with salad leaves and naan bread.

14

SERVES 4

chicken & corn empanadas

Preheat the oven to 200°C/400°F/Gas Mark 6. Place the chicken, sweetcorn, onion, olives, coriander, Tabasco, cinnamon and salt and pepper, to taste, in a bowl and mix together.

Roll out the pastry on a lightly floured work surface. Using a 15-cm/6-inch saucer as a guide, cut out 4 rounds.

Place an equal quantity of filling on 1 half of each pastry round. Brush the edge of each round with beaten egg, fold the pastry over the filling and press the edges together to seal. Crimp the edges with a fork and prick the tops.

Place on a baking sheet, brush with beaten egg and sprinkle lightly with salt. Bake in the preheated oven for 20 minutes, or until golden brown and piping hot in the centre.

ingredients

400 g/14 oz cooked chicken, diced
400 g/14 oz canned creamed-style
   sweetcorn kernels
1 small onion, finely chopped
8 pimento-stuffed green olives,
   finely chopped
2 tbsp finely chopped fresh
   coriander
1 tsp Tabasco sauce, or to taste
1 tsp cinnamon
salt and pepper
350 g/12 oz ready-made puff pastry,
   thawed if frozen
plain flour, for dusting
beaten egg, for sealing and glazing

sticky ginger marmalade loaf

Preheat the oven to 180°C/350°F/Gas Mark 4. Grease and line the base and ends of a 900-g/2-lb loaf tin. Place 1 tablespoon of the ginger marmalade in a small saucepan and reserve. Place the remaining marmalade in a bowl with the butter, sugar and eggs.

Sift in the flour, baking powder and ground ginger and beat together until smooth. Stir in three-quarters of the nuts. Spoon the mixture into the prepared loaf tin and smooth the top. Sprinkle with the remaining nuts and bake in the preheated oven for 1 hour, or until well risen and a skewer inserted into the centre comes out clean.

Leave to cool in the tin for 10 minutes, then turn out and peel off the lining paper. Transfer to a wire rack to cool until warm. Set the saucepan of reserved marmalade over a low heat to warm, then brush over the loaf and serve in slices.

ingredients

175 g/6 oz butter, softened, plus
extra for greasing

125 g/4½ oz ginger marmalade

175 g/6 oz light muscovado sugar

3 eggs, beaten

225 g/8 oz self-raising flour

½ tsp baking powder

1 tsp ground ginger

100 g/3½ oz pecan nuts, roughly
chopped

COOK'S TIP

*If the loaf begins to brown too much
before it has cooked, lightly cover
with a piece of foil.*

vegetarian fajitas

SERVES 4

Heat the oil in a heavy-based frying pan. Add the onions and garlic and cook over a low heat, stirring occasionally, for 5 minutes, or until softened. Stir in the green and red peppers, chillies and coriander and cook, stirring occasionally, for 10 minutes.

Meanwhile, dry-fry the tortillas, one at a time, for 30 seconds on each side in a separate frying pan. Alternatively, stack the tortillas and heat in a microwave oven according to the packet instructions.

Add the mushrooms to the vegetable mixture and cook, stirring constantly, for 1 minute. Season to taste with salt and pepper. Divide the vegetables between the tortillas, roll up and serve immediately.

ingredients

2 tbsp corn oil

2 onions, thinly sliced

2 garlic cloves, finely chopped

2 green peppers, deseeded and
    sliced

2 red peppers, deseeded and sliced

4 fresh green chillies, deseeded and
    sliced

2 tsp chopped fresh coriander

12 wheat tortillas

225 g/8 oz mushrooms, sliced

salt and pepper

glazed turnips

SERVES 4–6

ingredients

900 g/2 lb young turnips, peeled and
    quartered

55 g/2 oz butter

1 tbsp brown sugar

150 ml/¼ pint vegetable stock

1 sprig fresh rosemary

salt and pepper

Put the turnip into a saucepan of boiling salted water, bring back to the boil and simmer for 10 minutes. Drain well.

Melt the butter in the rinsed-out saucepan over a gentle heat, add the turnip and sugar and mix to coat well.

Add the stock with the rosemary and bring to the boil. Reduce the heat and simmer for 15–20 minutes with the lid off the pan so that the juices reduce and the turnips are tender and well glazed.

Remove the pan from the heat, discard the rosemary and season with salt and pepper to taste.

Serve immediately with roast lamb, pork, or duck.

balti prawns

Deseed and thinly slice 2 of the chillies and reserve for the garnish. Place the whole chillies, onions, lemon juice, tomato purée, 2 tablespoons of the fresh coriander, the ground coriander, chilli powder, turmeric and salt in a food processor and process until a smooth paste forms. If necessary, thin with the water.

Heat the sunflower oil in a preheated wok or large, heavy-based frying pan. Add the spice paste and cook, stirring constantly, for 4 minutes, or until thickened.

Add the prawns and cook, stirring constantly, for 4–5 minutes, or until they have changed colour. Transfer to a warmed serving plate, garnish with the sliced chillies and remaining fresh coriander and serve immediately.

ingredients

4 fresh green chillies

2 onions, roughly chopped

2 tbsp lemon juice

2 tbsp tomato purée

3 tbsp chopped fresh coriander

1 tsp ground coriander

1 tsp chilli powder

½ tsp ground turmeric

pinch of salt

1 tbsp water (optional)

3 tbsp sunflower oil

32 large raw prawns, peeled and
  deveined

JANUARY

18

SERVES 4

COOK'S TIP

For a cucumber raita, beat 300 ml/10 fl oz natural yogurt, then stir in ¼ diced cucumber, 1 chopped fresh chilli, ¼ teaspoon ground cumin and salt to taste. Chill before serving.

SERVES 4

cauliflower cheese

Cook the cauliflower in a saucepan of boiling salted water for 4–5 minutes. It should still be firm. Drain, place in a hot 1.4-litre/ 2½-pint gratin dish and keep warm.

Melt the butter in the rinsed-out saucepan over a medium heat and stir in the flour. Cook for 1 minute, stirring continuously.

Remove from the heat and stir in the milk gradually until you have a smooth consistency.

Return to a low heat and continue to stir while the sauce comes to the boil and thickens. Reduce the heat and simmer gently, stirring constantly, for about 3 minutes until the sauce is creamy and smooth.

Remove from the heat and stir in the Cheddar cheese and a good grating of the nutmeg. Taste and season well with salt and pepper.

Pour the hot sauce over the cauliflower, top with the Parmesan and place under a hot grill to brown. Serve immediately with perhaps a tomato, green salad and some crusty bread.

ingredients

1 cauliflower, trimmed and cut into
   florets (675 g/1½ lb prepared
   weight)
40 g/1½ oz butter
40 g/1½ oz plain flour
450 ml/16 fl oz milk
115 g/4 oz Cheddar cheese, finely
   grated
whole nutmeg, for grating
salt and pepper
1 tbsp grated Parmesan cheese

TO SERVE

1 small tomato
green salad
crusty bread

tagliarini with gorgonzola

Melt the butter in a heavy-based pan. Stir in 175 g/6 oz of the cheese and melt, over a low heat, for about 2 minutes.

Add the double cream, wine and cornflour and beat with a whisk until fully incorporated.

Stir in the sage and season to taste with salt and white pepper. Bring to the boil over a low heat, whisking constantly, until the sauce thickens. Remove from the heat and set aside while you cook the pasta.

Bring a large saucepan of lightly salted water to the boil. Add the tagliarini and 1 tbsp of the olive oil. Cook the pasta for 8–10 minutes, or until just tender, then drain thoroughly and toss in the remaining olive oil. Transfer the pasta to a serving dish and keep warm.

Reheat the sauce over a low heat, whisking constantly. Spoon the Gorgonzola sauce over the tagliarini, generously sprinkle over the remaining cheese and serve immediately.

ingredients

25 g/1 oz butter

225 g/8 oz Gorgonzola cheese, roughly crumbled

150 ml/5 fl oz double cream

2 tbsp dry white wine

1 tsp cornflour

4 fresh sage sprigs, finely chopped

400 g/14 oz dried tagliarini

2 tbsp olive oil

salt and white pepper

COOK'S TIP

When buying Gorgonzola always check that it is creamy yellow with delicate green veining. Avoid hard or discoloured cheese. It should have a rich, piquant aroma, not a bitter smell.

chicken-noodle soup

Put the chicken breasts and water in a saucepan over a high heat and bring to the boil. Lower the heat to its lowest setting and simmer, skimming the surface until no more foam rises. Add the onion, garlic, ginger, peppercorns, cloves, star anise and a pinch of salt and continue to simmer for 20 minutes, or until the chicken is tender and cooked through. Meanwhile, grate the carrot along its length on the coarse side of a grater so you get long, thin strips.

Strain the chicken, reserving about 1.2 litres/2 pints stock, but discarding any flavouring ingredients. (At this point you can leave the stock to cool and refrigerate overnight, so any fat solidifies and can be lifted off and discarded.) Return the stock to the rinsed-out saucepan with the carrot, celery, baby corn cobs and spring onions and bring to the boil. Boil until the baby corn cobs are almost tender, then add the noodles and continue boiling for 2 minutes.

Meanwhile, chop and add the chicken to the pan and continue cooking for about 1 minute longer until the chicken is reheated and the noodles are soft. Add seasoning to taste.

ingredients

2 skinless chicken breasts

2 litres/3½ pints water

1 onion, with skin left on, cut in half

1 large garlic clove, cut in half

1-cm/½-inch piece fresh root ginger, peeled and sliced

4 black peppercorns, lightly crushed

4 cloves

2 star anise

salt and pepper

1 carrot, peeled

1 celery stick, chopped

100 g/3½ oz baby corn cobs, cut in half lengthways and chopped

2 spring onions, finely shredded

115 g/4 oz dried rice vermicelli noodles

griddled pork with orange sauce

Mix the orange juice, vinegar and garlic together in a shallow, non-metallic dish and season to taste with pepper. Add the pork, turning to coat. Cover and leave in the refrigerator to marinate for up to 3 hours.

Meanwhile, mix all the gremolata ingredients together in a small mixing bowl, cover with clingfilm and leave to chill in the refrigerator until required.

Heat a non-stick griddle pan and brush lightly with olive oil. Remove the pork from the marinade, add to the pan and cook over a medium–high heat for 5 minutes on each side, or until the juices run clear when the meat is pierced with a skewer.

Meanwhile, pour the marinade into a small saucepan and simmer over a medium heat for 5 minutes, or until slightly thickened. Transfer the pork to a serving dish, pour the orange sauce over it and sprinkle with the gremolata. Serve immediately.

ingredients

4 tbsp freshly squeezed orange juice

4 tbsp red wine vinegar

2 garlic cloves, finely chopped

pepper

4 pork steaks, trimmed of all visible fat

olive oil, for brushing

GREMOLATA

3 tbsp finely chopped fresh parsley

grated rind of 1 lime

grated rind of ½ lemon

1 garlic clove, very finely chopped

bœuf stroganof

Heat the oil in a large frying pan. Add the onion and cook, stirring, for 5 minutes, until softened and lightly coloured. Add the mushrooms and mustard to the pan and fry, stirring occasionally, for a further 4–5 minutes, or until lightly coloured.

Add the beef to the pan and fry, stirring occasionally, for 5 minutes, or until tender. Add the crème fraîche and salt and pepper, then heat, stirring all the time, until hot. Serve garnished with the chopped parsley.

ingredients

2 tbsp vegetable oil

1 onion, sliced roughly

225 g/8 oz button mushrooms, sliced thinly

1 tsp French mustard

450 g/1 lb rump or sirloin steak, sliced thinly

300 ml/10 fl oz reduced-fat crème fraîche

salt and pepper

chopped fresh parsley, to garnish

garlic-crusted haddock with mash

Preheat the oven to 230°C/450°F/Gas Mark 8.

Cut the potatoes into chunks and cook in a saucepan of lightly salted water for 15 minutes, or until tender. Drain well. Mash in the saucepan until smooth. Set over a low heat and beat in the milk, butter and salt and pepper to taste.

Put the haddock fillets in a roasting tin and brush the fish with the oil. Sprinkle the garlic on top, add salt and pepper to taste, then spread with the mashed potatoes. Roast in the oven for 8–10 minutes, or until the fish is just tender.

Meanwhile, preheat the grill. Transfer the fish to the grill and cook for about 2 minutes, or until golden brown. Sprinkle with the parsley and serve immediately.

ingredients

900 g/2 lb floury potatoes

salt and pepper

125 ml/4 fl oz milk

55 g/2 oz butter

4 haddock fillets, about 225 g/8 oz each

1 tbsp sunflower oil

4 garlic cloves, finely chopped

2 tbsp chopped fresh parsley, to garnish

VARIATION

If you prefer, you can cook the potatoes unpeeled, but do scrub them first. Peel them as soon as they are cool enough to handle, then mash as above. This helps to preserve the vitamins and minerals that lie just beneath the skin.

SERVES 4

neeps & tatties

Cook the swede and potato in a large saucepan of boiling salted water for 20 minutes until soft. Test with the point of a knife and if not cooked return to the heat for a further 5 minutes.

Drain well, return to the rinsed-out pan and heat for a few moments to ensure they are dry. Mash using a potato masher until smooth. Season well with the salt and pepper and add the butter. Grate as much of the nutmeg into the mash as you like and serve piping hot, garnished with the parsley.

ingredients

450 g/1 lb swedes, peeled and diced

250 g/9 oz floury potatoes, such as
    King Edwards, Maris Piper or
    Desirée, peeled and diced

salt and pepper

55 g/2 oz butter

whole nutmeg, for grating

fresh parsley sprigs, to garnish

sunshine risotto

Place the sun-dried tomatoes in a heatproof bowl and pour over enough boiling water to cover. Set aside to soak for 30 minutes, or until soft and supple. Drain and pat dry with kitchen paper, then shred finely and set aside.

Bring the stock to the boil in a saucepan, then reduce the heat and keep simmering gently over a low heat while you are cooking the risotto.

Heat the olive oil in a deep saucepan over a medium heat. Add the onion and cook, stirring occasionally, for 2 minutes, or until beginning to soften. Add the garlic and cook for a further 15 seconds.

Reduce the heat, add the rice and mix to coat in the oil. Cook, stirring constantly, for 2–3 minutes, or until the grains are translucent.

Gradually add the hot stock, a ladle at a time. Stir constantly and add more liquid as the rice absorbs each addition. Increase the heat to medium so that the liquid bubbles. After about 15 minutes, stir in the sun-dried tomatoes.

Continue adding the stock, stirring constantly, until the risotto has been cooking for 20 minutes, or until all the liquid is absorbed and the rice is creamy.

Remove the saucepan from the heat and stir in the chopped parsley and half the pecorino. Spoon the risotto onto 6 warmed plates. Drizzle with extra virgin olive oil and sprinkle the remaining pecorino on top. Serve immediately.

ingredients

about 12 sun-dried tomatoes
1.5 litres/2¾ pints chicken or
   vegetable stock
2 tbsp olive oil
1 large onion, finely chopped
4–6 garlic cloves, finely chopped
400 g/14 oz risotto rice
2 tbsp chopped fresh flat-leaved
   parsley
115 g/4 oz freshly grated aged
   pecorino cheese
extra virgin olive oil, for drizzling

ingredients

3 tbsp olive oil

1 onion, chopped

1 red pepper, deseeded and diced

1 orange pepper, deseeded and
   diced

800 g/1 lb 12 oz canned chopped
   tomatoes

1 tbsp sun-dried tomato paste

1 tsp paprika

225 g/8 oz pepperoni sausage,
   sliced

2 tbsp chopped fresh flat-leaved
   parsley, plus extra to garnish

salt and pepper

450 g/1 lb dried garganelli

mixed salad leaves, to serve

pepperoni pasta

Heat 2 tablespoons of the oil in a large, heavy-based frying pan. Add the onion and cook over a low heat, stirring occasionally, for 5 minutes, or until softened. Add the red and orange peppers, tomatoes and their can juices, sun-dried tomato paste and paprika and bring to the boil.

Add the pepperoni and parsley and season to taste with salt and pepper. Stir well, bring to the boil, then reduce the heat and simmer for 10–15 minutes.

Meanwhile, bring a large, heavy-based saucepan of lightly salted water to the boil. Add the pasta, return to the boil and cook for 8–10 minutes, or until tender but still firm to the bite. Drain well and transfer to a warmed serving dish. Add the remaining olive oil and toss. Add the sauce and toss again. Sprinkle with parsley and serve immediately with mixed salad leaves.

scallops with herb butter

Cut away any discoloured parts from the scallops. Dry well and season with salt and pepper.

Heat a heavy-based frying pan or griddle and brush with the oil. When the oil is smoking, add the scallops and cook for 1 minute, then turn and cook on the other side for 1 minute. It is a good idea to cook the scallops in 2 batches as, if you try to cook them all at once, you might end up with them stewing rather than frying. The scallops should have a good golden colour and a slight crust at the edges. Transfer to a warm plate and keep warm.

To make the herb butter, melt the butter in a saucepan and fry the garlic for a few seconds. Add the parsley and, while still foaming, pour over the scallops.

Serve at once with plenty of bread to mop up the juices.

ingredients

12 large shelled scallops, cleaned

salt and pepper

1 tbsp vegetable oil

crusty bread, to serve

HERB BUTTER

25 g/1 oz unsalted butter

2 garlic cloves, finely chopped

2 tbsp chopped fresh parsley

bread & butter pudding

Preheat the oven to 180°C/350°F/Gas Mark 4.

Use a little of the butter to grease a 20 x 25-cm/8 x 10-inch baking dish and butter the slices of bread. Cut the bread into quarters and arrange half overlapping in the dish.

Scatter half the fruit and peel over the bread, cover with the remaining bread slices and add the remaining fruit and peel.

In a mixing jug, whisk the eggs well and mix in the milk, cream and sugar. Pour this over the pudding and leave to stand for 15 minutes to allow the bread to soak up some of the egg mixture. Tuck in most of the fruit as you don't want it to burn in the oven. Grate the nutmeg over the top, according to taste, and sprinkle over the demerara sugar.

Place the pudding on a baking tray and bake at the top of the oven for 30–40 minutes until just set and golden brown.

Remove from the oven and serve warm with a little cream.

ingredients

85 g/3 oz butter, softened

6 slices of thick white bread

55 g/2 oz mixed fruit (sultanas,
   currants and raisins)

25 g/1 oz candied peel

3 large eggs

300 ml/½ pint milk

150 ml/¼ pint double cream

55 g/2 oz caster sugar

whole nutmeg, for grating

1 tbsp demerara sugar

cream, to serve

VARIATIONS

Try dried apricots instead of mixed fruit and spread apricot jam on the buttered bread. Alternatively, add a sliced banana and sprinkle with cinnamon or add sliced pear to slices of panettone, mixing a little vanilla extract into the egg. For a grown-up pudding, pour a small glass of rum or whisky into the egg.

chicken & vegetable bake

To make the filling, pour the stock into a large saucepan and bring to the boil. Add the chicken and mushrooms, lower the heat, cover the pan and simmer for 25–30 minutes. Butter a 1.2-litre/2-pint ovenproof pie dish. Remove the pan from the heat, lift out the chicken and mushrooms and place in the prepared pie dish. Reserve the stock.

Preheat the oven to 200°C/400°F/Gas Mark 6. In a bowl, mix the cornflour with enough of the milk to make a smooth paste, then stir in the remaining milk. Pour the mixture into the dish, add the stock, carrots and rosemary and season.

To make the topping, put the mash into a bowl and mix in the onion and half the cheese. Spoon over the chicken filling, level the surface, then scatter over the remaining cheese. Bake for 30 minutes until golden. Remove from the oven and garnish with the rosemary.

ingredients

300 ml/10 fl oz chicken stock
450 g/1 lb boneless chicken, chopped
100 g/3½ oz button mushrooms
1 tbsp cornflour
150 ml/5 fl oz milk
200 g/7 oz carrots, peeled, blanched and chopped
1 tbsp chopped fresh rosemary
salt and pepper
900 g/2 lb potatoes, peeled, cooked and mashed
1 onion, grated
100 g/3½ oz Cheddar cheese, grated
sprigs of fresh rosemary, to garnish

braised beef in red wine

Put the flour and pepper in a polythene bag, add the meat and shake well to coat each piece. Heat the oil in a large flameproof casserole. Add the meat and fry, in batches, for 5–10 minutes, stirring constantly, until browned on all sides. Remove with a slotted spoon and set aside.

Add the whole onions, the garlic and carrots to the casserole and fry for 5 minutes until beginning to soften. Return the meat to the casserole.

Pour in the wine, stirring in any glazed bits from the bottom, then add the stock, the tomatoes with their juice, lemon rind, bay leaf, parsley, basil, thyme, salt and pepper. Bring to the boil then cover the casserole.

Cook in a preheated oven, 180°C/350°F/Gas Mark 4, for about 2 hours, until the meat is tender. Serve hot with rice.

ingredients

25 g/1 oz plain white flour
salt and pepper
900 g/2 lb stewing beef or veal, cubed
4 tbsp olive oil
350 g/12 oz button onions
2 garlic cloves, chopped finely
350 g/12 oz carrots, sliced
300 ml/½ pint dry red wine
150 ml/¼ pint beef or chicken stock
400 g/14 oz canned chopped tomatoes with herbs in juice
pared rind of 1 lemon
1 bay leaf
1 tbsp chopped fresh parsley
1 tbsp chopped fresh basil
1 tsp chopped fresh thyme
freshly cooked rice, to serve

February

quick clam chowder

Heat the oil in a heavy-based saucepan. Add the bacon and cook over a medium heat, stirring, for 5 minutes, or until the fat runs and it begins to crisp. Remove from the saucepan, drain on kitchen paper and reserve.

Add the butter to the saucepan and stir to melt. Add the onion, celery and potatoes with a pinch of salt. Cover and cook over a low heat, stirring occasionally, for 10 minutes, or until soft.

Stir in the leek, the tomatoes and all their juices and 2 tablespoons of the parsley. Pour in the stock, bring to the boil, reduce the heat and simmer for 10–15 minutes, or until the vegetables are tender. Season to taste with salt and pepper and stir in the clams. Heat the soup through gently for 2–3 minutes, then ladle into warmed bowls, garnish with the remaining parsley and reserved bacon and serve.

ingredients

2 tsp sunflower oil

115 g/4 oz rindless streaky bacon, diced

25 g/1 oz butter

1 onion, chopped

2 celery sticks, chopped

2 potatoes, chopped

salt and pepper

2 leeks, sliced

400 g/14 oz canned chopped tomatoes

3 tbsp chopped fresh parsley

1.2 litres/2 pints fish stock

550 g/1 lb 4 oz canned clams, drained and rinsed

veal with prosciutto & sage

Place the veal escalopes between 2 sheets of clingfilm and pound with the flat end of a meat mallet or the side of a rolling pin until they are very thin. Transfer to a plate and sprinkle with the lemon juice. Set aside for 30 minutes, spooning the juice over them occasionally.

Pat the escalopes dry with kitchen paper, season with salt and paper and rub with half the sage. Place a slice of prosciutto on each escalope and secure with a cocktail stick.

Melt the butter in a large, heavy-based frying pan. Add the remaining sage and cook over a low heat, stirring constantly, for 1 minute. Add the escalopes and cook for 3–4 minutes on each side, until golden brown. Pour in the wine and cook for a further 2 minutes.

Transfer the escalopes to a warmed serving dish and pour the pan juices over them. Remove and discard the cocktail sticks and serve immediately.

ingredients

4 veal escalopes

2 tbsp lemon juice

salt and pepper

1 tbsp chopped fresh sage leaves

4 slices prosciutto

55 g/2 oz unsalted butter

3 tbsp dry white wine

hot cheese soup

Melt the butter in a large, heavy-based saucepan. Sprinkle in the flour and cook, stirring constantly, for 1 minute. Remove the saucepan from the heat and gradually stir in the chicken stock and milk. Return to the heat and bring to the boil, stirring constantly, then simmer for 3–4 minutes, or until the soup is thickened and smooth. Add the grated carrot and simmer for 3 minutes, then stir in the grated cheese.

When the cheese has melted, season to taste with salt and pepper. Ladle the soup into warmed soup bowls and serve immediately with crusty bread.

ingredients

55 g/2 oz butter

55 g/2 oz plain flour

425 ml/15 fl oz chicken stock

300 ml/10 fl oz milk

2 carrots, grated

175 g/6 oz Cheddar cheese, grated

salt and pepper

crusty bread, to serve

beef stew with herb dumplings

Preheat the oven to 150°C/300°F/Gas Mark 2.

Heat 1 tablespoon of the oil in a large frying pan and fry the onion and garlic until soft and brown. Remove from the pan using a slotted spoon and place in a large casserole dish.

Trim the meat and cut into thick strips. Using the remaining oil, fry the meat in the frying pan over a high heat, stirring well until it is brown all over. Sprinkle in the flour and stir well to prevent lumps. Season well.

Over a medium heat, pour in the stock, stirring all the time to make a smooth sauce, then continue to heat until boiling.

Carefully turn the contents of the frying pan into the casserole dish. Add the bouquet garni and the wine. Cover and cook gently for 2–2½ hours.

Start making the dumplings 20 minutes before the stew is ready. Place all the ingredients except the water in a bowl and mix well. Just before adding the dumplings to the stew, add enough of the water to the mixture to form a firm but soft dough. Break the dough into 12 pieces and roll them into round dumplings (you might need some flour on your hands for this).

Remove the stew from the oven, check the seasoning, discard the bouquet garni and add the dumplings, pushing them down under the liquid. Cover and return the dish to the oven, continuing to cook for 15 minutes until the dumplings have doubled in size.

Serve piping hot with the parsley scattered over the top.

ingredients

3 tbsp olive oil

2 onions, finely sliced

2 garlic cloves, chopped

1 kg/2 lb 4 oz good-quality braising steak

2 tbsp plain flour

salt and pepper

300 ml/½ pint beef stock

bouquet garni (bunch of mixed fresh herbs)

150 ml/¼ pint red wine

1 tbsp chopped fresh parsley, to garnish

HERB DUMPLINGS

115 g/4 oz self-raising flour, plus extra for shaping

55 g/2 oz suet

1 tsp mustard

1 tbsp chopped fresh parsley

1 tsp chopped fresh sage

salt and pepper

4 tbsp cold water

chicken liver pâté

Melt half the butter in a large frying pan over a medium heat and cook the onion for 3–4 minutes until soft and transparent. Add the garlic and continue to cook for a further 2 minutes.

Check the chicken livers and remove any discoloured parts using a pair of scissors. Add the livers to the frying pan and cook over quite a high heat for 5–6 minutes until they are brown in colour.

Season well with salt and pepper and add the mustard and brandy, if using.

Process the pâté in a blender or food processor until smooth. Add the remaining butter cut into small pieces and process again until creamy.

Press the pâté into a serving dish or 4 small ramekins, smooth the surface and cover. If it is to be kept for more than 2 days, you could cover the surface with a little clarified butter. Serve accompanied by toast fingers.

ingredients

140 g/5 oz butter
1 onion, finely chopped
1 garlic clove, finely chopped
250 g/9 oz chicken livers
salt and pepper
½ tsp Dijon mustard
2 tbsp brandy (optional)
brown toast fingers, to serve

ingredients

butter, for greasing

900 g/2 lb white fish fillets, such as
plaice, skinned

salt and pepper

150 ml/¼ pint dry white wine

1 tbsp chopped fresh parsley,
tarragon or dill

175 g/6 oz small mushrooms, sliced

110 g/3½ oz butter

175 g/6 oz cooked peeled prawns

40 g/1½ oz plain flour

125 ml/4 fl oz double cream

900 g/2 lb floury potatoes, such as
King Edwards, Maris Piper or
Desirée, peeled and cut into
chunks

fisherman's pie

Preheat the oven to 180°C/350°F/Gas Mark 4. Butter a 1.7-litre/3-pint baking dish.

Fold the fish fillets in half and place in the dish. Season well with salt and pepper, pour over the wine and scatter over the herbs.

Cover with foil and bake for 15 minutes until the fish starts to flake. Strain off the liquid and reserve for the sauce. Increase the oven temperature to 220°C/425°F/Gas Mark 7.

Sauté the mushrooms in a frying pan with 15 g/½ oz of the butter and spoon over the fish. Scatter over the prawns.

Heat 55 g/2 oz of the butter in a saucepan and stir in the flour. Cook for a few minutes without browning, remove from the heat, then add the reserved cooking liquid gradually, stirring well between each addition.

Return to the heat and gently bring to the boil, still stirring to ensure a smooth sauce. Add the cream and season to taste with salt and pepper. Pour over the fish in the dish and smooth over the surface.

Make the mashed potato by cooking the potatoes in boiling salted water for 15–20 minutes. Drain well and mash with a potato masher until smooth. Season to taste with salt and pepper and add the remaining butter, stirring until melted.

Pile or pipe the potato onto the fish and sauce and bake for 10–15 minutes until golden brown.

salmon ramen

While you heat a grill to high, bring the stock to the boil with the garlic clove and soy sauce in a saucepan, and bring another pan of water to the boil for cooking the noodles.

Mix the ingredients for the teriyaki glaze together and brush one surface of each salmon fillet with the glaze. Lightly brush the grill rack with oil and grill the salmon fillets for 4 minutes on one side only. The flesh should flake easily and the centre should remain a bright pink. Remove the fish from the grill and set aside.

Boil the noodles for 3 minutes until soft. Alternatively, cook according to the packet instructions. Drain and rinse.

Remove the garlic from the stock, then bring the stock back to the boil. Drop in the spinach leaves and spring onions and leave them to boil until the leaves are just wilted. Use a slotted spoon to remove the spinach and spring onions and divide them among 4 large bowls. Divide the noodles among the bowls, then add a salmon fillet to each. Carefully pour the boiling stock into each bowl.

Sprinkle with the beansprouts, chilli slices and coriander leaves to serve.

ingredients

1 litre/1¾ pints fish or vegetable
   stock
1 large garlic clove
½ tsp light soy sauce
4 salmon fillets, 140 g/ 5 oz each,
   skinned
groundnut or sunflower oil, for
   grilling
140 g/5 oz dried ramen or thin
   Chinese egg noodles
100 g/3½ oz baby spinach leaves
4 spring onions, chopped

TERIYAKI GLAZE
2½ tbsp sake
2½ tbsp dark soy sauce
2 tbsp mirin or sweet sherry
½ tbsp soft light brown sugar
½ garlic clove, very finely chopped
0.5-cm/¼-inch piece fresh root
   ginger, peeled and very finely
   chopped

TO SERVE
100 g/3½ oz beansprouts
1 fresh green chilli, deseeded and
   sliced
fresh coriander leaves

COOK'S TIP

Dried ramen noodles are the ones you find wrapped together in tight bundles, often labelled simply as 'stir-fry noodles'. But, if you can't find any, just substitute any Japanese or Chinese egg noodles.

maple pecan pies

MAKES 12

To make the pastry, sift the flour into a mixing bowl and rub in the butter with the fingertips until the mixture resembles breadcrumbs. Add the sugar and egg yolks and mix to form a soft dough. Wrap the dough and chill in the refrigerator for 30 minutes. Preheat the oven to 200°C/400°F/Gas Mark 6.

On a lightly floured work surface, roll out the pastry thinly, cut out 12 circles and use to line 12 tartlet tins. Prick the bases with a fork. Line each tin with baking paper and fill with baking beans. Bake in the preheated oven for 10–15 minutes until light golden. Remove the paper and beans and bake for a further 2–3 minutes. Leave to cool on a wire rack.

Mix half the maple syrup and half the cream in a bowl. Put the sugar, cream of tartar and water in a saucepan and heat gently until the sugar dissolves. Bring to the boil and boil until light golden. Remove from the heat and stir in the maple syrup and cream mixture.

Return the saucepan to the heat and cook to the soft ball stage (116°C/240°F): that is, when a little of the mixture dropped into a bowl of cold water forms a soft ball. Stir in the remaining cream and leave until cool. Brush the remaining maple syrup over the edges of the pies. Put the chopped pecan nuts in the pastry cases and spoon in the toffee. Top each pie with a pecan half. Leave to cool completely before serving.

ingredients

PASTRY

140 g/5 oz plain flour, plus extra
   for dusting

85 g/3 oz butter, cut into small
   pieces

55 g/2 oz golden caster sugar

2 egg yolks

FILLING

2 tbsp maple syrup

150 ml/5 fl oz double cream

115 g/4 oz golden caster sugar

pinch of cream of tartar

6 tbsp water

115 g/4 oz shelled pecan nuts,
   chopped

12 pecan nut halves, to decorate

cheese toasts

Toast the bread under a medium grill on one side only.

Put the cheese into a saucepan and add the butter and beer. Heat slowly over a low heat, stirring continuously. Add some salt and pepper and the mustard powder and stir well until the mixture is thick and creamy. Allow to cool slightly before adding the egg.

Spread the mixture over the untoasted side of the bread and place under the hot grill until golden and bubbling. Serve at once.

ingredients

4 slices of bread

225 g/8 oz mature Cheddar cheese, grated

25 g/1 oz butter

3 tbsp beer

salt and pepper

½ tsp dry mustard powder

1 egg, beaten

SERVES 4

chicken with pistachio nuts

Combine the chicken stock, soy sauce and sherry with 1 teaspoon of cornflour. Stir well and set aside.

Combine the egg white, salt, 2 tablespoons of the oil and 2 teaspoons of cornflour. Toss and coat the chicken in the mixture.

In a wok or frying pan, heat the remaining vegetable oil until hot. Add the chicken in batches and stir-fry until golden. Remove from the pan, drain on kitchen paper and set aside to keep warm.

Add more oil to the pan if needed and stir-fry the mushrooms, then add the broccoli and cook for 2–3 minutes.

Return the chicken to the pan and add the beansprouts, water chestnuts and pistachio nuts. Stir-fry until all the ingredients are thoroughly warm. Add the chicken stock mixture and cook, stirring continuously until thickened.

Serve immediately over a bed of rice and garnish with the extra pistachios, if using.

ingredients

50 ml/2 fl oz chicken stock

2 tbsp soy sauce

2 tbsp dry sherry

3 tsp cornflour

1 egg white, beaten

½ tsp salt

4 tbsp peanut or vegetable oil

450 g/1 lb chicken breast, cut into strips

450 g/1 lb mushrooms, sliced thinly

1 head of broccoli, cut into florets

150 g/5½ oz beansprouts

100 g/3½ oz canned water chestnuts, drained and sliced thinly

175 g/6 oz pistachio nuts, plus extra to garnish (optional)

freshly cooked rice, to serve

SERVES 4

ginger chicken with
toasted sesame seeds

SERVES 4

In a medium dish, combine the soy sauce with the water and toss and coat the chicken strips in the marinade. Cover the dish with clingfilm and refrigerate for 1 hour.

Remove the chicken from the marinade with a slotted spoon. Heat the oil in a frying pan or wok, and stir-fry the chicken and leek until the chicken is browned and the leek is beginning to soften.

Stir in the remaining vegetables, the ginger and wine. Reduce the heat, cover and simmer for 5 minutes.

Place the sesame seeds on a baking sheet under a hot grill. Stir once to make sure they toast evenly. Set aside to cool.

In a small bowl, combine the cornflour with 1 tablespoon of water and whisk until smooth. Gradually add the liquid to the frying pan, stirring constantly until thickened.

Pile the chicken on a bed of hot rice, top with the sesame seeds and serve.

ingredients

MARINADE

4 tbsp soy sauce

4 tbsp water

STIR-FRY

500 g/1 lb 2 oz chicken breasts, skinned, cut into strips

2 tbsp groundnut oil

1 leek, sliced thinly

1 head of broccoli, cut into small florets

2 carrots, sliced thinly

1 cauliflower, cut into small florets

1 tsp grated fresh root ginger

5 tbsp white wine

2 tbsp sesame seeds

1 tbsp cornflour

1 tbsp water

freshly cooked rice, to serve

grilled mushroom
& spinach-stuffed trout

Clean the trout, trim the fins with a pair of scissors and wipe the inside of the fish with kitchen paper. Leave the head and tail on and slash the skin of each fish on both sides about 5 times. Brush with the oil and season well with salt and pepper, both inside and out.

To make the stuffing, melt the butter in a small saucepan and gently soften the shallots for 2–3 minutes. Add the mushrooms and continue to cook for a further 2 minutes. Add the spinach and heat until it is just wilted.

Remove from the heat and add the herbs, lemon rind and a good grating of nutmeg. Allow to cool.

Fill the trout with the mushroom and spinach stuffing, then reshape them as neatly as you can.

Grill under a medium grill for 10–12 minutes, turning once. The skin should be brown and crispy. Alternatively, barbecue for 6–8 minutes on each side, depending on the heat.

To make the tomato salsa, mix together all the ingredients and season well with the salt and pepper.

Serve the trout hot with the tomato salsa spooned over them.

ingredients

2 whole trout, about 350 g/12 oz
    each, gutted
1 tbsp vegetable oil
salt and pepper

STUFFING
25 g/1 oz butter
2 shallots, finely chopped
55 g/2 oz mushrooms, finely
    chopped
55 g/2 oz baby spinach
1 tbsp chopped fresh parsley
    or tarragon
grated rind of 1 lemon
whole nutmeg, for grating

TOMATO SALSA
2 tomatoes, peeled, deseeded
    and finely diced
10-cm/4-inch piece of cucumber,
    finely diced
2 spring onions, finely chopped
1 tbsp olive oil
salt and pepper

quick pork & pasta stir-fry

Heat the oil in a large frying pan or wok over a medium heat and add the chilli powder, garlic and red cabbage. Stir-fry for 2–3 minutes.

Stir in the rest of the vegetables and cook for a further 2 minutes. Add the meat, increase the heat and stir-fry for about 5 minutes, or until the pork is well cooked and the dish is piping hot.

Serve immediately over fettucine or vermicelli.

ingredients

1 tbsp groundnut oil
½ tsp chilli powder, or to taste
2 garlic cloves, crushed
½ red cabbage, shredded
2 leeks, sliced thinly
1 orange pepper, sliced thinly
1 carrot, sliced thinly
1 courgette, sliced thinly
350 g/12 oz pork tenderloin, cubed
freshly cooked fettucine or
    vermicelli, to serve

vanilla hearts

Lightly grease a baking tray with a little butter.

Sieve the flour into a large mixing bowl and rub in the butter with your fingertips until the mixture resembles fine breadcrumbs.

Stir in the caster sugar and vanilla essence and bring the mixture together with your hands to make a firm dough.

On a lightly floured surface, roll out the dough to a thickness of 2.5 cm/1 inch. Stamp out 12 hearts with a heart-shaped biscuit cutter measuring about 5 cm/ 2 inches across and 2.5 cm/1 inch deep.

Arrange the hearts on the prepared baking tray. Bake in a preheated oven, 180°C/350°F/Gas Mark 4, for about 15–20 minutes until the hearts are a light golden colour.

Transfer the vanilla hearts to a wire rack and leave to cool completely. Dust with a little caster sugar just before serving.

COOK'S TIP
Place a fresh vanilla pod in your caster sugar and keep it in a storage jar for several weeks to give the sugar a delicious vanilla flavour.

ingredients

150 g/5½ oz butter, cut into small
    pieces, plus extra for greasing
225 g/8 oz plain flour
125 g/4½ oz caster sugar, plus extra
    for dusting
1 tsp vanilla essence

mexican seafood stew

Preheat the oven to 200°C/400°F/Gas Mark 6. Place the pepper quarters skin-side up in a roasting tin with the tomatoes, chillies and garlic. Sprinkle with the dried oregano and drizzle with oil. Roast in the oven for 30 minutes, or until the peppers are well browned and softened.

Remove the roasted vegetables from the oven and let stand until cool enough to handle. Peel off the skins from the peppers, tomatoes and chillies and chop the flesh. Finely chop the garlic.

Heat the oil in a large pan. Add the onion and cook for about 5 minutes, or until softened. Add the peppers, tomatoes, chillies, garlic, stock, lime rind and juice, chopped coriander, bay leaf and salt and pepper to taste. Bring to the boil, then stir in the seafood. Reduce the heat, cover and let simmer gently for 10 minutes, or until the seafood is just cooked through. Discard the bay leaf, then garnish with chopped coriander before serving with warmed flour tortillas.

ingredients

1 each of yellow, red and orange
   peppers, cored, deseeded
   and quartered
450 g/1 lb ripe tomatoes
2 large fresh mild green chillies
6 garlic cloves, peeled
2 tsp dried oregano or dried
   mixed herbs
2 tbsp olive oil, plus extra
   for drizzling
1 large onion, finely chopped
475 ml/16 fl oz fish, vegetable or
   chicken stock
finely grated rind and juice of 1 lime
2 tbsp chopped fresh coriander,
   plus extra to garnish
1 bay leaf
salt and pepper
450 g/1 lb red snapper fillets,
   skinned and cut into chunks
225 g/8 oz raw prawns, shelled
225 g/8 oz cleaned squid, cut
   into rings
warmed flour tortillas, to serve

FEBRUARY

15

SERVES 4

rigatoni with spicy bacon & tomato sauce

Heat the oil and garlic in a large frying pan over a medium-low heat. Cook until the garlic is just beginning to colour. Add the bacon and cook until browned.

Stir in the tomatoes and chilli flakes. Season with a little salt and pepper. Bring to the boil, then simmer over a medium-low heat for 30-40 minutes, until the oil separates from the tomatoes.

Cook the pasta in plenty of boiling salted water until al dente. Drain and transfer to a warm serving dish.

Pour the sauce over the pasta. Add the basil and pecorino, then toss well to mix. Serve at once

ingredients

6 tbsp olive oil

3 garlic cloves, sliced thinly

75 g/2¾ oz streaky bacon, chopped

800 g/1 lb 12 oz canned chopped tomatoes

½ tsp dried chilli flakes

salt and pepper

450 g/1 lb rigatoni

10 fresh basil leaves, shredded

2 tbsp freshly grated pecorino

guinea fowl with cabbage

Preheat the oven to 240°C/475°F/Gas Mark 9.

Rub the guinea fowl with the oil and season to taste inside and out with salt and pepper. Add the apple and parsley sprigs to the guinea fowl's cavity and truss to tie the legs together. Place the guinea fowl in a roasting tin and roast in the oven for 20 minutes to colour the breasts. When the guinea fowl is golden brown, reduce the oven temperature to 160°C/325°F/Gas Mark 3.

Meanwhile, bring a large saucepan of salted water to the boil. Add the cabbage and blanch for 3 minutes. Drain, rinse in cold water and pat dry.

Place the lardons in a flameproof casserole over a medium-high heat and sauté until they give off their fat. Use a slotted spoon to remove the lardons from the casserole and set aside.

Add the onion to the fat left in the casserole and cook, stirring frequently, for 5 minutes, or until the onion is tender, but not brown. Stir the bouquet garni into the casserole with a very little salt and a pinch of pepper, then return the lardons to the casserole.

Remove the guinea fowl from the oven. Add the cabbage to the casserole, top with the guinea fowl and cover the surface with a piece of wet greaseproof paper. Cover the casserole and put it in the oven for 45 minutes–1 hour, or until the guinea fowl is tender and the juices run clear when a skewer is inserted into the thickest part of the meat.

Remove the guinea fowl from the casserole and cut into serving portions. Stir the parsley into the cabbage and onion, then taste and adjust the seasoning if necessary. Serve the guinea fowl portions on a bed of cabbage and onion.

ingredients

1 oven-ready guinea fowl, weighing
  1.25 kg/2 lb 12 oz
½ tbsp sunflower oil
salt and pepper
½ apple, peeled, cored and chopped
several fresh flat-leaved parsley
  sprigs, stems bruised
1½ tbsp chopped fresh flat-leaved
  parsley
1 large Savoy cabbage, coarse outer
  leaves removed, cored and
  quartered
1 thick piece of smoked belly of
  pork, weighing about 140 g/5 oz,
  rind removed and cut into thin
  lardons, or 140 g/5 oz unsmoked
  lardons
1 onion, sliced
1 bouquet garni

SERVES 4

COOK'S TIP
It is important not to add
too much salt to the onion
as the lardons will be salty.

jam roll

Sift the flour into a mixing bowl and add the salt and suet. Mix together well. Stir in the lemon rind and the sugar.

Make a well in the centre and add the liquid to give a light, elastic dough. Knead lightly until smooth. If you have time, wrap the dough in clingfilm and leave it to rest for 30 minutes.

Roll the dough into a 20 x 25-cm/8 x 10-inch rectangle.

Spread the jam over the dough, leaving a 1 cm/½ inch border. Brush the border with the milk and roll up the dough carefully, like a Swiss roll, from one short end. Seal the ends.

Wrap the roly-poly loosely in greaseproof paper and then in foil, sealing the ends well.

Prepare a steamer by half filling it with water and putting it on to boil. Place the roly-poly in the steamer and steam over rapidly boiling water for 1½–2 hours, making sure you top up the water from time to time.

When cooked, remove from the steamer, unwrap and serve on a warm plate, cut into slices with warm custard or cream.

ingredients

225 g/8 oz self-raising flour

pinch of salt

115 g/4 oz suet

grated rind of 1 lemon

1 tbsp sugar

125 ml/4 fl oz mixed milk and water

4–6 tbsp strawberry jam

2 tablespoons milk

custard or cream, to serve

VARIATION

Use the same amount of mincemeat instead of jam to make a mincemeat roly-poly. Alternatively, use golden syrup instead of the jam and serve with extra hot syrup. Lemon curd or marmalade can also be used.

tarragon chicken

Season the chicken with salt and pepper and place in a single layer in a large, heavy-based frying pan. Pour in the wine and enough chicken stock just to cover and add the garlic and dried tarragon. Bring to the boil, reduce the heat and poach gently for 10 minutes, or until the chicken is cooked through and tender.

Remove the chicken with a slotted spoon or tongs, cover and keep warm. Sieve the poaching liquid into a clean frying pan and skim off any fat from the surface. Bring to the boil and cook until reduced by about two-thirds.

Stir in the cream, return to the boil and cook until reduced by about half. Stir in the fresh tarragon. Slice the chicken breasts and arrange on warmed plates. Spoon over the sauce, garnish with tarragon sprigs and serve immediately.

ingredients

4 skinless, boneless chicken
   breasts, about 175 g/6 oz each
salt and pepper
125 ml/4 fl oz dry white wine
225–300 ml/8–10 fl oz chicken stock
1 garlic clove, finely chopped
1 tbsp dried tarragon
175 ml/6 fl oz double cream
1 tbsp chopped fresh tarragon
fresh tarragon sprigs, to garnish

italian cod

Preheat the oven to 200°C/400°F/Gas Mark 6.

Melt the butter in a large saucepan over a low heat, stirring constantly. Remove the pan from the heat and add the breadcrumbs, walnuts, the rind and juice of 1 lemon, half the rosemary and half the parsley, stirring to mix.

Press the breadcrumb mixture over the top of the cod fillets. Place the cod fillets in a shallow foil-lined roasting tin.

Roast the fish in the oven for 25–30 minutes.

Mix the garlic, the remaining lemon rind and juice, rosemary, parsley and the chilli together in a bowl. Beat in the oil and mix to combine. Drizzle the dressing over the cod steaks as soon as they are cooked.

Transfer the fish to warmed serving plates and serve immediately with salad leaves.

ingredients

25 g/1 oz butter

50 g/1¾ oz fresh wholemeal
  breadcrumbs

25 g/1 oz chopped walnuts

grated rind and juice of 2 lemons

2 fresh rosemary sprigs, stalks
  removed

2 tbsp chopped fresh parsley

4 cod fillets, about 150 g/ 5½ oz
  each

1 garlic clove, crushed

1 small fresh red chilli, diced

3 tbsp walnut oil

mixed salad leaves, to serve

VARIATION

If preferred, the walnuts may be omitted from the crust. In addition, extra virgin olive oil can be used instead of walnut oil, if you like.

sweet-&-sour red cabbage

Cut the cabbage into quarters, remove the centre stalk and shred finely.

Pour the oil into a large saucepan and add the red cabbage, onion, garlic and apple.

Sprinkle on the sugar, cinnamon and juniper berries and grate a quarter of the nutmeg into the pan.

Pour over the red wine vinegar and orange juice and add the orange rind.

Stir well and season with the salt and pepper. The saucepan will be quite full but the volume of the cabbage will reduce during cooking.

Cook over medium heat, stirring well from time to time, until the cabbage is just tender but still has 'bite'. This will take 10–15 minutes depending on how finely the cabbage is sliced.

Stir in the redcurrant jelly and add more salt and pepper if necessary. Serve hot.

ingredients

1 red cabbage, about
    750 g/1 lb 10 oz
2 tbsp olive oil
2 onions, finely sliced
1 garlic clove, chopped
2 small cooking apples, peeled,
    cored and sliced
2 tbsp muscovado sugar
½ tsp ground cinnamon
1 tsp crushed juniper berries
whole nutmeg, for grating
2 tbsp red wine vinegar
grated rind and juice of 1 orange
salt and pepper
2 tbsp redcurrant jelly

COOK'S TIP

Red cabbage is a traditional accompaniment for game and meat dishes.It is also truly delicious served with sausages for a simple supper.

creamy carrot & parsnip soup

Melt the butter in a large saucepan over a low heat. Add the onion and cook, stirring, for 3 minutes, until slightly softened. Add the carrots and parsnips, cover the pan and cook, stirring occasionally, for about 15 minutes, until the vegetables have softened a little. Stir in the ginger, orange rind and stock. Bring to the boil, then reduce the heat, cover the pan and simmer for 30–35 minutes until the vegetables are tender. Remove from the heat and leave to cool for 10 minutes.

Transfer the soup into a food processor and blend until smooth (you may need to do this in batches). Return the soup to the saucepan, stir in the cream and season well with salt and pepper. Warm through gently over a low heat.

Remove from the heat and ladle into soup bowls. Garnish each bowl with a swirl of cream and a sprig of fresh coriander and serve the soup with crusty rolls.

ingredients

4 tbsp butter

1 large onion, chopped

450 g/1 lb carrots, peeled and
chopped

2 large parsnips, peeled and
chopped

1 tbsp grated fresh root ginger

1 tsp grated orange rind

600 ml/1 pint vegetable stock

125 ml/4 fl oz single cream

salt and pepper

crusty rolls, to serve

GARNISH

single cream

sprigs of fresh coriander

spicy sweetcorn fritters

Place the sweetcorn, chillies, garlic, lime leaves, coriander, egg and polenta in a large mixing bowl and stir to combine.

Add the green beans to the ingredients in the bowl and mix well, using a wooden spoon.

Divide the mixture into small, evenly sized balls. Flatten the balls of mixture between the palms of your hands to form rounds.

Heat a little groundnut oil in a preheated wok or large frying pan until really hot. Cook the fritters, in batches, until brown and crispy on the outside, turning occasionally.

Leave the fritters to drain on absorbent kitchen paper while frying the remaining fritters. Transfer the drained fritters to warm serving plates and serve immediately.

ingredients

225 g/8 oz canned or frozen
sweetcorn kernels

2 red chillies, seeded and finely
chopped

2 cloves garlic, crushed

10 lime leaves, finely chopped

2 tbsp chopped fresh coriander

1 large egg

75 g/2¾ oz polenta

100 g/3½ oz fine green beans,
finely sliced

groundnut oil, for frying

quick chocolate mousse

Heat the cream in a saucepan over a low heat for about
3–4 minutes until almost boiling.

Break up or chop the chocolate into small pieces and place
in a blender.

Pour the hot cream into the blender and then blend together
until smooth.

Pour in the eggs and blend again until well mixed. Add the
Marsala and give the mixture a final blend.

Pour into 6 ramekin dishes and allow to cool. Cover with
clingfilm and chill for about 2 hours. Serve decorated with
the grated white chocolate.

ingredients

300 ml/10 fl oz single cream

200 g/7 oz continental dark
    chocolate (should have at least
    52% cocoa solids), such as
    Meunier

2 eggs, lightly beaten

2 tbsp Marsala

2 tbsp grated white chocolate,
    to decorate

lamb tagine

Heat the sunflower oil in a large, heavy-based frying pan or flameproof casserole. Add the onion and lamb cubes and cook over a medium heat, stirring frequently, for 5 minutes, or until the meat is lightly browned all over. Add the garlic, vegetable stock, orange rind and juice, honey, cinnamon stick and ginger. Bring to the boil, then reduce the heat, cover and simmer for 45 minutes.

Using a sharp knife, halve the aubergine lengthways and slice thinly. Add to the frying pan with the chopped tomatoes and apricots. Cover and cook for a further 45 minutes, or until the lamb is tender.

Stir in the coriander, season to taste with salt and pepper and serve immediately, straight from the frying pan, with the freshly cooked couscous.

ingredients

1 tbsp sunflower or corn oil

1 onion, chopped

350 g/12 oz boneless lamb,
    trimmed of all visible fat and
    cut into 2.5-cm/1-inch cubes

1 garlic clove, finely chopped

600 ml/1 pint Vegetable Stock
    grated rind and juice of 1 orange

1 tsp clear honey

1 cinnamon stick

1-cm/½-inch piece fresh root
    ginger, finely chopped

1 aubergine

4 tomatoes, peeled and chopped

115 g/4 oz no-soak dried apricots

2 tbsp chopped fresh coriander

salt and pepper

freshly cooked couscous, to serve

moules marinières

Clean the mussels by scrubbing or scraping the shells and pulling off any beards. Discard any with broken shells or any that refuse to close when tapped with a knife. Rinse the mussels under cold running water.

Pour the wine into a large, heavy-based saucepan, add the shallots and bouquet garni and season to taste with pepper. Bring to the boil over a medium heat. Add the mussels, cover tightly and cook, shaking the saucepan occasionally, for 5 minutes. Remove and discard the bouquet garni and any mussels that remain closed.

Divide the mussels between 4 soup plates with a slotted spoon. Tilt the casserole to let any sand settle, then spoon the cooking liquid over the mussels and serve immediately with crusty bread.

ingredients

2 kg/4 lb 8 oz live mussels

300 ml/10 fl oz dry white wine

6 shallots, finely chopped

1 bouquet garni

pepper

crusty bread, to serve

COOK'S TIP

*Never eat mussels that you have
collected from the beach yourself,
as they may have been polluted
and could cause serious illness.*

peanut butter cookies

Preheat the oven to 180°C/350°F/Gas Mark 4, then grease 3 baking sheets. Mix together the butter and peanut butter in a large bowl. Beat in the caster and muscovado sugars, then gradually beat in the egg and the vanilla essence. Sift in the flour, bicarbonate of soda, baking powder and salt and stir in the oats.

Drop spoonfuls of the mixture on to the baking sheets, spaced well apart to allow for spreading. Flatten slightly with a fork. Bake for 12 minutes until lightly brown. Cool for 2 minutes, then transfer to wire racks to cool completely.

ingredients

115 g/4 oz butter, softened, plus
   extra for greasing
115 g/4 oz crunchy peanut butter
115 g/4 oz golden caster sugar
115 g/4 oz light muscovado sugar
1 egg, beaten
½ tsp vanilla essence
85 g/3 oz plain flour
½ tsp bicarbonate of soda
½ tsp baking powder
pinch of salt
115 g/4 oz rolled oats

VARIATION
You can use smooth peanut butter
rather than crunchy peanut butter
if you prefer.

MAKES 26

lemon & ricotta pancakes

Place the ricotta cheese, sugar and egg yolks in a large bowl and mix together. Stir in the lemon rind and melted butter. Sift in the flour and fold in. Place the egg whites in a separate, spotlessly clean bowl and whisk until soft peaks form. Gently fold the egg whites into the ricotta mixture.

Set a large, non-stick frying pan over a medium heat and add heaped tablespoonfuls of mixture, allowing room for them to spread. Cook for 1–2 minutes, or until the underside is coloured, then turn over with a palette knife and cook on the other side for a further 2 minutes.

Wrap in a clean tea towel to keep warm until all the pancakes are cooked. Serve with the warmed conserve.

ingredients

250 g/9 oz ricotta cheese

5 tbsp golden caster sugar

3 large eggs, separated

finely grated rind of 1 lemon

2 tbsp melted butter

55 g/2 oz plain flour

warmed cherry or blueberry
   conserve, to serve

COOK'S TIP

Do not spread the pancake mixture too thinly in the frying pan. The finished pancakes should be about 10–13 cm/4–5 inches across.

macaroni with sausage, pepperoncini & olives

Heat the oil in a large frying pan over a medium heat. Add the onion and fry for 5 minutes until soft. Add the garlic and fry for a few seconds until just beginning to colour. Add the sausage and fry until evenly browned.

Stir in the pepperoncini, tomatoes, oregano and stock. Season with salt and pepper. Bring to the boil, then simmer over a medium heat for 10 minutes, stirring occasionally.

Cook the macaroni in plenty of boiling salted water until al dente. Drain and transfer to a warm serving dish.

Add the olives and half the cheese to the sauce, then stir until the cheese has melted.

Pour the sauce over the pasta. Toss well to mix. Sprinkle with the remaining cheese and serve at once.

ingredients

1 tbsp olive oil

1 large onion, chopped finely

2 garlic cloves, chopped very finely

450 g/1 lb pork sausage, peeled and
   chopped coarsely

3 canned pepperoncini, or other hot
   red peppers, drained and sliced

400 g/14 oz canned chopped
   tomatoes

2 tsp dried oregano

125 ml/4 fl oz chicken stock or
   red wine

salt and pepper

450 g/1 lb dried macaroni

15 black olives, pitted and quartered

75 g/2¾ oz freshly grated cheese,
   such as Cheddar or Gruyère

CHAPTER
3

March

pot roasted leg of lamb

Wipe the lamb all over with kitchen paper, trim off any excess fat and season to taste with salt and pepper, rubbing well in. Lay the sprigs of rosemary over the lamb, cover evenly with the bacon rashers and tie securely in place with kitchen string.

Heat the oil in a frying pan and fry the lamb over a medium heat for 10 minutes, turning several times. Remove from the pan.

Preheat the oven to 160°C/325°F/Gas Mark 3. Transfer the oil from the frying pan to a large flameproof casserole and cook the garlic and onions for 3–4 minutes until the onions are beginning to soften. Add the carrots and celery and cook for a further few minutes.

Lay the lamb on top of the vegetables and press down to partly submerge. Pour the wine over the lamb, add the tomato purée and simmer for 3–4 minutes. Add the stock, tomatoes and herbs and season to taste with salt and pepper. Return to the boil for a further 3–4 minutes.

Cover the casserole tightly and cook in the oven for 2–2½ hours until very tender.

Remove the lamb from the casserole and, if you like, remove the bacon and herbs together with the string. Keep the lamb warm. Strain the juices, skimming off any excess fat, and serve in a jug. The vegetables may be put around the joint or in a dish. Garnish with sprigs of rosemary.

ingredients

1 leg of lamb, weighing
   1.6 kg/3 lb 8 oz
salt and pepper
3–4 fresh rosemary sprigs
115 g/4 oz streaky bacon rashers
4 tbsp olive oil
2–3 garlic cloves, crushed
2 onions, sliced
2 carrots, sliced
2 celery sticks, sliced
300 ml/10 fl oz dry white wine
1 tbsp tomato purée
300 ml/10 fl oz lamb or chicken
   stock
3 medium tomatoes, peeled,
   quartered and deseeded
1 tbsp chopped fresh parsley
1 tbsp chopped fresh oregano or
   marjoram
fresh rosemary sprigs, to garnish

chocolate fondue

Prepare the fruit according to type, cutting it into bite-sized pieces. Brush apples, pears and bananas with a little lemon juice to prevent them from discolouring. Cut the sponge cake into cubes. Arrange the fruit and cake on several serving plates.

Place the chocolate and cream in the top of a double boiler and heat gently, stirring constantly, until melted and smooth. Alternatively, melt the chocolate and cream in a heatproof bowl set over a saucepan of barely simmering water. Remove the saucepan or bowl from the heat.

Stir in the rum and sugar. Pour the mixture into a ceramic fondue pot set over a burner and hand round the fruit and cake separately. Each guest can then spear their chosen morsel and dip it in the hot chocolate mixture.

ingredients

selection of fresh fruit, such as
    apples, bananas, pears, seedless
    grapes, peaches and oranges
juice of 1 lemon
small sponge or Madeira cake
225 g/8 oz plain chocolate, broken
    into pieces
6 tbsp double cream
2 tbsp dark rum
55 g/2 oz icing sugar

SERVES 4

COOK'S TIP
Make sure that the chocolate is melted over a very low heat. If the chocolate is too hot, then it may burn and turn grainy. Do not let any water splash on to the chocolate, otherwise it will seize and is unusuable.

VARIATION
Use white chocolate instead of plain chocolate and use other types of fruit, such as strawberries, grapes, or mango and pineapple chunks.

chickpeas and chorizo

Heat the oil in a large skillet or heavy-based frying pan over a medium heat. Add the onion and garlic and fry, stirring occasionally, until the onion is softened, but not browned. Stir in the chorizo and continue frying until it is heated through.

Tip the mixture into a bowl and stir in the chickpeas and pimientos. Splash with sherry vinegar and season with salt and pepper to taste. Serve hot or at room temperature, generously sprinkled with parsley, with plenty of crusty bread.

ingredients

4 tbsp olive oil

1 onion, chopped finely

1 large garlic clove, crushed

250 g/9 oz chorizo sausage, casing
    removed and cut into small dice

400 g/14 oz canned chickpeas,
    drained and rinsed

6 pimientos del piquillo, drained,
    patted dry and sliced

1 tbsp sherry vinegar, or to taste

salt and pepper

chopped fresh parsley, to garnish

crusty bread, to serve

COOK'S TIP

If you can't find these pimientos del piquillo you can roast the peppers yourself. Use 6 of the long, sweet Mediterranean variety if possible.

grilled sardines with lemon sauce

Peel the lemon. Remove all the bitter pith and discard. Using a small, serrated knife, cut between the membranes and ease out the flesh segments, discarding any pips. Chop finely and set aside.

Melt 25 g/1 oz of the butter in a small saucepan and season with salt and pepper. Brush the sardines all over with the melted butter and cook under a preheated grill or on a barbecue, turning once, for 5–6 minutes, until cooked through.

Meanwhile, melt the remaining butter, then remove the saucepan from the heat. Stir in all the chopped lemon and fennel.

Transfer the sardines to a warmed platter, pour the sauce over them and serve immediately.

ingredients

1 large lemon

85 g/3 oz unsalted butter

salt and pepper

20 fresh sardines, cleaned and
    heads removed

1 tbsp chopped fresh fennel leaves

COOK'S TIP

Sardines are delicious if they are very fresh, but quite unpleasant if they are not. If you are in any doubt about the freshness, use another small, oily fish, such as sprats.

roast chicken with oregano

Weigh the chicken and calculate the cooking time, allowing 20 minutes per 450 g/1 lb plus 20 minutes.

Grate the rind from the lemon and cut the lemon in half. Put the chicken in a large roasting tin and squeeze the lemon juice from 1 lemon half into the cavity. Add the lemon rind, 3 tablespoons of the oregano, and the garlic. Rub the butter, the juice from the remaining lemon half, and the oil over the chicken. Sprinkle with the remaining oregano, salt and pepper. Put the squeezed lemon halves inside the chicken cavity.

Roast the chicken in a preheated oven, 190°C/ 375°F/Gas Mark 5, for the calculated cooking time, basting occasionally, until golden brown and tender. (To test if the chicken is cooked, pierce the thickest part of a thigh with a skewer. If the juices run clear it is ready.)

Allow the chicken to rest in a warm place for 5–10 minutes then carve into slices or serving pieces. Stir the remaining juices in the tin and serve spooned over the chicken.

ingredients

1.6–1.8 kg/3½–4 lb whole chicken

1 lemon

4 tbsp chopped fresh oregano

1 garlic clove, crushed

25 g/1 oz butter

3 tbsp olive oil

salt and pepper

beef & bean soup

Heat the oil in a large saucepan over a medium heat. Add the onion and garlic and cook, stirring frequently, for 5 minutes, or until softened. Add the pepper and carrots and cook for a further 5 minutes.

Meanwhile, drain the beans, reserving the liquid from the can. Place two-thirds of the beans, reserving the remainder, in a food processor or blender with the bean liquid and process until smooth.

Add the mince to the saucepan and cook, stirring constantly, to break up any lumps, until well browned. Add the spices and cook, stirring, for 2 minutes. Add the cabbage, tomatoes, stock and puréed beans and season to taste with salt and pepper. Bring to the boil, then reduce the heat, cover and simmer for 15 minutes, or until the vegetables are tender.

Stir in the reserved beans, cover and simmer for a further 5 minutes. Ladle the soup into warmed soup bowls and serve.

ingredients

2 tbsp vegetable oil

1 large onion, finely chopped

2 garlic cloves, finely chopped

1 green pepper, deseeded and
   sliced

2 carrots, sliced

400 g/14 oz canned black-eyed
   beans

225 g/8 oz fresh beef mince

1 tsp each of ground cumin, chilli
   powder and paprika

¼ cabbage, sliced

225 g/8 oz tomatoes, peeled and
   chopped

600 ml/1 pint beef stock

salt and pepper

lobster risotto

SERVES 2

To prepare the lobster, remove the claws by twisting them. Crack the claws using the back of a large knife and set aside. Split the body lengthways. Remove and discard the intestinal vein, the stomach sac and the spongy gills. Remove the meat from the tail and roughly chop. Set aside with the claws.

Bring the stock to the boil in a saucepan, then reduce the heat and keep simmering gently over a low heat while you are cooking the risotto.

Heat the oil with half the butter in a large saucepan over a medium heat. Add the onion and cook, stirring occasionally, for 5 minutes until softened. Add the garlic and cook for a further 30 seconds. Stir in the thyme.

Reduce the heat, add the rice and mix to coat in butter and oil. Cook, stirring constantly, for 2–3 minutes, or until the grains are translucent.

Stir in the wine and cook, stirring constantly, for 1 minute until reduced. Gradually add the hot stock, a ladle at a time. Stir constantly and add more liquid as the rice absorbs each addition. Increase the heat to medium so that the liquid bubbles. Cook for 20 minutes, or until all the liquid is absorbed and the rice is creamy.

Five minutes before the end of cooking time, add the lobster meat and claws.

Remove the saucepan from the heat and stir in the peppercorns, remaining butter and the parsley. Spoon onto warmed plates and serve immediately.

ingredients

1 cooked lobster, about
   400–450 g/14 oz–1 lb
600 ml/1 pint fish stock
1 tbsp olive oil
55 g/2 oz butter
½ onion, finely chopped
1 garlic clove, finely chopped
1 tsp chopped fresh thyme leaves
175 g/6 oz risotto rice
150 ml/5 fl oz sparkling white wine
1 tsp green or pink peppercorns
   in brine, drained and roughly
   chopped
1 tbsp chopped fresh parsley

VARIATION

For a slightly less extravagant version, you could substitute 450 g/1 lb Mediterranean prawns for the lobster. If you peel them yourself, you can use the heads and shells to make a delicately flavoured shellfish stock.

tiny meatballs with tomato sauce

Heat 1 tablespoon of oil in a frying pan over a medium heat. Add the onion and fry for 5 minutes until soft, but not brown. Remove the pan from the heat and set aside to cool. In a bowl, mix the onion with the lamb, egg, lemon juice, cumin, cayenne, mint and salt and pepper. Use your hands to squeeze the ingredients together. Fry a tiny piece and taste to see if the seasoning needs adjusting. With wet hands, shape the mixture into about sixty 2-cm/¾-inch balls. Place on a tray and chill for at least 20 minutes.

To make the tomato sauce, heat the oil in a flameproof casserole over a medium heat. Add the garlic, shallots and peppers and fry for 10 minutes, stirring occasionally, until the peppers are soft, but not brown. Add the tomatoes and juices, orange rind and salt and pepper and bring to the boil. Reduce the heat to as low as possible and simmer, uncovered, for 45 minutes, or until the sauce thickens. Purée the sauce through a mouli. Alternatively, purée in a food processor, then use a wooden spoon to press through a fine sieve. Taste and adjust the seasoning if necessary.

When ready to cook, heat a little oil in 1 or 2 frying pans. Arrange the meatballs in a single layer, without overcrowding, and fry over a medium-high heat for 5 minutes until brown on the outside, but pink inside. Work in batches if necessary and keep the cooked meatballs warm. Reheat the tomato sauce and serve with the meatballs to dip.

COOK'S TIP

This is an ideal tapas to serve at a drinks party because the meatballs can be made ahead and both the sauce and meatballs can be served at room temperature. If you freeze the meatballs, allow 3 hours for them to thaw at room temperature.

ingredients

olive oil

1 red onion, chopped very finely

500 g/1 lb 2 oz minced lamb

1 large egg, beaten

2 tsp freshly squeezed lemon juice

½ tsp ground cumin

pinch of cayenne pepper, to taste

2 tbsp finely chopped fresh mint

salt and pepper

TOMATO SAUCE

2 tbsp olive oil

5 large garlic cloves

70 g/2½ oz shallots, chopped

2 red peppers, cored, deseeded
   and chopped

600 g/1 lb 5 oz good-quality canned
   chopped tomatoes

2 thin strips pared orange rind

breakfast muffins

Preheat the grill to medium. Cut the muffins in half and lightly toast them under the hot grill for 1–2 minutes on the open side. Transfer to a warmed plate and keep warm.

SERVES 4

Using a sharp knife, trim off all visible fat from the bacon and cook under the preheated hot grill for 2–3 minutes on each side, until cooked through. Drain on kitchen paper and keep warm.

Place 4 egg-poaching rings in a frying pan, then pour in enough water to cover the base of the frying pan. Bring to the boil and reduce the heat to a simmer. Break 1 egg into each ring and cook for 6 minutes, or until set.

Cut the tomatoes into 8 thick slices in total and arrange on foil on a grill rack. Grill under the preheated hot grill for 2–3 minutes, or until just cooked. Season to taste with salt and pepper. Peel and thickly slice the mushrooms. Place in a saucepan with the vegetable stock, bring to the boil, cover and simmer for 4–5 minutes. Drain and keep warm. Arrange the tomato and mushroom slices on the toasted muffins and top each with 2 bacon rashers. Carefully place a poached egg on top of each and sprinkle with a little pepper. Garnish with snipped fresh chives and serve.

ingredients

2 wholemeal muffins

8 lean back bacon rashers,
    rinds removed

4 medium eggs

2 large tomatoes

salt and pepper

2 large flat mushrooms

4 tbsp vegetable stock

1 small bunch of fresh chives,
    snipped, to garnish

VARIATION

Omit the bacon for a vegetarian version and use more tomatoes and mushrooms instead. Alternatively, include a grilled low-fat tofu burger.

raisin coleslaw & tuna-filled pitta breads

Mix the carrot, cabbage, yogurt, vinegar and raisins together in a bowl. Lightly stir in the tuna and half the pumpkin seeds and season to taste with pepper.

Lightly toast the pitta breads under a preheated hot grill or in a toaster, then leave to cool slightly. Using a sharp knife, cut each pitta bread in half. Divide the filling evenly among the pitta breads and sprinkle the remaining pumpkin seeds over the filling. Core and cut the apples into wedges, then serve immediately with the filled pitta breads.

ingredients

85 g/3 oz grated carrot

55 g/2 oz white cabbage, thinly sliced

85 g/3 oz low-fat natural yogurt

1 tsp cider vinegar

25 g/1 oz raisins

200 g/7 oz canned tuna steak in water, drained

2 tbsp pumpkin seeds

freshly ground black pepper

4 wholemeal or white pitta breads

4 dessert apples, to serve

---

noodles with chicken satay sauce

Heat the oil in a large frying pan over a medium heat. Add the chicken and fry for 5–7 minutes until no longer pink. Add the pepper and spring onions. Fry for 3 minutes until just soft. Remove from the heat.

Cook the pasta in plenty of boiling salted water until al dente. Drain and return to the pan.

Put the peanut butter, ginger, soy sauce and chicken stock in a large saucepan. Simmer over a medium-low heat, stirring, until bubbling. Add the chicken mixture and pasta to the peanut sauce. Toss gently until coated with the sauce. Transfer to a warm serving dish and serve immediately.

ingredients

2 tbsp vegetable oil

450 g/1 lb boneless, skinless chicken breasts, cubed

1 red pepper, seeded and sliced

4 spring onions, green part included, sliced diagonally

225 g/8 oz dried vermicelli or spaghettini

125 g/4½ oz smooth peanut butter

1 tsp grated fresh ginger root

2 tbsp soy sauce

125 ml/4 fl oz chicken stock

rhubarb crumble

Preheat the oven to 190°C/375°F/Gas Mark 5.

Cut the rhubarb into 2.5-cm/1-inch lengths and place in a 1.7-litre/3-pint ovenproof dish with the caster sugar and the orange rind and juice.

Make the crumble by placing the flour in a mixing bowl and rubbing in the butter until the mixture resembles breadcrumbs. Stir in the brown sugar and the ginger.

Spread the crumble evenly over the fruit and press down lightly using a fork.

Bake in the centre of the oven on a baking tray for 25–30 minutes until the crumble is golden brown.

Serve warm with cream or yogurt.

ingredients

900 g/2 lb rhubarb
115 g/4 oz caster sugar
grated rind and juice of 1 orange
225 g/8 oz plain or wholemeal flour
115 g/4 oz butter
115 g/4 oz soft brown sugar
1 tsp ground ginger
cream or yogurt, to serve

MARCH

12

SERVES 6

SERVES 4–6

sausages with lentils

Heat the oil in a large, preferably non-stick, lidded frying pan over a medium-high heat. Add the sausages and cook, stirring frequently, for about 10 minutes until they are brown all over and cooked through; remove from the frying pan and set aside.

Pour off all but 2 tablespoons of oil from the frying pan. Add the onion and peppers and cook for about 5 minutes until soft, but not brown. Add the lentils and thyme or marjoram and stir until coated with oil.

Stir in the stock and bring to the boil. Reduce the heat, cover and simmer for about 30 minutes until the lentils are tender and the liquid is absorbed. If the lentils are tender, but too much liquid remains, uncover the frying pan and simmer until it evaporates. Season to taste with salt and pepper.

Return the sausages to the frying pan and reheat. Stir in the parsley. Serve the sausages with lentils on the side, then splash a little red wine vinegar over each portion.

ingredients

2 tbsp olive oil

12 merguez sausages

2 onions, chopped finely

2 red peppers, cored, deseeded
  and chopped

1 orange or yellow pepper, cored,
  deseeded and chopped

280 g/10 oz small green lentils,
  rinsed

1 tsp dried thyme or marjoram

450 ml/16 fl oz vegetable stock

salt and pepper

4 tbsp chopped fresh parsley

red wine vinegar, to serve

bacon & polenta muffins

MARCH

14

Preheat the oven to 200°C/400°F/Gas Mark 6 and preheat the grill to medium. Line 12 holes of 1 or 2 muffin trays with paper muffin cases. Cook the pancetta under the preheated grill until crisp and then crumble into pieces. Reserve until required.

Sift the flour, baking powder and salt into a bowl, then stir in the polenta and sugar. Place the butter, eggs and milk in a separate bowl. Add the wet ingredients to the dry ingredients and mix until just blended. Fold in the pancetta, then divide the mixture between the paper cases and bake in the preheated oven for 20–25 minutes, or until risen and golden. Serve the muffins warm or cold.

ingredients

150 g/5½ oz pancetta

150 g/5½ oz self-raising flour

1 tbsp baking powder

1 tsp salt

250 g/9 oz fine polenta

55 g/2 oz golden granulated sugar

100 g/3½ oz butter, melted

2 eggs, beaten

300 ml/10 fl oz milk

MAKES 12

COOK'S TIP

Pancetta is thin Italian bacon. If it is unavailable, you can use thinly sliced rashers of streaky bacon instead.

clam & leek linguine

MARCH

15

Drain the clams, reserving the liquid. Heat the oil in a frying pan over a medium-low heat. Add the leeks and garlic and fry gently for 3–4 minutes until the leeks are tender-crisp. Stir in the wine and cook for 1–2 minutes until evaporated. Add the bay leaf, clams and the reserved liquid. Season with salt and pepper. Simmer for 5 minutes, then remove from the heat.

Cook the pasta in plenty of boiling salted water until al dente. Drain and transfer to a warm serving dish.

Briefly reheat the sauce and pour over the pasta. Add the parsley and toss well to mix. Serve immediately.

ingredients

400 g/14 oz clams in brine (in jar)

3 tbsp olive oil

2 large leeks (white part only), cut
　into thin 5 cm/2 inch strips

2 garlic cloves, chopped very finely

4 tbsp dry white wine

1 bay leaf

salt and pepper

350 g/12 oz dried linguine or
　spaghetti

3 tbsp chopped fresh flat-leaved
　parsley, to garnish

SERVES 4

cappuccino squares

Preheat the oven to 180°C/350°F/Gas Mark 4. Grease and line the base of a shallow 28 x 18-cm/11 x 7-inch tin. Sift the flour, baking powder and cocoa into a bowl and add the butter, sugar, eggs and coffee. Beat well, by hand or with an electric whisk, until smooth, then spoon into the prepared tin and smooth the top. Bake in the oven for 35–40 minutes, or until risen and firm. Leave to cool in the tin for 10 minutes, then turn out on to a wire rack and peel off the lining paper. Leave to cool completely.

To make the frosting, place the chocolate, butter and milk in a bowl set over a saucepan of simmering water and stir until the chocolate has melted. Remove the bowl from the saucepan and sift in the icing sugar. Beat until smooth, then spread over the cake. Dust the top of the cake with sifted cocoa powder, then cut into squares.

ingredients

225 g/8 oz butter, softened,
   plus extra for greasing
225 g/8 oz self-raising flour
1 tsp baking powder
1 tsp cocoa powder, plus extra
   for dusting
225 g/8 oz golden caster sugar
4 eggs, beaten
3 tbsp instant coffee granules
   dissolved in 2 tbsp hot water
cocoa powder, for dusting

WHITE CHOCOLATE FROSTING

115 g/4 oz white chocolate,
   broken into pieces
55 g/2 oz butter, softened
3 tbsp milk
175 g/6 oz icing sugar

irish soda bread

Preheat the oven to 230°C/450°F/Gas Mark 8, then dust a baking sheet with flour. Sift the white flour, wholemeal flour, bicarbonate of soda and salt into a bowl and stir in the sugar. Make a well in the centre and pour in enough of the buttermilk to make a dough that is soft but not too wet and sticky. Add a little more buttermilk, if needed. Turn the dough out on to a floured work surface and knead very briefly into a large round 5 cm/2 inches thick. Dust lightly with flour and, using a sharp knife, mark the top of the loaf with a deep cross.

Place the loaf on the baking sheet and bake in the preheated oven for 15 minutes. Reduce the oven temperature to 200°C/400°F/Gas Mark 6 and bake for 20–25 minutes more, or until the loaf sounds hollow when tapped on the bottom. Transfer to a wire rack to cool, and eat while still warm.

ingredients

280 g/10 oz plain white flour,
   plus extra for dusting
280 g/10 oz wholemeal flour
1½ tsp bicarbonate of soda
1 tsp salt
1 tsp dark muscovado sugar
about 425 ml/15 fl oz buttermilk

COOK'S TIP
Buttermilk is available in most large supermarkets, but if you cannot find it, you can substitute ordinary milk instead.

leek & potato soup

Melt the butter in a large saucepan over a medium heat, add the prepared vegetables and sauté gently for 2–3 minutes until soft but not brown. Pour in the stock, bring to the boil, then reduce the heat and simmer, covered, for 15 minutes.

Remove from the heat and liquidise the soup in the saucepan using a hand-held stick blender if you have one. Otherwise, pour into a blender, liquidise until smooth and return to the rinsed-out saucepan.

Heat the soup, season with salt and pepper to taste and serve in warm bowls, swirled with the cream, if using, and garnished with chives.

ingredients

55 g/2 oz butter

1 onion, chopped

3 leeks, sliced

225 g/8 oz potatoes, peeled and
    cut into 2-cm/¾-inch cubes

850 ml/1½ pints vegetable stock

salt and pepper

150 ml/5 fl oz single cream, optional

2 tbsp snipped fresh chives, to
    garnish

SERVES 4

hunter's chicken

Melt the butter with the olive oil in a flameproof casserole. Add the chicken pieces and cook, turning frequently, for 5–10 minutes, until golden brown all over. Transfer the pieces to a plate, using a slotted spoon. Preheat the oven to 160°C/325°F/ Gas Mark 3,

Add the onions and garlic to the casserole and cook over a low heat, stirring occasionally, for 10 minutes, until golden. Add the tomatoes with the juice from the can, the parsley, basil leaves, tomato purée and wine and season to taste with salt and pepper. Bring to the boil, then return the chicken pieces to the casserole, pushing them down into the sauce.

Cover and cook in the preheated oven for 50 minutes. Add the mushrooms and cook for a further 10 minutes, until the chicken is cooked through and tender. Serve immediately.

ingredients

15 g/½ oz unsalted butter

2 tbsp olive oil

1.8 kg/4 lb skinned chicken
  portions, bone in

2 red onions, sliced

2 garlic cloves, chopped finely

400 g/14 oz canned tomatoes,
  chopped

2 tbsp chopped fresh flat-leaved
  parsley

6 fresh basil leaves, torn

1 tbsp sun-dried tomato purée

150 ml/¼ pint red wine

salt and pepper

225 g/8 oz mushrooms, sliced

VARIATION

Substitute Marsala for the red wine and add 1 green pepper, deseeded and sliced, with the onion in step 2.

springtime pasta

Fill a bowl with cold water and add the lemon juice. Prepare the artichokes one at a time. Cut off the stems and trim away any tough outer leaves. Cut across the tops of the leaves. Slice in half lengthways and remove the central fibrous chokes, then cut lengthways into 5-mm/¼-inch thick slices. Immediately place the slices in the bowl of acidulated water to prevent discoloration.

Heat 5 tablespoons of the olive oil in a heavy-based frying pan. Drain the artichoke slices and pat dry with kitchen paper. Add them to the frying pan with the shallots, garlic, parsley and mint and cook over a low heat, stirring frequently, for 10–12 minutes, until tender.

Meanwhile, bring a large saucepan of lightly salted water to the boil. Add the pasta, bring back to the boil and cook for 8–10 minutes, until tender, but still firm to the bite.

Peel the prawns, cut a slit along the back of each and remove and discard the dark vein. Melt the butter in a small frying pan, cut the prawns in half and add them to the frying pan. Cook, stirring occasionally, for 2–3 minutes, until they have changed colour. Season to taste with salt and pepper.

Drain the pasta and tip it into a bowl. Add the remaining olive oil and toss well. Add the artichoke mixture and the prawns and toss again. Serve immediately.

ingredients

2 tbsp lemon juice

4 baby globe artichokes

7 tbsp olive oil

2 shallots, chopped finely

2 garlic cloves, chopped finely

2 tbsp chopped fresh flat-leaved
   parsley

2 tbsp chopped fresh mint

350 g/12 oz dried rigatoni or other
   tubular pasta

12 large uncooked prawns

25 g/1 oz unsalted butter

salt and pepper

COOK'S TIP

The large Mediterranean prawns, known as gamberoni in Italy, have a superb flavour and texture that is superior to that of the very big tiger prawns, but they may be difficult to obtain.

SERVES 4

spicy chickpea snack

Using a sharp knife, cut the potatoes into dice. Place them in a saucepan, add water just to cover and bring to the boil. Cover and simmer over a medium heat for 10 minutes until cooked through. Test by inserting the tip of a knife into the potatoes – they should feel soft. Drain and set aside.

Using a sharp knife, finely chop the onion. Set aside until required. Put the chickpeas into a bowl.

Combine the tamarind paste and water. Add the chilli powder, sugar and 1 teaspoon salt and mix again. Pour the mixture over the chickpeas.

Add the onion and the diced potatoes to the chickpeas, and stir to mix. Season to taste with pepper.

Transfer to a serving bowl and garnish with tomato, chilli and coriander leaves.

ingredients

2 medium potatoes

1 medium onion

400 g/14 oz can chickpeas, drained

2 tbsp tamarind paste

6 tbsp water

1 tsp chilli powder

2 tsp sugar

salt and pepper

TO GARNISH

1 tomato, sliced

2 fresh green chillies, chopped

fresh coriander leaves

amaretto coffee

Pour the Amaretto into the cup of coffee and stir so the flavour mixes in well with the coffee.

Hold a teaspoon, rounded side upward, against the side of the cup with the tip just touching the surface of the coffee. Pour the cream over the back of the spoon so that it floats on top of the coffee. Serve immediately.

ingredients

30 ml/1 fl oz Amaretto
1 cup hot black coffee
1 tbsp double cream

SERVES 1

roasted sea bass

Preheat the oven to 200°C/400°F/Gas Mark 6.

Remove any scales from the fish and rinse it thoroughly both inside and out. If you like, trim off the fins with a pair of scissors. Using a sharp knife, make five or six cuts diagonally into the flesh of the fish on both sides. Season well with salt and pepper, both inside and out.

Mix the onion, garlic, herbs and anchovies together in a bowl.

Stuff the fish with half the mixture and spoon the remainder into a roasting tin. Place the sea bass on top.

Spread the butter over the fish, pour over the wine and place in the oven. Roast for 30–35 minutes until the fish is cooked through and the flesh flakes easily.

Using a fish slice, carefully remove the sea bass from the tin to a warmed serving platter. Place the roasting tin over a medium heat and stir the onion mixture and juices together. Add the crème fraîche, mix well and pour into a warmed serving bowl.

Serve the sea bass whole and divide at the table. Spoon a little sauce on the side.

ingredients

1 whole sea bass, about
    1.3–1.8 kg/3–4 lb, cleaned
salt and pepper
1 small onion, finely chopped
2 garlic cloves, finely chopped
2 tbsp finely chopped fresh
    herbs, such as parsley, chervil
    and tarragon
25 g/1 oz anchovy fillets, finely
    chopped
25 g/1 oz butter
150 ml/5 fl oz white wine
2 tbsp crème fraîche

SERVES 4

ingredients

two 400 ml/14 fl oz cans sweetened
  condensed milk
6 tbsp butter, melted
150 g/5½ oz digestive biscuits,
  crushed into crumbs
50 g/1¾ oz almonds, toasted
  and ground
50 g/1¾ oz hazelnuts, toasted
  and ground
4 ripe bananas
1 tbsp lemon juice
1 tsp vanilla essence
75 g/2¾ oz chocolate, grated
450 ml/16 fl oz thick double
  cream, whipped

banoffee pie

Place the cans of milk in a large saucepan and cover them with water. Bring to the boil, then reduce the heat and simmer for 2 hours. Ensure the water is topped up regularly to keep the cans covered. Carefully lift out the hot cans and leave to cool.

Preheat the oven to 180°C/350°F/Gas Mark 4. Grease a 23-cm/9-inch flan tin with butter. Put the remaining butter into a bowl and add the biscuits and nuts. Mix together well, then press the mixture evenly into the base and sides of the flan tin. Bake for 10–12 minutes, then remove from the oven and leave to cool.

Peel and slice the bananas and put them into a bowl. Sprinkle over the lemon juice and vanilla essence and mix gently. Spread the banana mixture over the biscuit crust in the tin, then open the cans of condensed milk and spoon the contents over the bananas. Sprinkle over 50 g/1¾ oz of the chocolate, then top with a thick layer of whipped cream. Scatter over the remaining chocolate and serve.

peking duck salad

Begin by preparing the Peking duck. Remove the crisp skin and cut it into thin strips, then slice the meat and set both aside separately. The noodles won't need any cooking, but rinse them under lukewarm water to separate them, then leave them to drain. Meanwhile, mix the hoisin and plum sauces together in a large bowl and add the noodles after any excess water has dripped off. Add the duck skin to the bowl, and stir together.

Cut the cucumber in half lengthways, then use a teaspoon to scoop out the seeds and cut into half-moon slices and add to the noodles. Next slice the spring onions on the diagonal and add to the bowl. Use your hands to mix all the ingredients together until they are well coated with the sauce.

SERVES 4

Transfer the noodles to a large platter and arrange the duck meat on top.

ingredients

½ Peking duck, bought from a
    Chinese takeaway

450 g/1 lb fresh Hokkien noodles

5 tbsp bottled hoisin sauce

5 tbsp bottled plum sauce

1 small cucumber

4 spring onions

COOK'S TIP

If you can't find Hokkien noodles, any thick noodles, such as udon or many brands of ready-to-use noodles sold in the Asian food sections of supermarkets, are equally suitable. Or boil dried thick Chinese egg noodles for 5 minutes, or according to the packet instructions, and use them.

lemon curd

You will need 2 jam jars or 3–4 small jars with lids and waxed discs. To sterilize the jars, make sure they are washed in soapy water and rinsed well and then heat in a moderate oven for 5 minutes.

Carefully grate the rind from each of the lemons using a fine grater. Make sure you only take the yellow rind and not the bitter white pith.

Cut the lemons in half and squeeze out all the juice, then sieve to remove the pips.

Place a medium heatproof bowl over a saucepan of simmering water and add the lemon rind, juice and sugar. Mix together well until the sugar has dissolved.

Add the eggs and the butter cut into small pieces and continue to stir for 25–30 minutes until the butter has melted and the mixture begins to thicken. Beat well and turn into the jars. Cover and label before storing. Once opened the lemon curd will keep for up to 2 months in the refrigerator.

ingredients

3 unwaxed lemons

350 g/12 oz caster sugar

3 eggs, beaten

175 g/6 oz butter

VARIATIONS

To make orange curd, use 3 Seville oranges instead of the lemons, and for lime prepare 5 limes for the same amount of the other ingredients. Blackberries and blackcurrants can also be made into curd by stewing the fruit first and sieving to make a purée.

ingredients

2 tbsp olive oil, plus extra for
    greasing
350 g/12 oz strong white flour
½ tsp salt
1 sachet easy-blend dried yeast
250 ml/9 fl oz lukewarm water
115 g/4 oz stoned green or black
    olives, halved

TOPPING

2 red onions, sliced
2 tbsp olive oil
1 tsp sea salt
1 tbsp thyme leaves

SERVES 4

VARIATION
Use this quantity of dough to make
1 large focaccia, if you prefer.

mini focaccia

Lightly oil several baking sheets. Sift the flour and salt into a large mixing bowl, then stir in the yeast. Pour in the olive oil and lukewarm water and mix everything together to form a dough.

Turn the dough out on to a lightly floured surface and knead it for about 5 minutes. Alternatively, use an electric mixer with a dough hook.

Place the dough in a greased bowl, cover and set aside in a warm place for about 1–1½ hours or until it has doubled in size. Knock back the dough by kneading it again for 1–2 minutes.

Knead half of the olives into the dough. Divide the dough into quarters and then shape the quarters into rounds. Place them on the baking sheets and push your fingers into the dough to create a dimpled effect.

To make the topping, sprinkle the red onions and remaining olives over the rounds. Drizzle over the oil and sprinkle with sea salt and thyme leaves. Cover and set aside to rise for 30 minutes.

Bake in a preheated oven, 190°C/375°F/Gas Mark 5, for 20-25 minutes or until the focaccia are golden.

Transfer to a wire rack to cool completely before serving.

goujons with garlic mayonnaise

Combine the mayonnaise and garlic in a small dish. Cover with clingfilm and refrigerate while you cook the fish.

Cut the fish into 2.5 cm/1 inch strips. Dip in the egg, then drain and dredge in flour. Meanwhile heat the oil. Fry the pieces of fish quickly in the oil until they are golden brown. This should take only 3–4 minutes. Remove the cooked fish from the oil and drain on a dish lined with kitchen paper.

Remove the garlic mayonnaise from the refrigerator, stir once. Set the drained fish on a dish, garnish with lemon wedges, and serve with the mayonnaise on the side for dipping.

ingredients

6 tbsp mayonnaise
2 garlic cloves, peeled and crushed
2 large white fish fillets, skinned
1 egg, beaten
3 heaped tbsp plain flour
oil for deep frying
lemon wedges, to garnish

chinese-style marinated beef with vegetables

To make the marinade, mix the sherry, soy sauce, cornflour, sugar, garlic and sesame oil in a bowl. Add the beef to the mixture, cover with clingfilm and set aside to marinate for 30 minutes.

Heat 1 tablespoon of the sesame oil in a frying pan or wok. Stir-fry the beef without its marinade for 2 minutes until medium-rare. Discard the marinade. Remove the beef from the pan and set aside.

Combine the cornflour and soy sauce in a bowl and set aside. Pour the remaining 2 tablespoons of sesame oil into the pan, add the broccoli, carrots and mangetouts and stir-fry for 2 minutes.

Add the stock, cover the pan and steam for 1 minute. Stir in the spinach, beef and the cornflour mixture. Cook until the juices boil and thicken.

Serve over rice or noodles and garnish with fresh coriander.

ingredients

MARINADE
1 tbsp dry sherry
½ tbsp soy sauce
½ tbsp cornflour
½ tsp caster sugar
2 garlic cloves, chopped finely
1 tbsp sesame oil

STIR-FRY
500 g/1 lb 2 oz rump steak, cut
   into thin strips
3 tbsp sesame oil
½ tbsp cornflour
½ tbsp soy sauce
1 head of broccoli, cut into florets
2 carrots, cut into thin strips
125 g/4 oz mangetouts
125 ml/4 fl oz beef stock
250 g/9 oz baby spinach, shredded
fresh coriander, to garnish
freshly cooked white rice or
   noodles, to serve

gnocchi with tuna, garlic, lemon, capers & olives

Cook the gnocchi in plenty of boiling salted water. Drain and return to the pan.

Heat the olive oil and half the butter in a frying pan over a medium–low heat. Add the garlic and cook for a few seconds until just beginning to colour. Reduce the heat to low. Add the tuna, lemon juice, capers and olives. Stir gently until all the ingredients are heated through.

Transfer the pasta to a warm serving dish. Pour the tuna mixture over the pasta. Add the parsley and remaining butter. Toss well to mix. Serve immediately.

ingredients

350 g/12 oz gnocchi

4 tbsp olive oil

4 tbsp butter

3 large garlic cloves, sliced thinly

200 g/7 oz canned tuna, drained
  and broken into chunks

2 tbsp lemon juice

1 tbsp capers, drained

10–12 black olives, pitted and sliced

2 tbsp chopped fresh flat-leaved
  parsley, to serve

SERVES 4

MARCH
31

MAKES 10–12 SLICES

ingredients

100 g/3½ oz raisins

finely grated rind and juice of
    1 orange

175 g/6 oz butter, diced, plus extra
    for greasing the tin

100 g/3½ oz plain chocolate, at least
    70% cocoa solids,broken up

4 large eggs, beaten

100 g/3½ oz caster sugar

1 tsp vanilla essence

55 g/2 oz plain flour

55 g/2 oz ground almonds

½ tsp baking powder

pinch salt

55 g/2 oz blanched almonds, lightly
    toasted and chopped

icing sugar, sifted, to decorate

rich chocolate cake

Put the raisins in a small bowl, add the orange juice and leave to soak for 20 minutes. Line a deep 25-cm/10-inch round cake tin with a removable base with greaseproof paper and grease the paper; set aside.

Melt the butter and chocolate together in a small saucepan over a medium heat, stirring. Remove from the heat and set aside to cool.

Using an electric mixer beat the eggs, sugar and vanilla together for about 3 minutes until light and fluffy. Stir in the cooled chocolate mixture.

Drain the raisins if they haven't absorbed all the orange juice. Sift over the flour, ground almonds, baking powder and salt. Add the raisins, orange rind and almonds and fold everything together.

Spoon into the cake tin and smooth the surface. Bake in a preheated oven, 180°C/350°F/Gas Mark 4, for about 40 minutes, or until a cocktail stick inserted into the centre comes out clean and the cake starts to come away from the side of the tin. Leave to cool in the tin for 10 minutes, then remove from the tin and allow to cool completely on a wire rack. Dust the surface with icing sugar before serving.

CHAPTER

4

April

easter biscuits

Preheat the oven to 180°C/350°F/Gas Mark 4, then grease 2 large baking sheets. Place the butter and sugar in a bowl and beat until light and fluffy. Gradually beat in the egg and milk. Stir in the mixed peel and currants, then sift in the flour and mixed spice. Mix together to make a firm dough. Knead lightly until smooth. On a floured work surface, roll out the dough to 5 mm/¼ inch thick and use a 5-cm/2-inch round biscuit cutter to stamp out the biscuits. Re-roll the dough trimmings and stamp out more biscuits until the dough is used up. Place the biscuits on the prepared baking sheets and bake in the preheated oven for 10 minutes.

Remove from the oven to glaze. Brush with the egg white and sprinkle with the caster sugar, then return to the oven for a further 5 minutes, or until lightly browned. Leave to cool on the baking sheets for 2 minutes, then transfer to wire racks to cool completely.

ingredients

175 g/6 oz butter, softened, plus
   extra for greasing
175 g/6 oz golden caster sugar
1 egg, beaten
2 tbsp milk
55 g/2 oz chopped mixed peel
115 g/4 oz currants
350 g/12 oz plain flour, plus extra
   for dusting
1 tsp mixed spice

GLAZE

1 egg white, lightly beaten
2 tbsp golden caster sugar

spaghetti with parsley chicken

Heat the olive oil in a heavy-based saucepan. Add the lemon rind and cook over a low heat, stirring frequently, for 5 minutes. Stir in the ginger and sugar, season to taste with salt and cook, stirring constantly, for a further 2 minutes. Pour in the chicken stock, bring to the boil, then cook for 5 minutes, or until the liquid has reduced by half.

Meanwhile, bring a large heavy-based saucepan of lightly salted water to the boil. Add the pasta, return to the boil and cook for 8–10 minutes, or until tender but still firm to the bite.

Meanwhile, melt half the butter in a frying pan. Add the chicken and onion and cook, stirring frequently, for 5 minutes, or until the chicken is light brown all over. Stir in the lemon and ginger mixture and cook for 1 minute. Stir in the parsley leaves and cook, stirring constantly, for a further 3 minutes. Drain the pasta and transfer to a warmed serving dish, then add the remaining butter and toss well. Add the chicken sauce, toss again and serve.

ingredients

1 tbsp olive oil
thinly pared rind of 1 lemon,
   cut into julienne strips
1 tsp finely chopped fresh
   root ginger
1 tsp sugar
salt
225 ml/8 fl oz chicken stock
250 g/9 oz dried spaghetti
55 g/2 oz butter
225 g/8 oz skinless, boneless
   chicken breasts, diced
1 red onion
leaves from 2 bunches of
   flat-leaved parsley

ingredients

1 kg/2 lb 4 oz fresh spinach, tough
    stalks removed
350 g/12 oz ricotta cheese
115 g/4 oz freshly grated Parmesan
    cheese
3 eggs, beaten lightly
pinch of freshly grated nutmeg
salt and pepper
115–175 g/4–6 oz plain flour, plus
    extra for dusting

HERB BUTTER

115 g/4 oz unsalted butter
2 tbsp chopped fresh oregano
2 tbsp chopped fresh sage

spinach & ricotta dumplings

Wash the spinach, then place it in a saucepan with just the water clinging to its leaves.
Cover and cook over a low heat for 6–8 minutes, until just wilted. Drain well and set aside
to cool.

Squeeze or press out as much liquid as possible from the spinach, then chop finely or
process in a food processor or blender. Place the spinach in a bowl and add the ricotta, half
the Parmesan, the eggs and nutmeg and season to taste with salt and pepper. Beat until
thoroughly combined. Begin by sifting in 115 g/4 oz of the flour and lightly work it into the
mixture, adding more, if necessary, to make a workable mixture. Cover with clingfilm and
chill for 1 hour.

With floured hands, break off small pieces of the mixture and roll them into walnut-sized
balls. Handle them as little as possible, as they are quite delicate. Lightly dust the dumplings
with flour.

Bring a large saucepan of lightly salted water to the boil. Add the dumplings and cook for
2–3 minutes, until they rise to the surface. Remove them from the saucepan with a slotted
spoon, drain well and set aside.

Meanwhile, make the herb butter. Melt the butter in a large, heavy-based frying pan. Add
the oregano and sage and cook over a low heat, stirring frequently, for 1 minute. Add the
dumplings and toss gently for 1 minute to coat. Transfer to a warmed serving dish and
sprinkle with the remaining Parmesan and serve.

COOK'S TIP

*A good way to remove
the liquid from cooked
spinach is to put it in a
sieve and use a potato
masher to press out the
unwanted water.*

jansson's temptation

SERVES 4

Preheat the oven to 200°C/400°F/Gas Mark 6. Generously grease an ovenproof dish with butter. Cut each anchovy fillet into 4 pieces. Layer the grated potatoes, onion slices, garlic, parsley and anchovies in the dish, ending with a layer of potatoes, seasoning each layer with pepper. Pour half the cream over the top and dot with the butter.

Bake in the preheated oven for 35–40 minutes, or until the potatoes are just coloured, then pour over the remaining cream and bake for a further 20–25 minutes until the topping is golden and tender. Serve garnished with the parsley sprigs.

ingredients

40 g/1½ oz butter, plus extra
   for greasing
14 anchovy fillets
450 g/1 lb potatoes, grated
2 onions, sliced
1 garlic clove, finely chopped
1 tbsp chopped fresh parsley
pepper
300 ml/10 fl oz single cream
   fresh parsley sprigs, to garnish

COOK'S TIP

If you use canned anchovy fillets, you can drizzle a little of the oil over the potatoes before adding the cream. If using salted anchovy fillets, soak them in water or milk before cutting them up.

ingredients

25 g/1 oz butter

2 carrots, cut into thin batons

1 small onion, finely chopped

225 g/8 oz skinless, boneless
   chicken breast, diced

225 g/8 oz mushrooms, quartered

125 ml/4 fl oz dry white wine

125 ml/4 fl oz chicken stock

2 garlic cloves, finely chopped

salt and pepper

2 tbsp cornflour

4 tbsp water

2 tbsp single cream

125 ml/4 fl oz natural yogurt

2 tsp fresh thyme leaves

115 g/4 oz rocket

350 g/12 oz dried penne

fresh thyme sprigs, to garnish

APRIL

5

SERVES 3–4

penne with chicken & rocket

Melt the butter in a heavy-based frying pan. Add the carrots and cook over a medium
heat, stirring frequently, for 2 minutes. Add the onion, chicken, mushrooms, wine,
chicken stock and garlic and season to taste with salt and pepper. Mix the cornflour and
water together in a bowl until a smooth paste forms, then stir in the cream and yogurt.
Stir the cornflour mixture into the frying pan with the thyme, cover and simmer for
5 minutes. Place the rocket on top of the chicken, but do not stir in, cover and cook for
5 minutes, or until the chicken is tender.

Sieve the cooking liquid into a clean saucepan, then transfer the chicken and
vegetables to a dish and keep warm. Heat the cooking liquid, whisking occasionally,
for 10 minutes, or until reduced and thickened.

Meanwhile, bring a large heavy-based saucepan of lightly salted water to the boil. Add
the pasta, return to the boil and cook for 8–10 minutes, or until tender but still firm to
the bite. Return the chicken and vegetables to the thickened cooking liquid and stir to
coat. Drain the pasta well, transfer to a warmed serving dish and spoon the chicken
and vegetable mixture on top. Garnish with thyme sprigs and serve immediately.

VARIATION
Replace the rocket with
the same amount of fresh
watercress or baby spinach
leaves, if you prefer.

chorizo & scallop soup

Put the chorizo in a clean, dry frying pan and cook over a medium heat for about 5–8 minutes. Lift out with a slotted spoon and drain on kitchen paper. Put the peas in a colander and rinse under cold running water. Leave to drain.

Heat the oil in a large saucepan over a medium heat. Add the shallots and cook for about 4 minutes, until slightly softened. Add the carrots, leeks and garlic and cook for another 3 minutes.

Add the drained peas to the pan, then the stock and oregano. Bring to the boil, then add the chorizo and season with salt and pepper. Lower the heat, cover and simmer for 1–1¼ hours. Just before the end of the cooking time, add the scallops and cook for about 2 minutes.

Remove the saucepan from the heat. Ladle the soup into serving bowls, garnish with chopped fresh parsley and serve with slices of fresh wholemeal bread.

ingredients
125 g/4½ oz lean chorizo, skinned and chopped
450 g/1 lb split yellow peas
1 tbsp vegetable oil
2 shallots, chopped
2 carrots, chopped
2 leeks, trimmed and chopped
2 garlic cloves, chopped
1.5 litres/2¾ pints vegetable stock
½ tsp dried oregano
salt and pepper
225 g/8 oz scallops
fresh flat-leaved parsley, chopped, to garnish
slices of fresh wholemeal bread, to serve

storecupboard tuna

Preheat the oven to 180°C/350°F/Gas Mark 4. Melt the butter in a large, heavy-based saucepan. Sprinkle in the flour and cook, stirring constantly, for 1 minute. Remove the saucepan from the heat and gradually whisk in the milk. Return to the heat, bring to the boil and cook, whisking constantly, for 2 minutes.

Remove the saucepan from the heat and stir in the grated cheese. Flake the tuna and add it to the mixture with the oil from the can. Stir in the sweetcorn and season to taste with salt and pepper.

Lightly grease a large ovenproof dish. Line the dish with the tomato slices, then spoon in the tuna mixture. Crumble the crisps over the top and bake in the preheated oven for 20 minutes. Serve.

ingredients
25 g/1 oz butter, plus extra for greasing
25 g/1 oz plain flour
300 ml/10 fl oz milk
55 g/2 oz Cheddar cheese, grated
200 g/7 oz canned tuna in oil
325 g/11½ oz canned sweetcorn, drained
salt and pepper
2 tomatoes, thinly sliced
70 g/2½ oz plain crisps

roast lamb with orzo

If necessary, untie the leg of lamb and open out. Place the lemon slices down the middle, sprinkle over half the oregano, the chopped garlic, salt and pepper. Roll up the meat and tie with string. Using the tip of a sharp knife, make slits in the lamb and insert the garlic slices.

Weigh the meat and calculate the cooking time, allowing 25 minutes per 450 g/1 lb plus 25 minutes.

Put the tomatoes and their juice, 150 ml/¼ pint cold water, the remaining oregano, the sugar and the bay leaf in a large roasting tin. Place the lamb on top, drizzle over the olive oil and season with salt and pepper.

Roast the lamb in a preheated oven, 180°C/350°F/ Gas Mark 4, for the calculated cooking time. Fifteen minutes before the lamb is cooked, stir 150 ml/¼ pint boiling water and the orzo into the tomatoes. Add a little extra water if the sauce seems too thick. Return to the oven for a further 15 minutes, until the lamb and orzo are tender and the tomatoes reduced to a thick sauce.

To serve, carve the lamb into slices and serve hot with the orzo and the tomato sauce.

ingredients

about 750 g/1 lb 10 oz boned leg
   or shoulder of lamb

½ lemon, sliced thinly

1 tbsp chopped fresh oregano

4 large garlic cloves, 2 chopped
   finely and 2 sliced thinly

salt and pepper

800 g/1 lb 12 oz canned chopped
   tomatoes in juice

pinch of sugar

1 bay leaf

2 tbsp olive oil

225 g/8 oz orzo or short grain rice

ingredients

4 salmon fillets, about
   200 g/7 oz each
125 ml/4 fl oz teriyaki marinade
1 shallot, sliced
2-cm/³⁄₄-inch piece fresh root ginger,
   finely chopped
2 carrots, sliced
115 g/4 oz closed-cup
   mushrooms, sliced
1.2 litres/2 pints vegetable stock
250 g/9 oz dried medium egg
   noodles
115 g/4 oz frozen peas
175 g/6 oz Chinese leaves,
   shredded
4 spring onions, sliced

teriyaki salmon fillets
with chinese noodles

Wipe off any fish scales from the salmon skin. Arrange the salmon fillets, skin-side up, in a dish just large enough to fit them in a single layer. Mix the teriyaki marinade with the shallot and ginger in a small bowl and pour over the salmon. Cover and leave to marinate in the refrigerator for at least 1 hour, turning the salmon over halfway through the marinating time.

Put the carrots, mushrooms and stock into a large saucepan. Arrange the salmon, skin-side down, on a shallow baking tray. Pour the fish marinade into the saucepan of vegetables and stock and bring to the boil. Reduce the heat, cover and simmer for 10 minutes.

Meanwhile, preheat the grill to medium. Cook the salmon under the preheated grill for 10–15 minutes, depending on the thickness of the fillets, until the flesh turns pink and flakes easily. Remove from the grill and keep warm.

Add the noodles and peas to the stock and return to the boil. Reduce the heat, cover and simmer for 5 minutes, or until the noodles are tender. Stir in the Chinese leaves and spring onions and heat through for 1 minute.

Carefully drain off 300 ml/10 fl oz of the stock into a small heatproof jug and reserve. Drain and discard the remaining stock. Divide the noodles and vegetables between 4 warmed serving bowls and top each with a salmon fillet. Pour the reserved stock over each meal and serve immediately.

filo chicken pie

Put the chicken in a large saucepan and add the halved onion, carrot, celery, bay leaf, lemon rind and peppercorns. Pour in enough cold water to just cover the chicken legs and bring to the boil. Cover with a lid and simmer for 1 hour. (To test if the chicken is cooked, pierce a thigh with a skewer. If the juices run clear it is ready.) Remove the chicken from the saucepan, reserving the stock, and set aside to cool. When the chicken is cool enough to handle, remove the flesh, discarding the skin and bones. Cut the flesh into small bite-sized pieces.

Bring the stock to the boil and boil until reduced to about 600 ml/1 pint. Strain and reserve the stock.

To make the filling, heat 55 g/2 oz of the butter in a saucepan, add the chopped onions and fry for 5–10 minutes, until softened. Stir in the flour and cook gently, stirring, for 1–2 minutes. Remove from the heat and gradually stir in the reserved stock and the milk. Return to the heat, bring to the boil, stirring constantly, then simmer for 1–2 minutes until thick and smooth.

Remove the saucepan from the heat, stir in the chicken, and season with salt and pepper. Leave to cool. When the mixture has cooled, stir in the cheese and eggs and mix well together.

Melt the remaining butter and use a little to lightly grease a deep 30 x 20 cm/12 x 8 inch roasting tin. Cut the pastry sheets in half widthways. Take a sheet of pastry and cover the remaining sheets with a damp tea towel. Use the sheet to line the tin and brush with a little of the melted butter. Repeat with half of the pastry sheets, brushing each with butter.

Spread the chicken filling over the pastry, then top with the remaining pastry sheets, brushing each with butter and tucking down the edges. Using a sharp knife, score the top layers of the pastry into 6 squares.

Bake the pie in a preheated oven, 190°C/375°F/Gas Mark 5, for about 50 minutes, until golden brown. Remove from the oven and leave in a warm place for 5–10 minutes then serve hot, cut into squares.

ingredients

1.5 kg/3 lb 5 oz whole chicken

1 small onion, halved, and 3 large
    onions, chopped finely

1 carrot, sliced thickly

1 celery stick, sliced thickly

1 bay leaf

pared rind of 1 lemon

10 peppercorns

155 g/5½ oz butter

55 g/2 oz plain white flour

150 ml/¼ pint milk

salt and pepper

25 g/1 oz pecorino or kefalotiri
    cheese, grated

3 eggs, beaten

225 g/8 oz ready-made filo pastry

APRIL
11

SERVES 4–6

ingredients

2 tbsp olive oil

1 onion, chopped finely

2 garlic cloves, chopped finely

650 g/1 lb 7 oz lean minced lamb or beef

400 g/14 oz canned chopped tomatoes
in juice

pinch of sugar

2 tbsp chopped fresh flat-leaved parsley

1 tbsp chopped fresh marjoram

1 tsp ground cinnamon

½ tsp grated nutmeg

¼ tsp ground cloves

salt and pepper

225 g/8 oz long, hollow macaroni or
other short pasta

2 eggs, beaten

300 ml/½ pint Greek yogurt

55 g/2 oz feta cheese, grated

25 g/1 oz kefalotiri or pecorino
cheese, grated

baked pasta with spicy meat sauce

Heat the oil in a saucepan, add the onion and garlic and fry for 5 minutes, until softened.
Add the lamb or beef and fry for about 5 minutes, until browned all over, stirring frequently
and breaking up the meat.

Add the tomatoes to the saucepan, the sugar, parsley, marjoram, cinnamon, nutmeg,
cloves, salt and pepper. Bring to the boil then simmer, uncovered, for 30 minutes,
stirring occasionally.

Meanwhile, cook the macaroni in a large saucepan of boiling salted water for about
10–12 minutes or as directed on the packet, until tender, then drain well. Beat together the
eggs, yogurt and feta cheese. Season with salt and pepper.

When the meat is cooked, transfer it to a large ovenproof dish. Add the macaroni in a layer
to cover the meat then pour over the sauce. Sprinkle over the kefalotiri or pecorino cheese.

Bake in a preheated oven, 190°C/375°F/Gas Mark 5, for 30–45 minutes, until golden brown.
Serve hot or warm, cut into portions.

roast monkfish with romesco sauce

Preheat the oven to 220°C/425°F/Gas Mark 7.

For the sauce, put the pepper, garlic and tomatoes in a roasting tin and toss with 1 tablespoon of the oil. Roast in the oven for 20–25 minutes, then remove from the oven, cover with a tea towel and set aside for 10 minutes. Peel off the skins and place the vegetables in a food processor.

Heat 1 tablespoon of the remaining oil in a frying pan. Add the bread cubes and almonds and cook over a low heat, stirring frequently, until golden. Remove with a slotted spoon and drain on kitchen paper. Add the chilli, shallots and paprika to the frying pan and cook, stirring occasionally, for 5 minutes.

Transfer the bread and chilli mixtures to the food processor, add the vinegar, sugar and water and process to a paste. With the motor running, add the remaining oil through the feeder tube. Set aside.

Reduce the oven temperature to 200°C/400°F/Gas Mark 6. Rinse the monkfish tail and pat it dry. Wrap the ham around the monkfish and brush lightly with oil. Season to taste with salt and pepper. Put the fish on a baking sheet.

Roast the monkfish in the oven for 20 minutes until the flesh is opaque and flakes easily. Test by lifting off the ham along the central bone and cut a small amount of the flesh away from the bone to see if it flakes.

Cut through the ham to remove the central bone and produce 2 thick fillets. Cut each fillet into 2 or 3 pieces and arrange on plates with a spoonful of Romesco Sauce. Serve immediately.

ingredients

1 monkfish tail, about 900 g/2 lb,
    membrane removed
2–3 slices serrano ham
olive oil, for brushing
salt and pepper

ROMESCO SAUCE

1 red pepper, halved and deseeded
4 garlic cloves, unpeeled
2 tomatoes, halved
125 ml/4 fl oz olive oil
1 slice white bread, diced
4 tbsp blanched almonds
1 fresh red chilli, deseeded and
    chopped
2 shallots, chopped
1 tsp paprika
2 tbsp red wine vinegar
2 tsp sugar
1 tbsp water

SERVES 4–6

13

SERVES 4

pan-fried pork with mozzarella

Trim any excess fat from the meat, then slice it crossways into 12 pieces, each about 2.5 cm/1 inch thick. Stand each piece on end and beat with the flat end of a meat mallet or the side of a rolling pin until thoroughly flattened. Rub each piece all over with garlic, transfer to a plate and cover with clingfilm. Set aside in a cool place for 30 minutes to 1 hour.

Cut the mozzarella into 12 slices. Season the pork to taste with salt and pepper, then place a slice of cheese on top of each slice of meat. Top with a slice of prosciutto, allowing it to fall in folds. Place a sage leaf on each portion and secure with a cocktail stick.

Melt the butter in a large, heavy-based frying pan. Add the pork, in batches if necessary, and cook for 2–3 minutes on each side, until the meat is tender and the cheese has melted. Remove with a slotted spoon and keep warm while you cook the remaining batch.

Remove and discard the cocktail sticks. Transfer the pork to 4 warmed individual plates, garnish with parsley and lemon slices and serve immediately with mostarda di Verona, if using.

ingredients

450 g/1 lb loin of pork

2–3 garlic cloves, chopped finely

175 g/6 oz mozzarella di bufala, drained

salt and pepper

12 slices prosciutto

12 fresh sage leaves

55 g/2 oz unsalted butter

mostarda di Verona, to serve (optional)

TO GARNISH

flat-leaved parsley sprigs

lemon slices

COOK'S TIP

Mostarda di Verona is made with apple purée and is available from some good Italian delicatessens.

marinated raw beef

Using a very sharp knife, cut the beef fillet into wafer-thin slices and arrange on 4 individual serving plates.

Pour the lemon juice into a small bowl and season to taste with salt and pepper. Whisk in the olive oil, then pour the dressing over the meat. Cover the plates with clingfilm and set aside for 10–15 minutes to marinate.

Remove and discard the clingfilm. Arrange the Parmesan shavings in the centre of each serving and sprinkle with parsley. Garnish with lemon slices and serve with fresh bread.

ingredients

200 g/7 oz fillet of beef, in 1 piece
2 tbsp lemon juice
salt and pepper
4 tbsp extra virgin olive oil
55 g/2 oz Parmesan cheese, shaved
   thinly
4 tbsp chopped fresh flat-leaved
   parsley
lemon slices, to garnish
ciabatta or focaccia, to serve

COOK'S TIP
You need extremely thin slices of meat for this recipe. If you place the beef in the freezer for about 30 minutes, you will find it easier to slice.

VARIATION
To make Carpaccio di Tonno, substitute fresh, uncooked tuna for the fillet of beef. Do not use thawed frozen fish, and eat on the day of purchase.

SERVES 4

warm chicken liver salad

Arrange the salad leaves on serving plates.

Heat the oil in a non-stick frying pan, add the onion and cook for 5 minutes, or until softened. Add the chicken livers, tarragon and mustard and cook for 3–5 minutes, stirring, until tender. Put on top of the salad leaves.

Add the vinegar, salt and pepper to the pan and heat, stirring all the time, until all the sediment has been lifted from the pan. Pour over the chicken livers and serve warm.

ingredients

salad leaves
1 tbsp olive oil
1 small onion, chopped finely
450 g/1 lb frozen chicken livers, thawed
1 tsp chopped fresh tarragon
1 tsp wholegrain mustard
2 tbsp balsamic vinegar
salt and pepper

SERVES 6-8

french country casserole

Preheat the oven to 180°C/350°F/Gas Mark 4. Heat the oil in a large, flameproof casserole. Add the lamb in batches and cook over a medium heat, stirring, for 5–8 minutes, or until browned. Transfer to a plate.

Add the sliced leeks to the casserole and cook, stirring occasionally, for 5 minutes, or until softened. Sprinkle in the flour and cook, stirring, for 1 minute. Pour in the wine and stock and bring to the boil, stirring. Stir in the tomato purée, sugar, chopped mint and apricots and season to taste with salt and pepper.

Return the lamb to the casserole and stir. Arrange the potato slices on top and brush with the melted butter. Cover and bake in the preheated oven for 1½ hours. Increase the oven temperature to 200°C/400°F/Gas Mark 6, uncover the casserole and bake for a further 30 minutes, or until the potato topping is golden brown. Serve immediately, garnished with fresh mint sprigs.

ingredients

2 tbsp sunflower oil
2 kg/4 lb 8 oz boneless leg of lamb, cut into 2.5-cm/1-inch cubes
6 leeks, sliced
1 tbsp plain flour
150 ml/5 fl oz rosé wine
300 ml/10 fl oz chicken stock
1 tbsp tomato purée
1 tbsp sugar
2 tbsp chopped fresh mint
115 g/4 oz dried apricots, chopped
salt and pepper
1 kg/2 lb 4 oz potatoes, sliced
3 tbsp melted unsalted butter
fresh mint sprigs, to garnish

VARIATION
Use a light red wine instead of rosé if you would prefer a slightly heavier flavour in this country casserole.

COOK'S TIP
It is always a good idea to fry off meat to brown it before adding it to a casserole. This will ensure that it has an appetising colour in the finished dish.

ingredients

4 bananas

6 tbsp chopped mixed nuts,
    to decorate

VANILLA ICE CREAM

300 ml/10 fl oz milk

1 tsp vanilla essence

3 egg yolks

100 g/3½ oz caster sugar

300 ml/10 fl oz double cream,
    whipped

CHOCOLATE RUM SAUCE

125 g/4½ oz plain chocolate,
    broken into small pieces

2½ tbsp butter

6 tbsp water

1 tbsp rum

banana splits

To make the ice cream, heat the milk and vanilla essence in a saucepan until almost boiling. In a bowl, beat together the egg yolks and sugar. Remove the milk from the heat and stir a little into the egg mixture. Transfer the mixture to the pan. Stir over a low heat until thick. Do not boil. Remove from the heat. Cool for 30 minutes, fold in the cream, cover with clingfilm and chill for 1 hour. Transfer into an ice cream maker and process for 15 minutes. Alternatively, transfer into a freezerproof container and freeze for 1 hour, then place in a bowl and beat to break up the ice crystals. Put back in the container and freeze for 30 minutes. Repeat twice more, freezing for 30 minutes and whisking each time.

To make the sauce, melt the chocolate, butter and water together in a saucepan, stirring. Remove from the heat and stir in the rum. Peel the bananas, slice lengthways and arrange on 4 serving dishes. Top with ice cream and nuts and serve with the sauce.

plaice parcels with fresh herbs

Preheat the oven to 190°C/375°F/Gas Mark 5. Cut 4 large squares of aluminium foil, each large enough to hold a fish and form a parcel, and brush with oil.

Place each fish fillet on a foil sheet and sprinkle over the herbs, lemon rind and juice, onion, capers (if using), salt and pepper. Fold the foil to make a secure parcel and place on a baking sheet.

Bake the parcels in the oven for 15 minutes, or until tender.

Serve the fish piping hot, in their loosely opened parcels.

ingredients

vegetable oil

4 plaice fillets, skinned

6 tbsp chopped fresh herbs, such
as dill, parsley, chives, thyme
or marjoram

finely grated zest and juice
of 2 lemons

1 small onion, sliced thinly

1 tbsp capers (optional)

salt and pepper

chicken with pak choi

Break the broccoli into small florets and cook in a saucepan of lightly salted boiling water for 3 minutes. Drain and reserve.

Heat a wok over a high heat until almost smoking, add the oil and then add the ginger, chilli and garlic. Stir-fry for 1 minute. Add the onion and chicken and stir-fry for a further 3–4 minutes, or until the chicken is sealed on all sides.

Add the remaining vegetables, including the broccoli, and stir-fry for 3–4 minutes, or until tender.

Add the soy and Thai fish sauces and stir-fry for a further 1–2 minutes, then serve immediately sprinkled with the coriander and sesame seeds.

ingredients

175 g/6 oz broccoli

1 tbsp groundnut oil

2.5-cm/1-inch piece fresh root
ginger, finely grated

1 fresh red Thai chilli, deseeded
and chopped

2 garlic cloves, crushed

1 red onion, cut into wedges

450 g/1 lb skinless, boneless
chicken breast, cut into thin strips

175 g/6 oz pak choi, shredded

115 g/4 oz baby corn, halved

1 tbsp light soy sauce

1 tbsp Thai fish sauce

1 tbsp chopped fresh coriander

1 tbsp toasted sesame seeds

ingredients

MARINADE

75 ml/2½ fl oz vegetable stock

2 tsp cornflour

2 tbsp soy sauce

1 tbsp caster sugar

pinch of chilli flakes

STIR-FRY

250 g/9 oz firm tofu, rinsed and
    drained thoroughly and cut into
    1 cm/½ inch cubes

4 tbsp groundnut oil

1 tbsp grated fresh root ginger

3 garlic cloves, crushed

4 spring onions, sliced thinly

1 head of broccoli, cut into florets

1 carrot, cut into batons

1 yellow pepper, sliced thinly

250 g/9 oz shiitake mushrooms,
    sliced thinly

freshly cooked rice, to serve

spicy tofu

Blend the vegetable stock, cornflour, soy sauce, sugar and chilli flakes together in a
large bowl. Add the tofu and toss well to cover in the marinade. Set aside to marinate
for 20 minutes.

In a large frying pan or wok, heat 2 tablespoons of the groundnut oil and stir-fry the
tofu with its marinade until brown and crispy. Remove from the pan and set aside.

Heat the remaining 2 tablespoons of groundnut oil in the pan and stir-fry the ginger,
garlic and spring onions for 30 seconds. Add the broccoli, carrot, yellow pepper and
mushrooms to the pan and cook for 5–6 minutes. Return the tofu to the pan and
stir-fry to reheat. Serve immediately over steamed rice.

21

SERVES 4

ingredients

175 g/6 oz cherry tomatoes
225 g/8 oz mixed mushrooms,
    such as button, chestnut,
    shiitake and oyster
4 tbsp vegetable stock
small bunch of fresh thyme
4 eggs, separated
125 ml/4 fl oz water
4 egg whites
4 tsp olive oil
25 g/1 oz rocket leaves
salt and pepper
fresh thyme sprigs, to garnish

soufflé omelette

Halve the tomatoes and place them in a saucepan. Wipe the mushrooms with kitchen paper, trim if necessary and slice if large. Place the mushrooms in the pan with the tomato halves.

Add the stock and thyme, still tied together, to the pan. Bring to the boil, cover and simmer for 5–6 minutes until tender. Drain, remove the thyme and discard. Keep the mixture warm.

Meanwhile, separate the eggs and whisk the egg yolks with the water until frothy. In a clean, grease-free bowl, whisk the 8 egg whites until stiff and dry.

Spoon the egg yolk mixture into the egg whites and, using a metal spoon, fold together until well mixed. Take care not to knock out too much of the air.

For each omelette, brush a small omelette pan with 1 teaspoon of the oil and heat until hot. Pour in a quarter of the egg mixture and cook for 4–5 minutes until the mixture has set.

Finish cooking the omelette under a preheated medium grill for 2–3 minutes.

Transfer the omelette to a warm serving plate. Fill the omelette with a few rocket leaves and a quarter of the mushroom and tomato mixture. Flip over the top of the omelette, garnish with sprigs of thyme and serve.

home-made turkey burgers

Cook the rice in a large pan of boiling salted water for about 10 minutes, or until tender. Drain, rinse under cold running water, then drain well again.

Put the cooked rice, apple, garlic, herbs and spices in a large bowl and mix well together. With wet hands, shape the mixture into 8 thick burgers.

Pour a little oil into a large non-stick frying pan, add the burgers and cook for about 10 minutes, turning them over several times, until they are golden brown. Remove from the pan and serve hot, garnished with spring onion and lime.

ingredients

55 g/2 oz long grain white rice

salt and pepper

450 g/1 lb lean minced turkey

1 small cooking apple, peeled,
    cored and grated

1 small onion, chopped finely

1 garlic clove, chopped finely

1 tsp ground sage

½ tsp dried thyme

½ tsp ground allspice

vegetable oil, for frying

spring onion and lime, to garnish

APRIL

22

SERVES 4

sausages in batter

Preheat the oven to 220°C/425°F/Gas Mark 7.

Grease a 20 x 25-cm/8 x10-inch ovenproof dish or roasting tin.

Make the batter by sifting the flour and salt into a large bowl.
Make a well in the centre and add the beaten egg and half the
milk. Carefully mix the liquid into the flour until the mixture is
smooth. Gradually beat in the remaining milk. Leave to stand
for 30 minutes.

Prick the sausages and place them in the ovenproof dish.
Sprinkle over the oil and cook the sausages in the oven for
10 minutes until they are beginning to colour and the fat has
begun to run and is sizzling.

Remove from the oven and quickly pour the batter over the
sausages. Return to the oven and cook for 35–45 minutes,
or until the batter is well risen and golden brown.
Serve immediately.

ingredients

butter, for greasing

115 g/4 oz plain flour

pinch of salt

1 egg, beaten

300 ml/10 fl oz milk

450 g/1 lb good-quality sausages

1 tbsp vegetable oil

lamb steaks with herb noodles

Start by mixing together the flavourings for the herb noodles. Put the lime juice, nam pla, sweet chilli sauce, brown sugar and sesame oil in a small bowl and beat together, then set aside.

Heat a large ridged cast-iron griddle or frying pan over a high heat. Lightly brush the steaks or chops with oil on both sides and season with salt and pepper. Add them to the pan and cook for about 6 minutes for rare, or 10 minutes for well done, turning the meat over once.

Meanwhile, boil the noodles for 3 minutes, until soft. Alternatively, cook according to the packet instructions. Drain well and immediately transfer to a large bowl. Add the lime juice mixture and toss together, then stir in the chopped fresh herbs.

Serve the lamb steaks with the noodles on the side. Sprinkle with extra herbs, if you like, and lime wedges for squeezing over. This dish is equally good served hot straight from the hob or left to cool for tepid summer eating.

ingredients

4 lamb steaks or boneless
   chump chops
groundnut or sunflower oil
salt and pepper
fresh mint or coriander sprigs,
   to garnish
lime wedges, to serve

HERB NOODLES
juice of 1 lime
1 tbsp nam pla (Thai fish sauce)
½ tbsp sweet chilli sauce
1 tsp soft light brown sugar
½ tbsp sesame oil
250 g/9 oz dried thick Chinese egg
   noodles
5 tbsp finely chopped mint leaves
5 tbsp finely chopped coriander
   leaves

ingredients

1 tbsp melted butter

350 g/12 oz smoked fish, skinned

2 hard-boiled eggs, chopped

salt and pepper

25 g/1 oz butter

25 g/1 oz plain flour

300 ml/10 fl oz milk

55 g/2 oz Cheddar cheese, grated

pinch of cayenne pepper

1 tbsp freshly grated Parmesan
    cheese

brown toast slices, to serve

smoked fish pots

Preheat the oven to 180°C/350°F/Gas Mark 4.

Use the melted butter to grease 4 small soufflé dishes or ramekins.

Flake the fish onto a plate, mix with the chopped egg and season with a little pepper. Place the mixture into the prepared dishes.

Melt the butter in a saucepan over a medium heat and stir in the flour. Cook for 1 minute, stirring continuously. Remove from the heat and stir in the milk gradually until smooth. Return to a low heat and stir until the sauce comes to the boil and thickens. Reduce the heat and simmer gently, stirring constantly, until the sauce is creamy and smooth.

Add the grated cheese and stir until melted, then season with salt and pepper to taste and add the cayenne pepper. Pour the sauce over the fish and egg mixture and sprinkle over the Parmesan cheese.

Place the ramekins on a baking tray and cook in the oven for 10–15 minutes until bubbling and golden. Serve at once with brown toast.

ingredients

6 tbsp butter

1.3 kg/3 lb waxy potatoes, diced

3 garlic cloves, crushed

1 tsp paprika

2 tomatoes, peeled, deseeded
   and diced

12 eggs

pepper

FILLING

225 g/8 oz baby spinach

1 tsp fennel seeds

125 g/4½ oz feta cheese, diced
   (drained weight)

4 tbsp natural yogurt

feta & spinach omelette

Heat 1 tablespoon of the butter in a frying pan and cook the potatoes over a low heat, stirring, for 7–10 minutes until golden. Transfer to a bowl.

Add the garlic, paprika and tomatoes to the pan and cook for a further 2 minutes.

Whisk the eggs together and season with pepper. Pour the eggs into the potatoes and mix well.

Cook the spinach in boiling water for 1 minute until just wilted. Drain and refresh under cold running water. Pat dry with kitchen paper. Stir in the fennel seeds, feta cheese and the yogurt.

Heat a quarter of the remaining butter in a 15 cm/6 inch omelette pan. Ladle a quarter of the egg and potato mixture into the pan. Cook, turning once, for 2 minutes, until set.

Transfer the omelette to a serving plate. Spoon a quarter of the spinach mixture on to half of the omelette, then fold the omelette in half over the filling. Repeat to make 4 omelettes.

five-spice chicken with vegetables

Heat the oil in a preheated wok or large frying pan. Add the garlic and the sliced spring onions and stir-fry over a medium-high heat for 1 minute.

In a bowl, mix together the cornflour and rice wine, then add the mixture to the pan. Stir-fry for 1 minute, then add the chicken, five-spice powder, ginger and stock and cook for a further 4 minutes. Add the corn cobs and cook for 2 minutes, then add the beansprouts and cook for a further minute.

Remove from the heat, garnish with chopped spring onions, if using, and serve with freshly cooked jasmine rice.

ingredients

2 tbsp sesame oil

1 garlic clove, chopped

3 spring onions, trimmed and sliced

1 tbsp cornflour

2 tbsp rice wine

4 skinless chicken breasts, cut into strips

1 tbsp Chinese five-spice powder

1 tbsp grated fresh root ginger

125 ml/4 fl oz chicken stock

100 g/3½ oz baby corn cobs, sliced

300 g/10½ oz beansprouts

finely chopped spring onion, to garnish (optional)

freshly cooked jasmine rice, to serve

conchiglie with salmon, soured cream & mustard

Cook the pasta in plenty of boiling salted water until al dente. Drain and return to the pan. Add the soured cream, mustard, spring onions, smoked salmon and lemon peel to the pasta. Stir over a low heat until heated through. Season with pepper.

Transfer to a serving dish. Sprinkle with the chives. Serve warm or at room temperature.

ingredients

450 g/1 lb conchiglie or tagliatelle

300 ml/10 fl oz soured cream

2 tsp Dijon mustard

4 large spring onions, sliced finely

225 g/8 oz smoked salmon, cut into bite-sized pieces

finely grated peel of ½ lemon

pepper

2 tbsp chopped fresh chives

ingredients

115 g/4 oz baby sweetcorn

115 g/4 oz whole baby carrots

salt and pepper

175 g/6 oz shelled broad beans

175 g/6 oz whole green beans, cut
    into 2.5 cm/1 inch pieces

350 g/12 oz penne

300 ml/10 fl oz low-fat natural yogurt

1 tbsp chopped fresh parsley

1 tbsp snipped fresh chives

a few chives, to garnish

APRIL

29

SERVES 4

penne primavera

Cook the sweetcorn and carrots in boiling salted water for 5 minutes, or until tender,
then drain and rinse under cold running water. Cook the broad beans and green beans
in boiling salted water for 3–4 minutes, or until tender, then drain and rinse under cold
running water. If preferred, slip the skins off the broad beans.

Cook the pasta in a large saucepan of boiling salted water for 10 minutes or as directed
on the packet, until tender.

Meanwhile, put the yogurt, parsley, snipped chives, salt and pepper in a bowl and mix
them together.

Drain the cooked pasta and return to the pan. Add the vegetables and yogurt sauce, heat
gently and toss together, until hot.

Serve garnished with a few lengths of chives.

spicy pork risotto

SERVES 4

Cut off and discard the crust from the bread, then soak in the water or milk for 5 minutes to soften. Drain and squeeze well to remove all the liquid. Mix the bread, pork, garlic, onion, crushed peppercorns and salt together in a bowl. Add the egg and mix well.

Heat the corn oil in a frying pan over a medium heat. Form the meat mixture into balls and brown a few at a time in the oil. Remove from the pan, drain and set aside until all the meatballs are cooked.

Combine the tomatoes, tomato purée, oregano, fennel seeds and sugar in a heavy-based saucepan. Add the meatballs. Bring the sauce to the boil over a medium heat, then reduce the heat and simmer for 30 minutes, or until the meat is thoroughly cooked.

To make the risotto, bring the stock to the boil in a saucepan, then reduce the heat and keep simmering gently over a low heat while you are cooking the risotto.

Heat the olive oil with 25 g/1 oz of the butter in a deep saucepan over a medium heat until the butter has melted. Stir in the onion and cook, stirring occasionally, for 5 minutes, or until soft and starting to turn golden. Do not brown.

Reduce the heat, add the rice and mix to coat in oil and butter. Cook, stirring constantly, for 2–3 minutes, or until the grains are translucent.

Add the wine and cook, stirring constantly, for 1 minute until reduced. Gradually add the hot stock, a ladle at a time. Stir constantly and add more liquid as the rice absorbs each addition. Increase the heat to medium so that the liquid bubbles. Cook for 20 minutes, or until all the liquid is absorbed. Season to taste.

Lift out the cooked meatballs and add to the risotto. Remove the risotto from the heat and add the remaining butter. Mix well. Arrange the risotto and a few meatballs on plates. Drizzle with tomato sauce, garnish with basil and serve.

ingredients

1 thick slice white bread
water or milk, for soaking
450 g/1 lb fresh pork mince
2 garlic cloves, finely minced
1 tbsp finely chopped onion
1 tsp black peppercorns, lightly
  crushed
pinch of salt
1 egg
corn oil, for shallow-frying
400 g/14 oz canned chopped
  tomatoes
1 tbsp tomato purée
1 tsp dried oregano
1 tsp fennel seeds
pinch of sugar
1 litre/1¾ pints beef stock
1 tbsp olive oil
40 g/1½ oz butter
1 small onion, finely chopped
280 g/10 oz risotto rice
150 ml/5 fl oz red wine
salt and pepper
fresh basil leaves, to garnish

COOK'S TIP

For the best quality, it's always best to buy a lean, single piece of meat, trim off any fat and then mince it at home – either using a traditional mincer or in a food processor.

CHAPTER

5

May

eggs benedict with quick hollandaise sauce

Fill a wide frying pan three-quarters full with water and bring to the boil over a low heat. Reduce the heat to a simmer and add the vinegar. When the water is barely shimmering, carefully break the eggs into the pan. Leave for 1 minute, then, using a large spoon, gently loosen the eggs from the bottom of the pan. Leave to cook for a further 3 minutes, or until the white is cooked and the yolk is still soft, basting the top of the egg with the water from time to time.

Meanwhile, to make the hollandaise sauce, place the egg yolks in a blender or food processor. Melt the butter in a small saucepan until bubbling. With the motor running, gradually add the hot butter to the egg in a steady stream until the sauce is thick and creamy. Add the lemon juice, and a little warm water if the sauce is too thick, then season to taste with pepper. Transfer to a dish and keep warm.

Split the muffins and toast them on both sides. To serve, top each muffin with a slice of ham, a poached egg and a generous spoonful of hollandaise sauce.

ingredients

1 tbsp white wine vinegar

4 eggs

4 English muffins

4 slices good quality ham

QUICK HOLLANDAISE SAUCE

3 egg yolks

200 g/7 oz butter

1 tbsp lemon juice

pepper

COOK'S TIP

For best results when poaching eggs, break them into a cup first, then slide them into the hot water. Poach for a little longer than the suggested three minutes if you prefer firmer yolks.

CAUTION

Recipes using raw eggs should be avoided by infants, the elderly, pregnant women, convalescents, and anyone suffering from an illness.

ingredients

115 g/4 oz butter, plus extra
    for greasing
450 g/1 lb plain flour, plus extra
    for dusting
2 tsp ground ginger
1 tsp mixed spice
2 tsp bicarbonate of soda
100 g/3½ oz golden syrup
115 g/4 oz light muscovado sugar
1 egg, beaten

TO DECORATE

currants
glacé cherries
85 g/3 oz icing sugar
3–4 tsp water

MAY

2

MAKES 20

COOK'S TIP

*At Christmas, cut out star and bell
shapes. When the biscuits come out
of the oven, pierce a hole in each
with a skewer. Thread through
ribbons and hang on the tree.*

gingerbread people

Preheat the oven to 160°C/325°F/Gas Mark 3, then grease 3 large baking sheets. Sift
the flour, ginger, mixed spice and bicarbonate of soda into a large bowl. Place the butter,
syrup and sugar in a saucepan over a low heat and stir until melted. Pour on to the dry
ingredients and add the egg. Mix together to make a dough. The dough will be sticky
to begin with, but will become firmer as it cools.

On a lightly floured work surface, roll out the dough to about 3 mm/⅛ inch thick and stamp
out gingerbread people shapes. Place on the prepared baking sheets. Re-knead and re-roll
the trimmings and cut out more shapes until the dough is used up. Decorate with currants
for eyes and pieces of cherry for mouths. Bake in the oven for 15–20 minutes,
or until firm and lightly browned.

Remove from the oven and leave to cool on the baking sheets for a few minutes, then
transfer to wire racks to cool completely. Mix the icing sugar with the water to a thick
consistency. Place the icing in a small polythene bag and cut a tiny hole in one corner.
Pipe buttons or clothes shapes on to the cooled biscuits.

rösti with roasted vegetables

For the roasted vegetables, mix the oil, vinegar and honey together in a large, shallow dish. Add the red pepper, courgettes, onions, fennel, tomatoes, garlic and rosemary to the dish and toss in the marinade. Leave to marinate for at least 1 hour.

Preheat the oven to 200°C/400°F/Gas Mark 6. Cook the potatoes in a saucepan of lightly salted boiling water for 8–10 minutes, or until partially cooked. Leave to cool, then coarsely grate.

Transfer the vegetables, except the tomatoes and garlic, and the marinade to a roasting tin. Roast in the preheated oven for 25 minutes, then add the tomatoes and garlic and roast for a further 15 minutes, or until the vegetables are tender and slightly blackened around the edges.

Meanwhile, cook the rösti. Take each quarter of the potato mixture in your hands and form into a roughly shaped cake. Heat just enough oil to cover the base of a frying pan over a medium heat. Put the cakes, 2 at a time, into the pan and flatten with a spatula to form rounds about 2 cm/¾ inch thick.

Cook the rösti for 6 minutes on each side, or until golden brown and crisp. Mix the dressing ingredients. To serve, top each rösti with the roasted vegetables and drizzle with a little pesto dressing. Season to taste.

ingredients

900 g/2 lb potatoes, halved if large

salt

sunflower oil, for frying

ROASTED VEGETABLES

2 tbsp extra virgin olive oil

1 tbsp balsamic vinegar

1 tsp clear honey

1 red pepper, deseeded and
  quartered

2 courgettes, sliced lengthways

2 red onions, quartered

1 small fennel bulb, cut into thin
  wedges

16 vine-ripened tomatoes

8 garlic cloves

2 fresh rosemary sprigs

salt and pepper

PESTO DRESSING

2 tbsp pesto

1 tbsp boiling water

1 tbsp extra virgin olive oil

chicken livers in red wine & thyme

MAY

4

SERVES 4

Rinse the chicken livers under cold running water and pat dry with kitchen paper. Heat the lemon-flavoured oil in a frying pan. Add the garlic and cook, stirring, over a medium heat for 2 minutes. Add the chicken livers, wine and thyme. Season with salt and pepper and cook for 3 minutes.

Meanwhile, arrange the rocket leaves on a large serving platter. Remove the pan from the heat and spoon the chicken livers over the bed of rocket. Pour over the cooking juices, then garnish with sprigs of fresh thyme and serve with fresh crusty bread.

ingredients

250 g/9 oz fresh chicken livers

3 tbsp lemon-flavoured oil

2 garlic cloves, finely chopped

4 tbsp red wine

1 tbsp chopped fresh thyme

salt and pepper

sprigs of fresh thyme, to garnish

rocket leaves and fresh crusty
    bread, to serve

5

SERVES 4

ingredients

225 g/8 oz fresh young spinach
leaves
115 g/4 oz cooked ham
1 litre/1¾ pints chicken stock
1 tbsp olive oil
40 g/1½ oz butter
1 small onion, finely chopped
280 g/10 oz risotto rice
150 ml/5 fl oz dry white wine
50 ml/2 fl oz single cream
85 g/3 oz freshly grated Parmesan
or Grana Padano cheese
salt and pepper

shredded spinach & ham risotto

Wash the spinach well and slice into thin shreds. Cut the ham into thin strips.

Bring the stock to the boil in a saucepan, then reduce the heat and keep simmering gently over a low heat while you are cooking the risotto.

Heat the oil with 25 g/1 oz of the butter in a deep saucepan over a medium heat until the butter has melted. Add the onion and cook, stirring occasionally, for 5 minutes, or until soft and starting to turn golden. Do not brown.

Reduce the heat, add the rice and mix to coat in oil and butter. Cook, stirring constantly, for 2–3 minutes, or until the grains are translucent.

Add the wine and cook, stirring constantly, for 1 minute until reduced.

VARIATION
For a spicier flavour, you could substitute salami for the ham. Make sure that you peel off any rind before cutting the slices into strips.

Gradually add the hot stock, a ladle at a time. Stir constantly and add more liquid as the rice absorbs each addition. Increase the heat to medium so that the liquid bubbles. Cook for 20 minutes, or until all the liquid is absorbed and the rice is creamy. Add the spinach and ham with the last ladleful of stock.

Remove the risotto from the heat and add the remaining butter and the cream. Mix well, then stir in the Parmesan until it melts. Season to taste and serve immediately.

ingredients

450 g/1 lb undyed smoked haddock,
   skinned
2 tbsp olive oil
1 onion, finely chopped
1 tsp mild curry paste
175 g/6 oz long-grain rice
salt and pepper
55 g/2 oz butter
3 hard-boiled eggs
2 tbsp chopped fresh parsley,
   to garnish

MAY

6

SERVES 4

VARIATION
Kedgeree can also be made
with salmon.

spicy haddock rice

Place the fish in a large saucepan and cover with water. Bring the water to the boil, then turn down to a simmer and poach the fish for 8–10 minutes until it flakes easily.

Remove the fish and keep warm, reserving the water in a jug or bowl.

Add the oil to the saucepan and gently soften the onion for about 4 minutes. Stir in the curry paste and add the rice.

Measure 600 ml/1 pint of the haddock water and return to the saucepan. Bring to a simmer and cover. Cook for 10–12 minutes until the rice is tender and the water has been absorbed. Season to taste with salt and pepper.

Flake the fish and add to the saucepan with the butter. Stir very gently over a low heat until the butter has melted. Chop 2 of the hard-boiled eggs and add to the saucepan.

Turn the kedgeree into a serving dish, slice the remaining egg and use to garnish. Scatter the parsley over and serve at once.

7

stuffed peppers with cheese

Preheat the oven to 190°C/375°F/Gas Mark 5. Cut the peppers in half lengthways and deseed. Blanch in a large saucepan of boiling water for 5 minutes. Remove with a slotted spoon and drain upside down.

Pour the stock into a separate saucepan, add the rice and bring to the boil. Reduce the heat, cover and simmer for 15 minutes. Remove from the heat and reserve, covered, for 5 minutes, then drain. Heat the oil in a frying pan, add the onion and cook, stirring occasionally, for 5 minutes, or until softened. Add the garlic, mushrooms, tomatoes and carrot and season to taste. Cover and cook for 5 minutes.

Stir the rice, parsley, goat's cheese and pine kernels into the vegetable mixture. Place the pepper halves, cut-side up, in a roasting tin or ovenproof dish. Divide the rice and vegetable mixture between them. Sprinkle with Parmesan cheese and bake in the preheated oven for 20 minutes, or until the cheese is golden. Serve.

ingredients

4 large red, yellow or green peppers

450 ml/16 fl oz vegetable stock

200 g/7 oz long-grain rice

2 tbsp olive oil

1 onion, chopped

2 garlic cloves, finely chopped

115 g/4 oz chestnut mushrooms, chopped

4 tomatoes, peeled and chopped

1 carrot, diced

salt and pepper

1 tbsp chopped fresh parsley

100 g/3½ oz goat's cheese, crumbled

55 g/2 oz pine kernels

25 g/1 oz freshly grated Parmesan cheese

COOK'S TIP

The colour of peppers depends on what stage of development they are at when they are picked. If you prefer a sweeter taste, pick orange and red peppers, which are riper than young green peppers.

quick mackerel pâté

Remove and discard any remaining bones from the mackerel fillets and put the fish into a small bowl. Mash the fish with a fork and combine with the yogurt, parsley and lemon juice and rind. Season to taste with pepper.

Divide the pâté between 4 ramekins. Cover and refrigerate until required or serve immediately.

To serve, garnish the pâté with lemon wedges and parsley sprigs and serve with the prepared vegetables and toasted bread.

ingredients

250 g/9 oz skinless smoked
    mackerel fillets
150 g/51/2 oz low-fat natural yogurt
1 tbsp chopped fresh parsley
1 tbsp lemon juice
finely grated rind of 1/2 lemon
freshly ground black pepper

TO GARNISH

4 lemon wedges
few sprigs of fresh parsley

TO SERVE

1 red pepper, deseeded and cut into
    chunky strips
1 yellow pepper, deseeded and cut
    into chunky strips
2 carrots, cut into strips
2 celery sticks, cut into strips
slices wholemeal or white bread,
    toasted and cut into triangles

MAY
8

SERVES 4

crispy roast asparagus

Preheat the oven to 200°C/400°F/Gas Mark 6.

Choose asparagus spears of similar widths. Trim the base of the spears so that all the stems are approximately the same length.

Arrange the asparagus in a single layer on a baking sheet. Drizzle with the oil and sprinkle with the salt.

Place the baking sheet in the oven and roast the asparagus for 10–15 minutes, turning the spears once. Remove from the oven and transfer to a warmed dish. Serve immediately, sprinkled with grated Parmesan cheese.

ingredients

450 g/1 lb asparagus spears
2 tbsp extra virgin olive oil
1 tsp coarse sea salt
1 tbsp freshly grated Parmesan
    cheese, to serve

COOK'S TIP

As well as there being both green
and white varieties of asparagus,
there is considerable variation in
width, so it is important to try to find
spears of a similar size. Otherwise,
some will be tender while others
require further cooking. As a general
rule, the stems of green asparagus
rarely need peeling, but those of
white asparagus do.

MAY
9

SERVES 4

MAY 10

SERVES 4

spaghetti alla carbonara

Bring a large, heavy-based saucepan of lightly salted water to the boil. Add the pasta, return to the boil and cook for 8–10 minutes, or until tender but still firm to the bite.

Meanwhile, cook the bacon and garlic in a heavy-based, dry frying pan over a medium heat for 5 minutes, or until crisp-tender. Remove from the frying pan and drain on some kitchen paper.

Drain the pasta and return it to the saucepan, but do not return to the heat. Add the bacon and garlic and the eggs. Season to taste with salt and pepper. Toss thoroughly with 2 large forks. Add half the Parmesan cheese and toss again. Transfer to a warmed serving dish, sprinkle with the remaining Parmesan cheese and serve immediately.

ingredients

450 g/1 lb dried spaghetti

175 g/6 oz rindless streaky bacon, diced

1 garlic clove, finely chopped

3 eggs, lightly beaten

salt and pepper

4 tbsp fresh Parmesan cheese shavings

MAY 11

MAKES 1 X 250-ML/
9-FL OZ JAR

oven-dried tomatoes

Preheat the oven to 120°C/250°F/Gas Mark ½.

Using a sharp knife, cut each of the tomatoes into quarters.

Using a teaspoon, scoop out the seeds and discard. If the tomatoes are large, cut each quarter in half lengthways again.

Sprinkle sea salt in a roasting tin and arrange the tomato slices, skin-side down, on top. Roast in the oven for 2½ hours, or until the edges are just starting to look charred and the flesh is dry, but still pliable. The exact roasting time and yield will depend on the size and juiciness of the tomatoes. Check the tomatoes at 30-minute intervals after 1½ hours.

Remove the dried tomatoes from the roasting tin and leave to cool completely. Put in a 250-ml/9-fl oz preserving jar and pour over enough oil to cover. Seal the jar tightly and store in the refrigerator, where the tomatoes will keep for up to 2 weeks.

ingredients

1 kg/2 lb 4 oz large, juicy, full-flavoured tomatoes

extra virgin olive oil

sea salt

bacon with lamb's lettuce

Heat 2 teaspoons of the oil in a large, heavy-based frying pan. Add the bacon and cook over a medium heat for 5 minutes, or until crisp. Remove from the frying pan and drain on kitchen paper. Add the garlic and bread to the frying pan and cook, stirring and tossing frequently, until crisp and golden brown on all sides. Remove from the pan and drain on kitchen paper.

Place the red wine vinegar, balsamic vinegar, mustard and remaining sunflower oil in a screw-top jar and shake vigorously, then pour into a bowl. Alternatively, mix the vinegars and mustard together in a bowl and whisk in the oil until the dressing is creamy. Season with salt and pepper.

Add the lamb's lettuce and bacon to the dressing and toss to coat. Divide the salad among plates, sprinkle with the croûtons and serve.

ingredients

6–8 tbsp sunflower oil

225 g/8 oz rindless streaky bacon, diced

2 garlic cloves, finely chopped

4 slices of white bread, crusts removed, cut into 1-cm/½-inch cubes

5 tbsp red wine vinegar

1 tbsp balsamic vinegar

2 tsp wholegrain mustard

salt and pepper

225 g/8 oz lamb's lettuce

COOK'S TIP

If you buy lamb's lettuce with the root still attached, leave it to stand in a bowl of iced water for 1 hour to refresh (if you have time).

deep-fried green chillies

EACH BAG
OF CHILLIES
SERVES 4–6

ingredients

olive oil

sweet or hot green chillies

sea salt

Heat 7.5 cm/3 inches of oil in a heavy-based saucepan until it reaches 190°C/375°F/Gas Mark 5, or until a day-old cube of bread turns brown in 30 seconds.

Rinse the chillies and pat very dry with kitchen paper. Drop them in the hot oil for no longer than 20 seconds until they turn bright green and the skins blister.

Remove with a slotted spoon and drain well on crumpled kitchen paper. Sprinkle with sea salt and serve at once.

iced coffee with cream

Use the water and coffee granules to brew some hot coffee, then leave to cool to room temperature. Transfer to a jug, cover with clingfilm and chill in the refrigerator for at least 45 minutes.

When the coffee has chilled, pour it into a food processor. Add the sugar, and process until well combined. Add the ice cubes and process until smooth.

Pour the mixture into glasses. Float single cream on the top, decorate with whole coffee beans and serve.

ingredients
400 ml/14 fl oz water
2 tbsp instant coffee granules
2 tbsp brown sugar
6 ice cubes

DECORATION
single cream
whole coffee beans

MAY 14

SERVES 2

---

macaroni cheese

Put the milk, onion, peppercorns, and bay leaf in a pan and bring to a boil. Remove from the heat and let stand for 15 minutes.

Melt the butter in a pan and stir in the flour until well combined and smooth. Cook over medium heat, stirring constantly, for 1 minute. Remove from the heat. Strain the milk and stir a little into the butter and flour mixture until well incorporated. Return to the heat and gradually add the remaining milk, stirring constantly, until it has all been incorporated. Cook for an additional 3 minutes, or until the sauce is smooth and thickened, then add the nutmeg, cream, and pepper to taste. Add the Cheddar and Roquefort cheeses and stir until melted.

Meanwhile, bring a large pan of water to a boil. Add the macaroni, then return to a boil and cook for 8–10 minutes, or until just tender. Drain well and add to the cheese sauce. Stir well together.

Preheat the broiler to high. Spoon the macaroni cheese into an ovenproof serving dish, then scatter over the Gruyère cheese and cook under the broiler until bubbling and brown.

ingredients
2½ cups milk
1 onion
8 peppercorns
1 bay leaf
scant 4 tbsp butter
scant ⅓ cup all-purpose flour
½ tsp ground nutmeg
⅓ cup heavy cream
3½ oz/100 g sharp Cheddar cheese, grated
3½ oz/100 g Roquefort cheese, crumbled
12 oz/350 g dried macaroni
3½ oz/100 g Gruyère or Emmental cheese, grated
pepper

MAY 15

SERVES 4

artichoke heart soufflé

Preheat the oven to 190°C/375°F/Gas Mark 5. Grease a 1.7-litre/3-pint soufflé dish with butter, then tie a double strip of greaseproof paper around the dish so that it protrudes about 5 cm/2 inches above the rim.

Melt the butter in a large, heavy-based saucepan. Add the flour and cook, stirring constantly, for 2 minutes. Remove from the heat and gradually stir in the milk. Return to the heat and bring to the boil, whisking constantly, for 2 minutes, or until thickened and smooth. Remove from the heat, season with nutmeg, salt and pepper, then beat in the cream, cheese and artichoke hearts. Beat in the egg yolks, 1 at a time.

Whisk the egg-whites in a clean, greasefree bowl until stiff peaks form. Fold 2 tablespoons of the egg whites into the artichoke mixture to loosen, then gently fold in the remainder.

Carefully pour the mixture into the prepared soufflé dish and bake in the preheated oven for 35 minutes, or until the soufflé is well risen and the top is golden. Serve immediately.

ingredients

4 tbsp butter, plus extra
   for greasing
6 tbsp plain flour
300 ml/10 fl oz milk
pinch of freshly grated nutmeg
salt and pepper
2 tbsp single cream
55 g/2 oz Emmenthal cheese,
   grated
6 canned artichoke hearts,
   drained and mashed
4 egg yolks
5 egg whites

VARIATION

*For spinach soufflé, substitute
225 g/8 oz of cooked, drained
and chopped spinach for the
artichoke hearts.*

ingredients

250 g/9 oz plain flour, plus extra
for dusting
1 tsp baking powder
pinch of salt
150 g/5½ oz golden caster sugar
2 eggs, beaten
finely grated rind of 1 unwaxed
orange
100 g/3½ oz whole blanched
almonds, lightly toasted

VARIATION

*As an alternative to almonds, use
hazelnuts or a mixture of almonds
and pistachio nuts.*

almond biscotti

Preheat the oven to 180°C/350°F/Gas Mark 4, then lightly dust a baking sheet with flour.
Sift the flour, baking powder and salt into a bowl. Add the sugar, eggs and orange rind
and mix to a dough. Knead in the toasted almonds.

Roll out the dough into a ball, cut in half and roll out each portion into a log about
4 cm/1½ inches in diameter. Place on the floured baking sheet and bake in the oven
for 10 minutes. Remove from the oven and leave to cool for 5 minutes.

Using a serrated knife, cut the logs into 1-cm/½-inch thick diagonal slices. Arrange the
slices on the baking sheet and return to the oven for 15 minutes, or until slightly golden.
Transfer to a wire rack to cool and crispen.

mushroom bites with aîoli

Preheat the oven to 190°C/375°F/Gas Mark 5. To make the aïoli, put the garlic in a bowl, add a pinch of salt and mash with the back of a spoon. Add the egg yolks and beat with an electric whisk for 30 seconds, or until creamy. Start beating in the oil, one drop at a time. As the mixture begins to thicken, add the oil in a steady stream, beating constantly. Season to taste with salt and pepper, cover the bowl with clingfilm and chill in the refrigerator until required.

Line a large baking sheet with baking paper. Grate the bread into breadcrumbs and place them in a bowl with the Parmesan cheese and paprika. Lightly whisk the egg whites in a separate clean bowl, then dip each mushroom first into the egg whites, then into the breadcrumbs, and place on the prepared baking sheet.

Bake in the preheated oven for 15 minutes, or until the coating is crisp and golden. Serve immediately with the aîoli.

ingredients

115 g/4 oz fresh white bread

2 tbsp freshly grated Parmesan cheese

1 tsp paprika

2 egg whites

225 g/8 oz button mushrooms

AÏOLI

4 garlic cloves, crushed

salt and pepper

2 egg yolks

225 ml/8 fl oz extra virgin olive oil

VARIATION

For a herb cream dip, mix 4 tablespoons of chopped herbs with 200 ml/7 fl oz soured cream, 1 chopped garlic clove, lemon juice and seasoning to taste.

ingredients

4 duck legs, all visible fat trimmed
    off
800 g/1 lb 12 oz canned tomatoes,
    chopped
8 garlic cloves, peeled, but left
    whole
1 large onion, chopped
1 carrot, peeled and chopped finely
1 celery stick, peeled and chopped
    finely
3 sprigs fresh thyme
100 g/3½ oz Spanish green olives
    stuffed with pimientos in brine,
    rinsed
salt and pepper
1 tsp finely grated orange rind

MAY

19

SERVES 4

duck legs with olives

Put the duck legs in the bottom of a flameproof casserole or a large, heavy-based frying pan with a tight-fitting lid. Add the tomatoes, garlic, onion, carrot, celery, thyme and olives and stir together. Season with salt and pepper to taste.

Turn the heat to high and cook, uncovered, until the ingredients begin to bubble. Reduce the heat to low, cover tightly and simmer for 1¼–1½ hours until the duck is very tender. Check occasionally and add a little water if the mixture appears to be drying out.

When the duck is tender, transfer it to a serving platter, cover and keep hot in a preheated warm oven. Leave the casserole uncovered, increase the heat to medium and cook, stirring, for about 10 minutes until the mixture forms a sauce. Stir in the orange rind, then taste and adjust the seasoning if necessary.

Mash the tender garlic cloves with a fork and spread over the duck legs. Spoon the sauce over the top. Serve at once.

sweet chilli squid

Place the sesame seeds on a baking sheet, toast under a hot grill and set aside. Heat 1 tablespoon of oil in a frying pan over a medium heat. Add the squid and cook for 2 minutes. Remove from the pan and set aside.

Add the other tablespoon of oil to the pan and fry the peppers and shallots over a medium heat for 1 minute. Add the mushrooms and fry for another 2 minutes.

Return the squid to the pan and add the sherry, soy sauce, sugar, chilli flakes and garlic, stirring thoroughly. Cook for a further 2 minutes.

Sprinkle with the toasted sesame seeds, drizzle over the sesame oil and mix. Serve on a bed of rice.

ingredients

1 tbsp sesame seeds, toasted

2 tbsp sesame oil

280 g/10 oz squid, cut into strips

2 red peppers, sliced thinly

3 shallots, sliced thinly

85 g/3 oz mushrooms, sliced thinly

1 tbsp dry sherry

4 tbsp soy sauce

1 tsp sugar

1 tsp hot chilli flakes, or to taste

1 clove of garlic, crushed

1 tsp sesame oil

freshly cooked rice, to serve

chicken with forty cloves of garlic

Preheat the oven to 180°C/350°F/Gas Mark 4. Season the chicken inside and out with salt and pepper, then truss with fine string or elastic string. Place on a rack in a casserole dish and arrange the garlic and herbs around it.

Pour the wine over the chicken and cover with a tight-fitting lid. Cook in the oven for 1½–1¾ hours, or until tender and the juices run clear when a skewer is inserted into the thickest part of the meat.

Transfer the chicken and garlic to a dish and keep warm. Strain the cooking juices into a jug. Carve the meat. Skim off any fat on the surface of the cooking juices.

Divide the chicken and garlic among serving plates. Spoon over a little of the cooking juices. Serve immediately with freshly cooked green beans, handing round the remaining cooking juices separately.

ingredients

1 chicken, weighing 1.6 kg/3 lb 8 oz

salt and pepper

3 garlic bulbs, separated into cloves but unpeeled

6 fresh thyme sprigs

2 fresh tarragon sprigs

2 bay leaves

300 ml/10 fl oz dry white wine

freshly cooked beans, to serve

chicken tikka

Place the chicken in a large glass bowl. Add the garlic, ginger, yogurt, lemon juice, chilli powder, turmeric and coriander and stir well. Cover with clingfilm and leave to marinate in the refrigerator for up to 8 hours.

Preheat a griddle or barbecue. To make the raita, cut the cucumber into thick slices, then chop finely. Place the cucumber and chilli in a bowl and beat in the yogurt with a fork. Stir in the cumin and season to taste with salt. Cover and leave to chill in the refrigerator until required.

Thread the chicken cubes on to presoaked wooden skewers and brush with oil. Cook the chicken over medium heat, turning and brushing frequently with oil, until thoroughly cooked. Briefly heat the naan bread on the griddle or barbecue. Remove the chicken from the skewers and place on individual serving plates. Garnish with onion rings, coriander sprigs and lemon wedges and serve with the naan bread and the raita.

ingredients

500 g/1 lb 2 oz skinless, boneless
   chicken, cut into 5-cm/2-inch
   cubes
1 garlic clove, finely chopped
1-cm/½-inch piece fresh root
   ginger, finely chopped
150 ml/5 fl oz natural yogurt
4 tbsp lemon juice
1 tsp chilli powder
¼ tsp ground turmeric
1 tbsp chopped fresh coriander
vegetable oil, for brushing
naan bread, to serve

RAITA

½ cucumber
1 fresh green chilli, deseeded
   and finely chopped
300 ml/10 fl oz natural yogurt
¼ tsp ground cumin
salt

TO GARNISH

thinly sliced onion rings
fresh coriander sprigs
lemon wedges

COOK'S TIP

*Fresh chillies can burn the skin
several hours after chopping, so it
is advisable to wear gloves when
handling them. Alternatively, wash
your hands thoroughly afterwards.*

turkey with bamboo shoots & water chestnuts

Blend the sherry, lemon juice, soy sauce, ginger and garlic in a bowl, then add the turkey and stir. Cover the dish with clingfilm and refrigerate to marinate for 3–4 hours.

In a wok or frying pan, add the sesame oil and vegetable oil and heat slowly. Remove the turkey from the marinade with a slotted spoon (reserving the marinade) and stir-fry a few pieces at a time until browned. Remove the turkey from the pan and set aside.

Add the mushrooms, green pepper and courgette to the pan and stir-fry for 3 minutes. Add the spring onions and stir-fry for 1 minute more. Add the bamboo shoots and water chestnuts to the pan, then the turkey along with half of the reserved marinade. Stir over a medium-high heat for another 2–3 minutes, until the ingredients are evenly coated and the marinade has reduced.

Serve immediately over noodles or rice.

ingredients

MARINADE

4 tbsp sweet sherry

1 tbsp lemon juice

1 tbsp soy sauce

2 tsp grated fresh root ginger

1 clove garlic, crushed

STIR-FRY

450 g/1 lb turkey breast, cubed

1 tbsp sesame oil

2 tbsp vegetable oil

125 g/4½ oz small mushrooms, cut into halves

1 green pepper, cut into strips

1 courgette, sliced thinly

4 spring onions, cut into quarters

115 g/4 oz canned bamboo shoots, drained

115 g/4 oz canned sliced water chestnuts, drained

freshly cooked noodles, to serve

double chocolate chip cookies

Preheat the oven to 180°C/350°F/Gas Mark 4, then grease 3 baking sheets. Place the butter, granulated sugar and muscovado sugar in a bowl and beat until light and fluffy. Gradually beat in the egg and vanilla essence.

Sift the flour, cocoa and bicarbonate of soda into the mixture and stir in carefully. Stir in the chocolate chips and walnuts. Drop dessertspoonfuls of the mixture on to the prepared baking sheets, spaced well apart to allow for spreading.

Bake in the oven for 10–15 minutes, or until the mixture has spread and the cookies are beginning to feel firm. Leave to cool on the baking sheets for 2 minutes, then transfer to wire racks to cool completely.

MAY

24

MAKES 24

ingredients

115 g/4 oz butter, softened, plus
    extra for greasing
55 g/2 oz golden granulated sugar
55 g/2 oz light muscovado sugar
1 egg, beaten
½ tsp vanilla essence
115 g/4 oz plain flour
2 tbsp cocoa powder
½ tsp bicarbonate of soda
115 g/4 oz milk chocolate chips
55 g/2 oz walnuts, roughly chopped

chilli roast potatoes

Preheat the oven to 200°C/400°F/Gas Mark 6. Cook the potatoes in a large saucepan of boiling water for 10 minutes, then drain thoroughly.

Meanwhile, pour a little of the oil into a shallow roasting tin to coat the base. Heat the oil in the oven for 10 minutes, then remove the tin from the oven. Add the potatoes and brush them with the hot oil.

Mix the chilli powder, caraway seeds and salt together in a small bowl, then sprinkle the mixture evenly over the potatoes, turning them to coat. Add the remaining oil to the tin and return to the oven to roast for 15 minutes, or until the potatoes are cooked through and golden brown.

Using a slotted spoon, remove the potatoes from the tin, draining well, transfer to a large warmed serving dish and serve immediately.

MAY

25

SERVES 4

ingredients

500 g/1 lb 2 oz small new potatoes,
    scrubbed
150 ml/5 fl oz vegetable oil
1 tsp chilli powder
½ tsp caraway seeds
1 tsp salt

a spoonful of noodles

MAKES 12
SPOONFULS

Drop the noodles in a saucepan of boiling water and boil for 4 minutes, until soft. Alternatively, cook according to the packet instructions. Drain, rinse well to remove the excess starch and drain again.

Flake the crabmeat into a bowl. Stir in the parsley and 2 tablespoons of the lemon juice and add the salt, pepper and paprika. Add a little extra lemon juice, if you like. Toss the noodles with the crab salad.

Use only a small amount of noodles per spoon. Chinese soup spoons are inexpensive to buy from most Chinese food shops – use all one colour or a variety of Oriental patterns. If you don't have the spoons, serve bite-sized mounds of the noodle salad on slices of cucumber or radicchio leaves that are firm enough to pick up.

Using a fork, swirl the noodles and crab into a small mound, then place it in the spoon, with any loose ends tucked underneath. Continue until all the ingredients are used.

VARIATION
For an alternative flavour, toss the noodles with drained, flaked tuna, chopped capers, coriander and lime juice to taste.

You can make the salad and assemble it in the spoons in advance, but be sure to take them out of the refrigerator 15 minutes before you serve, so the flavours aren't dulled.

ingredients

55 g/2 oz dried thin buckwheat noodles, or any other thin noodles, such as Japanese somen

115 g/4 oz canned crabmeat (drained weight), any excess liquid squeezed out

2 tbsp very finely chopped fresh parsley

about 2 tbsp fresh lemon juice

salt and pepper

pinch of paprika

SERVES 4

layered vegetable bake

Preheat the oven to 180°C/350°F/Gas Mark 4. Brush a large ovenproof dish with a little of the olive oil. Prepare all the vegetables. Peel and thinly slice the potatoes, trim and slice the leeks and slice the tomatoes. Place a layer of potato slices in the base of the dish, sprinkle with half the basil leaves and cover with a layer of leeks. Top with a layer of tomato slices. Repeat these layers until all the vegetables are used up, ending with a layer of potatoes.

Stir the garlic into the vegetable stock and season to taste with salt and pepper. Pour the stock over the vegetables and brush the top with the remaining olive oil.

Bake in the preheated oven for 1½ hours, or until the vegetables are tender and the topping is golden brown. Serve immediately.

ingredients

1 tbsp olive oil, for brushing

675 g/1 lb 8 oz potatoes

2 leeks

2 beef tomatoes

8 fresh basil leaves

1 garlic clove, finely chopped

300 ml/10 fl oz vegetable stock

salt and pepper

chicken kebabs with yogurt sauce

To make the marinade, put the yogurt, garlic, lemon juice, herbs and salt and pepper in a large bowl and mix well together.

Cut the chicken breasts into chunks measuring about 4 cm/1½ inches square. Add to the yogurt mixture and toss well together until the chicken pieces are coated. Cover and leave to marinate in the fridge for about 1 hour. If you are using wooden skewers, soak them in cold water for 30 minutes.

Preheat the grill. Thread the pieces of chicken onto 8 flat, greased, metal kebab skewers, wooden skewers or rosemary stalks and place on a greased grill pan.

Cook the kebabs under the grill for about 15 minutes, turning and basting with the remaining marinade occasionally, until lightly browned and tender.

Pour the remaining marinade into a saucepan and heat gently but do not boil. Serve the kebabs on a bed of shredded lettuce and garnish with the lemon wedges. Accompany with the yogurt sauce.

ingredients

4 large skinned, boned chicken
 breasts
oil, for greasing
shredded Cos lettuce, to serve
lemon wedges, to garnish
YOGURT MARINADE
300 ml/½ pint Greek yogurt
2 garlic cloves, crushed
juice of ½ lemon
1 tbsp chopped fresh herbs such as
 oregano, dill, tarragon or parsley
salt and pepper

asparagus with poached eggs & parmesan

Bring 2 saucepans of water to the boil. Add the asparagus to 1 saucepan, return to a simmer and cook for 5 minutes, or until just tender.

Meanwhile, reduce the heat of the second saucepan to a simmer and carefully crack in the eggs, one at a time. Poach for 3 minutes, or until the whites are just set but the yolks are still soft. Remove with a slotted spoon.

Drain the asparagus and divide between 4 warmed plates. Top each plate of asparagus with an egg and shave over the cheese. Season to taste with pepper and serve immediately.

ingredients

300 g/10½ oz asparagus, trimmed
4 large eggs
85 g/3 oz Parmesan cheese
pepper

courgette pasta sauce
with lemon & rosemary

Heat the olive oil in a large frying pan over a medium–low heat. Add the onion and gently fry, stirring occasionally, for about 10 minutes until golden.

Raise the heat to medium–high. Add the garlic, rosemary and parsley. Cook for a few seconds, stirring.

Add the courgettes and lemon peel. Cook for 5–7 minutes, stirring occasionally, until the courgettes are just tender. Season with salt and pepper. Remove from the heat.

Cook the pasta in plenty of boiling salted water until al dente. Drain and transfer to a warm serving dish.

Briefly reheat the courgettes. Pour over the pasta and toss well to mix. Sprinkle with the Parmesan and serve immediately.

ingredients

6 tbsp olive oil

1 small onion, sliced very thinly

2 garlic cloves, chopped very finely

2 tbsp chopped fresh rosemary

1 tbsp chopped fresh flat-leaf
  parsley

450 g/1 lb small courgettes, cut into
  4 cm x 5 mm/1½ x ¼ inch strips

finely grated peel of 1 lemon

salt and pepper

450 g/1 lb fusilli

4 tbsp freshly grated Parmesan

SERVES 4

ingredients

2 pork fillets, weighing
    350 g/12 oz each

salt and pepper

2 thin slices of cooked ham or
    Parma ham

85 g/3 oz Lancashire cheese,
    crumbled

4 ready-to-eat prunes, cut in half

4 fresh sage leaves, chopped

25 g/1 oz butter

225 ml/8 fl oz cider or apple juice

1 tsp mild mustard

125 ml/4 fl oz single cream

lancashire cheese-stuffed pork fillet

Preheat the oven to 190°C/375°F/Gas Mark 5.

Cut the fillets down the centre, but do not cut right through. Spread them open and flatten out. You can bash the fillets with a rolling pin to flatten them out more if you wish.

Season the fillets well with salt and pepper and place a piece of ham on each one. Crumble over the cheese and arrange the prunes in between. Sprinkle over the sage leaves.

Fold the fillets over into neat sausage shapes and secure with cocktail sticks or tie with string to make sure they keep their shape.

Place in a small roasting tin, dot with the butter and pour over the cider.

Cover with foil and cook in the oven for 40–45 minutes, removing the foil for the last 10 minutes.

Remove the tin from the oven and place the pork on a warm plate. Remove the cocktail sticks or string and allow to rest for 10 minutes in a warm place.

Place the roasting tin on the stove over a medium heat and stir the juices well to mix. Add the mustard and bubble away until the sauce is quite thick. Stir in the cream and heat through.

Slice the pork across diagonally and serve the sauce separately.

CHAPTER
6

June

lemon granita

Heat the water in a heavy-based saucepan over a low heat. Add the sugar and stir until it has completely dissolved. Bring to the boil, remove the saucepan from the heat and set the syrup aside to cool.

Stir the lemon juice and rind into the syrup. Pour the mixture into a freezerproof container and place in the freezer for 3–4 hours.

To serve, remove the container from the freezer and dip the base into hot water. Turn out the ice block and chop coarsely, then place in a food processor and process until it forms small crystals (granita means 'granular'). Spoon into sundae glasses and serve immediately.

SERVES 4

ingredients

450 ml/16 fl oz water

115 g/4 oz white granulated sugar

225 ml/8 fl oz lemon juice

grated rind of 1 lemon

COOK'S TIP

An ordinary blender may not be sufficiently robust to process the ice as it can damage the blades. A good-quality food processor is recommended.

VARIATION

Many different fruit syrups can be used to flavour granitas – oranges, mandarins, pink grapefruit or mangoes. Simply substitute the juice in step 2. You can add extra flavour with a splash of liqueur or include herbs, such as lemon balm, or elderflower in the syrup in step 1 (strain before pouring into the freezer container). Coffee granita made with espresso coffee instead of fruit juice, with or without a dash of liqueur, is also delicious.

ingredients

4 boneless chicken breasts

1 bay leaf

1 small onion, sliced

1 carrot, sliced

salt and pepper

4 peppercorns

1 tbsp olive oil

2 shallots, finely chopped

2 tsp mild curry paste

2 tsp tomato purée

juice of ½ lemon

300 ml/10 fl oz mayonnaise

150 ml/5 fl oz natural yogurt

85 g/3 oz ready-to-eat dried apricots, chopped

2 tbsp chopped fresh parsley, to garnish

SERVES 6

coronation chicken

Place the chicken breasts in a large saucepan with the bay leaf, onion and carrot. Cover with water and add ½ teaspoon salt and the peppercorns. Bring to the boil over a medium heat, reduce the heat and simmer very gently for 20–25 minutes. Remove from the heat and allow to cool in the liquor. Reserve 150 ml/½ pint of the stock for the sauce.

Meanwhile, heat the oil in a frying pan and sauté the shallots gently for 2–3 minutes until soft but not coloured. Stir in the curry paste and continue to cook for a further minute. Stir in the reserved stock, the tomato purée and the lemon juice and simmer for 10 minutes until the sauce is quite thick. Cool.

Remove the chicken from the stock, take off the skin and slice into neat pieces.

Mix together the mayonnaise and the yogurt and stir into the sauce. Add the chopped apricots and season to taste with salt and pepper.

Stir the chicken into the sauce until well coated and turn into a serving dish. Allow to stand for at least 1 hour for the flavours to mingle. Serve garnished with the chopped parsley.

tagliatelle with asparagus & gorgonzola

Place the asparagus tips in a single layer in a shallow ovenproof dish. Sprinkle with a little olive oil. Season with salt and pepper. Turn to coat in the oil and seasoning.

Roast in a preheated oven at 230°C/450°F/Gas Mark 8 for 10–12 minutes until slightly browned and just tender. Set aside and keep warm.

Combine the crumbled cheese with the cream in a bowl. Season with salt and pepper.

Cook the pasta in plenty of boiling salted water until al dente. Drain and transfer to a warm serving dish.

Immediately add the asparagus and the cheese mixture. Toss well until the cheese has melted and the pasta is coated with the sauce. Serve at once.

ingredients

450 g/1 lb asparagus tips

olive oil

salt and pepper

225 g/8 oz Gorgonzola, crumbled

175 ml/6 fl oz double cream

350 g/12 oz dried tagliatelle
    or penne

crispy coated chicken breasts

Preheat the oven to 200°C/400°F/Gas Mark 6. To make the potato wedges, bring a large saucepan of water to the boil. Add the potatoes, cook over a medium heat for 5 minutes, then drain. Pour 2 tablespoons of the oil into a bowl and stir in the chilli powder. Add the potatoes and turn in the mixture until coated. Transfer to a baking sheet, drizzle over the remaining oil and bake for 35–40 minutes, turning frequently, until golden and cooked through.

About 15 minutes before the end of the cooking time, put the hazelnuts, breadcrumbs, cheese and parsley into a bowl, season and mix. Dip the chicken breasts into the egg, then coat in the breadcrumb mixture. Heat the oil in a frying pan. Add the chicken and cook over a medium heat for 3–4 minutes on each side until golden. Lift out and drain on kitchen paper. Remove the potatoes from the oven, divide between 4 serving plates, and add a chicken breast to each. Garnish with parsley and serve with lemon wedges.

ingredients

SWEET POTATO WEDGES

4 large sweet potatoes, peeled and
   cut into wedges

4 tbsp vegetable oil

1 tsp chilli powder

50 g/1¾ oz hazelnuts, toasted and
   ground

25 g/1 oz dried white or wholemeal
   breadcrumbs

2 tbsp freshly grated pecorino
   cheese

1 tbsp chopped fresh parsley

salt and pepper

4 skinless chicken breasts

1 egg, beaten

4 tbsp vegetable oil

sprigs of fresh flat-leaved parsley,
   to garnish

wedges of lemon, to serve

SERVES 4

baked fish & chips

Preheat the oven to 200°C/400°F/Gas Mark 6. Line 2 baking sheets with non-stick liner.

Rinse the chipped potatoes under cold running water, then dry well on a clean tea towel. Put in a bowl, spray with oil and toss together until coated. Spread the chips on a baking sheet and cook in the oven for 40–45 minutes, turning once, until golden. Meanwhile, put the flour on a plate, beat the egg in a shallow dish and spread the seasoned breadcrumbs on a large plate. Dip the fish fillets in the flour to coat, then the egg, allowing any excess to drip off, and finally the breadcrumbs, patting them firmly into the fish. Place the fish in one layer on a baking sheet.

Fifteen minutes before the chips have cooked, bake the fish fillets in the oven for 10–15 minutes, turning them once during cooking, until the fish is tender. Serve the fish with the chips.

ingredients
450 g/1 lb floury potatoes, peeled
    and cut into thick, even-sized
    chips
vegetable oil spray
55 g/2 oz plain white flour
1 egg
55 g/2 oz fresh white breadcrumbs,
    seasoned with salt and pepper
4 cod or haddock fillets

spaghetti olio e aglio

Bring a large, heavy-based saucepan of lightly salted water to the boil. Add the pasta, return to the boil and cook for 8–10 minutes, or until tender but still firm to the bite.

Meanwhile, heat the olive oil in a heavy-based frying pan. Add the garlic and a pinch of salt and cook over a low heat, stirring constantly, for 3–4 minutes, or until golden. Do not allow the garlic to brown or it will taste bitter. Remove the frying pan from the heat.

Drain the pasta and transfer to a warmed serving dish. Pour in the garlic-flavoured olive oil, then add the chopped parsley and season to taste with salt and pepper. Toss well and serve immediately.

ingredients
450 g/1 lb dried spaghetti
125 ml/4 fl oz extra virgin olive oil
3 garlic cloves, finely chopped
3 tbsp chopped fresh flat-leaved
    parsley
salt and pepper

strawberry baked alaska

Preheat the oven to 240°C/475°F/Gas Mark 9. Place the sponge cake in a large, shallow, ovenproof dish and sprinkle with the sherry or orange juice.

Whisk the egg whites in a spotlessly clean, greasefree bowl until stiff. Continue to whisk, gradually adding the sugar, until very stiff and glossy.

Working quickly, cover the top of the cake with the ice cream and then top with the strawberry halves. Spread the meringue over the cake, making sure that the ice cream is completely covered. Bake in the preheated oven for 3–5 minutes, or until the meringue is golden brown. Serve immediately, with whole strawberries.

ingredients

23-cm/9-inch round sponge cake

2 tbsp sweet sherry or orange juice

5 egg whites

140 g/5 oz caster sugar

600 ml/1 pint strawberry ice cream

175 g/6 oz fresh strawberries,
    halved, plus whole strawberries,
    to serve

JUNE

7

SERVES 4

COOK'S TIP

For the perfect meringue, bring the egg whites to room temperature before whisking. It is worth noting that the fresher the eggs, the greater the volume of the meringue.

fish roasted with lime

Preheat the oven to 180°C/350°F/Gas Mark 4.

Place the fish fillets in a non-metallic bowl and season to taste with salt and pepper. Squeeze the juice from the lime halves over the fish.

Heat the oil in a frying pan. Add the onion and garlic and cook, stirring frequently, for 2 minutes, or until softened. Remove the frying pan from the heat.

Place a third of the onion mixture and a little of the chillies and coriander in the base of a shallow ovenproof dish or roasting tin. Arrange the fish on top. Top with the remaining onion mixture, chillies and coriander.

Roast in the oven for 15–20 minutes, or until the fish has become slightly opaque and firm to the touch. Serve immediately, with lemon and lime wedges for squeezing over the fish.

ingredients

1 kg/2 lb 4 oz white fish fillets,
    such as bass, plaice or cod
salt and pepper
1 lime, halved
3 tbsp extra virgin olive oil
1 large onion, finely chopped
3 garlic cloves, finely chopped
2–3 pickled jalapeño chillies
    (jalapeños en escabeche),
    chopped
6–8 tbsp chopped fresh coriander
lemon and lime wedges, to serve

ingredients

300 g/10½ oz fresh or frozen
   shelled broad beans
olive oil
8 unboned chicken thighs, excess
   fat removed, skin on
1 large onion, sliced finely
1 large garlic clove, crushed
500 g/1 lb 2 oz chestnut
   mushrooms, wiped and sliced
   thickly
salt and pepper
500 ml/18 fl oz chicken stock
finely chopped fresh parsley, to
   garnish

JUNE

9

SERVES 4

chicken thighs with broad beans & mushrooms

To blanch the beans, bring a large saucepan of salted water to the boil, add the beans and continue boiling for 5–10 minutes until just tender. Drain and put in a bowl of cold water to stop further cooking. Peel off the outer skins; set aside.

Heat 2 tablespoons of the oil in a large, lidded frying pan or flameproof casserole over a medium-high heat. Add 4 chicken thighs, skin sides down, and fry for 5 minutes, or until the skins are crisp and golden. Remove from the frying pan and keep warm and fry the remaining thighs, adding a little extra oil if necessary.

Drain off all but 2 tablespoons of the fat in the frying pan. Add the onion and fry for 3 minutes, then add the garlic and continue frying for 5 minutes until the onion is golden. Stir in the mushrooms and salt and pepper to taste and continue frying for 2 minutes, or until the mushrooms absorb all the fat and begin to give off their juices.

Return the chicken thighs to the frying pan, skin sides up. Pour in the chicken stock and bring to the boil. Reduce the heat to low, cover tightly and simmer for 15 minutes.

Add the beans and continue simmering for 5 minutes until the beans are tender and the chicken juices run clear when a thigh is pierced. Taste and adjust the seasoning and sprinkle with parsley.

COOK'S TIP

*Unblanched broad beans
can take up to 20 minutes
to cook, depending on
their age. Frozen beans
can be added straight from
the freezer in Step 5 and
simmered for 5 minutes
until tender.*

10

california smoothie

Put the banana, strawberries, dates and honey into a blender and blend until smooth.

Add the orange juice and crushed ice cubes and blend again until smooth. Pour into a chilled Collins glass.

ingredients

1 banana, peeled and thinly sliced

60 g/2 oz strawberries

90 g/3 oz stoned dates

4½ tsp clear honey

250 ml/9 fl oz orange juice

4-6 crushed ice cubes

11

prawn cocktail

Divide the lettuce between 4 small serving dishes (traditionally, stemmed glass ones, but any small dishes will be fine).

Mix together the mayonnaise, cream and tomato ketchup in a bowl. Add Tabasco and lemon juice to your taste and season well with salt and pepper.

Divide the peeled prawns equally between the dishes and pour over the dressing. Chill for 30 minutes in the refrigerator.

Sprinkle a little paprika over the cocktails and garnish with a prawn and a slice of lemon on each dish. Serve with the slices of brown bread and butter.

ingredients

½ iceberg lettuce, finely shredded

150 ml/5 fl oz mayonnaise

2 tbsp single cream

2 tbsp tomato ketchup

few drops of Tabasco sauce

juice of ½ lemon

salt and pepper

175 g/6 oz cooked peeled prawns

TO GARNISH

dash of ground paprika

4 cooked prawns in their shells

4 lemon slices

thin buttered brown bread slices,
     to serve

VARIATIONS

Other fish cocktails can be made in the same way. Try using crabmeat, lobster or a mixture of seafood. A more modern approach is to serve the prawns with avocado or mango and to add lime juice and fish sauce as flavourings, omitting the mayonnaise.

ingredients

2 tsp mirin or sweet sherry

1½ tsp light soy sauce

1 tsp toasted sesame oil

½ tsp salt

115 g/4 oz cooked boneless lamb
   or chicken

55 g/2 oz mangetout

1 small red onion

1 red pepper

1 carrot

250 g/9 oz fresh udon or ramen
   noodles

100 g/3½ oz beansprouts

2 tbsp chopped fresh coriander

1 large egg

1 tsp oil

pink pickled ginger, sliced or
   shredded, to garnish

toasted sesame seeds, to garnish

hot wok noodles

Combine the mirin, soy sauce, sesame oil and salt in a large bowl, stirring until the salt dissolves. Set this mixture aside while you prepare the other ingredients, adding each one to the bowl as it is ready.

Remove excess fat from the lamb or any skin from the chicken, then thinly slice the flesh. Cut the mangetout into thin, long strips. Cut the onion in half crossways, then slice into half-moon shapes. Deseed and thinly slice the pepper. Peel and coarsely grate the carrot.

Add the noodles and beansprouts to the bowl, then use your hands to toss and coat all the ingredients. You can now cover and chill the bowl for up to 2 hours, or cook at once.

To make the omelette slices, beat the egg with ½ teaspoon water. Heat 1 teaspoon oil in a frying pan over a high heat. Pour in the egg and tilt the pan so it covers the base. Reduce the heat and cook until set. Slide the omelette out, roll up and slice thinly.

When it's time to cook, heat a wok or large frying pan over a high heat. Add the noodle mixture and stir-fry for 3 minutes, or until all the ingredients are hot and the vegetables are just tender. Stir in the coriander. Divide between 4 plates, then top with omelette slices, pickled ginger and toasted sesame seeds.

baked herb ricotta

Preheat the oven to 180°C/350°F/Gas Mark 4. Brush a 1-kg/2-lb 4 oz non-stick loaf tin with the oil.

Put the ricotta into a bowl and beat well. Add the eggs and stir until smooth, then stir in the herbs, pepper to taste and paprika.

Spoon the mixture into the prepared tin and put into a roasting tin half-filled with water. Bake in the preheated oven for 30–40 minutes, or until set. Remove from the oven and leave to cool.

Meanwhile, cut the crusts off the bread to make Melba toast. Toast each slice and cut widthways in half to create 2 thin slices. Cut each half diagonally into triangles. Arrange in a single layer on a baking sheet and bake in the oven for 10 minutes.

Turn the baked ricotta out on to a serving dish, drizzle with a little oil and sprinkle with paprika. Serve with the Melba toast and a green salad.

ingredients

1 tbsp olive oil, plus extra for
   drizzling
1 kg/2 lb 4 oz fresh ricotta cheese,
   drained
3 eggs, lightly beaten
3 tbsp chopped fresh herbs, such as
   tarragon, parsley, dill and chives
pepper
½ tsp paprika, plus extra for
   sprinkling
4 slices granary bread
green salad, to serve

eggs on vegetables

Heat the oil in a heavy-based frying pan over a medium-high heat. Add the peppers and onion and fry for 2 minutes, then add the garlic, chorizo and paprika and continue to fry for a further 3 minutes, or until the peppers and onion are soft, but not brown.

Stir in the tomatoes with their juices, the sugar and salt and pepper to taste and bring to the boil. Reduce the heat and simmer for about 10 minutes, uncovered.

Add the potatoes, beans and peas and continue simmering for 6–7 minutes until the potatoes are heated through and the beans and peas are cooked.

Divide the vegetable mixture between 4 small earthenware casseroles or individual oven-proof serving dishes and adjust the seasoning if necessary. Crack an egg on top of each. Put in a preheated oven, 180°C/350°F/Gas Mark 4, and bake for 10 minutes, or until the yolks are set as desired. Serve at once.

SERVES 4

ingredients

4 tbsp extra virgin olive oil

2 green peppers, cored, deseeded
    and chopped

1 large onion, chopped

2 garlic cloves, crushed

12 chorizo slices, each about
    5 mm/¼ inch thick, casings
    removed, if preferred

¼ tsp Spanish mild or smoked
    paprika

800 g/1 lb 12 oz canned chopped
    tomatoes

pinch of sugar

salt and pepper

225 g/8 oz new potatoes, cooked
    and chopped into 1-cm/½-inch
    cubes

100 g/3½ oz French or other green
    beans, chopped

100 g/3½ oz frozen or fresh shelled
    peas

4 large eggs

lemon & veal risotto

Bring the stock to the boil in a saucepan, then reduce the heat and keep simmering gently on a low heat while you are cooking the risotto.

Heat 1 tablespoon of the oil with 25 g/1 oz of the butter in a deep saucepan over a medium heat until the butter has melted. Add the onion and cook, stirring occasionally, for 5 minutes, or until soft and turning golden. Do not brown.

Reduce the heat, add the rice and mix to coat in oil and butter. Cook, stirring constantly, for 2–3 minutes, or until the grains are translucent.

Add 150 ml/5 fl oz of the wine and cook, stirring constantly, for 1 minute until reduced.

Gradually add the hot stock, a ladle at a time. Stir constantly and add more liquid as the rice absorbs each addition. Increase the heat to medium so that the liquid bubbles. Cook for 20 minutes, or until all the liquid is absorbed and the rice is creamy. Season to taste.

Meanwhile, sprinkle the remaining oil over the veal. Rub in the herbs and salt and pepper. Heat a non-stick frying pan over a high heat and brown the veal quickly, turning once. Pour over the lemon juice, remaining wine and the water. Bring to the boil, then reduce the heat. Cover and simmer gently for 15 minutes.

When the meat is cooked through, transfer to a serving dish and garnish with lemon rind.

Remove the risotto from the heat and add the remaining butter. Mix well, then stir in the Parmesan until it melts. Adjust the seasoning, if necessary, and serve immediately with the veal.

ingredients

1 litre/1 ¼ pints chicken stock
3 tbsp olive oil
40 g/1 ½ oz butter
1 small onion, finely chopped
280 g/10 oz risotto rice
200 ml/7 fl oz dry white wine
450 g/1 lb veal escalopes, beaten
   thin
1 tsp dried oregano
1 tsp dried thyme
salt and pepper
2 tbsp lemon juice
3 tbsp water
85 g/3 oz freshly grated Parmesan
   or Grana Padano cheese
2 thinly pared lemon rind, to garnish

COOK'S TIP

To prepare the veal, wrap in clingfilm and beat gently with the flat side of a meat mallet or the side of a rolling pin. Try to keep the thickness even.

SERVES 4–6

ingredients

225–300 g/8–10½ oz mixed soft
 fruits, such as blueberries and
 stoned fresh cherries
1½–2 tbsp Cointreau or orange
 flower water
250 g/9 oz mascarpone cheese
200 ml/7 fl oz crème fraîche
2–3 tbsp dark muscovado sugar

cheat's crème brûlée

Prepare the fruit, if necessary, and lightly rinse, then place in the bases of 4–6 x 150-ml/5-fl oz ramekin dishes. Sprinkle the fruit with the Cointreau or orange flower water.

Cream the cheese in a bowl until soft, then gradually beat in the crème fraîche.

Spoon the cheese mixture over the fruit, smoothing the surface and ensuring that the tops are level. Chill in the refrigerator for at least 2 hours.

Sprinkle the tops with the sugar. Using a chef's blow torch, grill the tops until caramelized (about 2–3 minutes). Alternatively, cook under a preheated grill, turning the dishes, for 3–4 minutes, or until the tops are lightly caramelized all over.

Serve immediately or chill in the refrigerator for 15–20 minutes before serving.

caesar salad

Bring a small, heavy-based saucepan of water to the boil. Meanwhile, heat 4 tablespoons of the olive oil in a heavy-based frying pan. Add the garlic and diced bread and cook, stirring and tossing frequently, for 4–5 minutes, or until the bread is crispy and golden all over. Remove from the frying pan with a slotted spoon and drain on kitchen paper.

While the bread is frying, add the egg to the boiling water and cook for 1 minute, then remove from the saucepan and reserve.

Arrange the lettuce leaves in a salad bowl. Mix the remaining olive oil and lemon juice together, then season to taste with salt and pepper. Crack the egg into the dressing and whisk to blend. Pour the dressing over the lettuce leaves, toss well, then add the croûtons and anchovies and toss the salad again. Sprinkle with Parmesan cheese shavings and serve.

ingredients

150 ml/5 fl oz olive oil

2 garlic cloves

5 slices white bread, crusts removed, cut into 1-cm/½-inch cubes

1 large egg

2 cos lettuces or 3 Little Gem lettuces

2 tbsp lemon juice

salt and pepper

8 canned anchovy fillets, drained and roughly chopped

85 g/3 oz fresh Parmesan cheese shavings

chicken with goat's cheese & basil

Using a sharp knife, slit along one long edge of each chicken breast then carefully open out each breast to make a small pocket. Divide the cheese equally between the pockets and tuck 3–4 basil leaves in each. Close the openings and season the breasts with salt and pepper.

Heat the oil in a frying pan, add the chicken breasts and fry gently for 15–20 minutes, turning several times, until golden and tender. Serve warm, garnished with a sprig of basil.

ingredients

4 skinned chicken breast fillets

100 g/3½ oz soft goat's cheese

small bunch fresh basil

salt and pepper

2 tbsp olive oil

blueberry & lemon drizzle cake

Preheat the oven to 180°C/350°F/Gas Mark 4, then grease and line the base of a 20-cm/8-inch square cake tin. Place the butter and sugar in a bowl and beat together until light and fluffy. Gradually beat in the eggs, adding a little flour towards the end to prevent curdling. Beat in the lemon rind, then fold in the remaining flour and almonds with enough of the lemon juice to give a good dropping consistency.

Fold in three-quarters of the blueberries and turn into the prepared tin. Smooth the surface, then scatter the remaining blueberries on top. Bake in the preheated oven for 1 hour, or until firm to the touch and a skewer inserted into the centre comes out clean.

To make the topping, place the lemon juice and sugar in a bowl and mix together. As soon as the cake comes out of the oven, prick it all over with a fine skewer and pour over the lemon mixture. Leave to cool in the tin until completely cold, then cut into 12 squares to serve.

ingredients

225 g/8 oz butter, softened,
 plus extra for greasing
225 g/8 oz golden caster sugar
4 eggs, beaten
250 g/9 oz self-raising flour, sifted
finely grated rind and juice of
 1 lemon
25 g/1 oz ground almonds
200 g/7 oz fresh blueberries

TOPPING
juice of 2 lemons
115 g/4 oz golden caster sugar

COOK'S TIP
If you warm a lemon gently in the microwave for a few seconds on High, it will yield more juice when you squeeze it.

20

SERVES 4

ingredients

1 tbsp olive oil

4 turkey escalopes or steaks

2 red peppers

1 red onion

2 garlic cloves, finely chopped

300 ml/10 fl oz passata

150 ml/5 fl oz medium white wine

1 tbsp chopped fresh marjoram

salt and pepper

400 g/14 oz canned cannellini beans, drained and rinsed

3 tbsp fresh white breadcrumbs

fresh basil sprigs, to garnish

VARIATION

Soak 15 g/½ oz of dried porcini mushrooms in boiling water to cover for 20 minutes. Drain and slice, then add with the onion and peppers in Step 2.

italian turkey steaks

Heat the oil in a flameproof casserole or heavy-based frying pan. Add the turkey escalopes and cook over a medium heat for 5–10 minutes, turning occasionally, until golden. Transfer to a plate.

Deseed and slice the red peppers. Slice the onion, add to the frying pan with the red peppers and cook over a low heat, stirring occasionally, for 5 minutes, or until softened. Add the garlic and cook for a further 2 minutes. Return the turkey to the frying pan and add the passata, wine and marjoram. Season to taste with salt and pepper. Bring to the boil, then reduce the heat, cover and simmer, stirring occasionally, for 25–30 minutes, or until the turkey is cooked through and tender.

Stir in the cannellini beans and simmer for a further 5 minutes. Sprinkle the breadcrumbs over the top and place under a preheated medium-hot grill for 2–3 minutes, or until golden. Serve, garnished with fresh basil sprigs.

hot sesame beef

Mix the beef strips with 1 tablespoon of the sesame seeds in a small bowl. In a separate bowl, whisk together the beef stock, soy sauce, ginger, garlic, cornflour and chilli flakes.

Heat 1 tablespoon of the sesame oil in a large frying pan or wok. Stir-fry the beef strips for 2–3 minutes. Remove and set aside.

Discard any remaining oil in the pan, then wipe with kitchen paper to remove any stray sesame seeds. Heat the remaining oil, add the broccoli, orange pepper, chilli and chilli oil (if desired) and stir-fry for 2–3 minutes. Stir in the beef stock mixture, cover and simmer for 2 minutes.

Return the beef to the pan and simmer until the juices thicken, stirring occasionally. Cook for another 1–2 minutes.

Sprinkle with the remaining sesame seeds. Serve over cooked wild rice and garnish with fresh coriander.

ingredients

500 g/1 lb 2 oz beef fillet,
    cut into thin strips
1½ tbsp sesame seeds
125 ml/4 fl oz beef stock
2 tbsp soy sauce
2 tbsp grated fresh root ginger
2 garlic cloves, chopped finely
1 tsp cornflour
½ tsp chilli flakes
3 tbsp sesame oil
1 large head of broccoli, cut
    into florets
1 orange pepper, sliced thinly
1 red chilli, deseeded and sliced
    finely
1 tbsp chilli oil, to taste
1 tbsp chopped fresh coriander,
    to garnish
freshly cooked wild rice, to serve

JUNE

21

SERVES 4

lemon butterfly cakes

Preheat the oven to 190°C/375°F/Gas Mark 5. Place 12 paper cases in a bun tin. Sift the flour and baking powder into a bowl. Add the butter, sugar, eggs, lemon rind and enough milk to give a medium-soft consistency. Beat the mixture thoroughly until smooth, then divide between the paper cases and bake in the preheated oven for 15–20 minutes, or until well risen and golden. Transfer to wire racks to cool.

To make the filling, place the butter in a bowl. Sift in the icing sugar and add the lemon juice. Beat well until smooth and creamy. When the cakes are quite cold, use a sharp-pointed vegetable knife to cut a circle from the top of each cake, then cut each circle in half. Spoon a little buttercream into the centre of each cake and press the 2 semi-circular pieces into it to resemble wings. Dust the cakes with sifted icing sugar before serving.

ingredients

115 g/4 oz self-raising flour
½ tsp baking powder
115 g/4 oz butter, softened
115 g/4 oz golden caster sugar
2 eggs, beaten
finely grated rind of ½ lemon
2–4 tbsp milk
icing sugar, for dusting

FILLING
55 g/2 oz butter
115 g/4 oz icing sugar
1 tbsp lemon juice

COOK'S TIP
If time is limited and you want to speed things up, then the cake mixture could be mixed in a food processor, rather than by hand.

VARIATION
To make these cakes extra special, place a few slices of strawberry on top of each one.

cheese aigrettes

Sift the flour, paprika and ½ teaspoon salt together on to a sheet of greaseproof paper or baking paper. Place the butter in a large, heavy-based saucepan, pour in the water and heat gently. The moment the butter has melted and the liquid begins to boil, tip in the flour mixture and beat vigorously with a wooden spoon until the dough comes away from the side of the saucepan.

Remove the saucepan from the heat and leave to cool for 5 minutes. Gradually beat in the eggs to give a stiff, dropping consistency – you may not need all of them. Stir in the Gruyère cheese.

Heat the sunflower oil to 180–190°C/350–375°F, or until a cube of bread browns in 30 seconds. Shape balls of choux dough between 2 teaspoons and drop them into the oil. Cook for 3–4 minutes, or until golden brown. Remove with a slotted spoon, drain on kitchen paper and keep warm until all the aigrettes are cooked. Pile on to a warmed serving dish, sprinkle with grated Parmesan cheese and serve immediately.

ingredients

100 g/3½ oz plain flour
½ tsp paprika
salt and pepper
6 tbsp butter, diced
200 ml/7 fl oz water
3 eggs, lightly beaten
85 g/3 oz Gruyère cheese, grated
sunflower oil, for deep-frying
55 g/2 oz freshly grated Parmesan
   cheese

COOK'S TIP

When deep-frying, either use a deep-fryer or a large, deep, heavy-based saucepan. Do not fill the deep-fryer more than half full with oil nor the saucepan more than a third full.

24

SERVES 4

prawn & garlic pasta sauce with cream

Heat the oil and butter in a saucepan over a medium–low heat. Add the garlic and red pepper. Fry for a few seconds until the garlic is just beginning to colour. Stir in the tomato purée and wine. Cook for 10 minutes, stirring.

Cook the pasta in plenty of boiling salted water until al dente. Drain and return to the pan.

Add the prawns to the sauce and raise the heat to medium–high. Cook for 2 minutes, stirring, until the prawns turn pink. Reduce the heat and stir in the cream. Cook for 1 minute, stirring constantly, until thickened. Season with salt and pepper.

Transfer the pasta to a warm serving dish. Pour the sauce over the pasta. Sprinkle with the parsley. Toss well to mix and serve at once.

ingredients

3 tbsp olive oil
3 tbsp butter
4 garlic cloves, chopped very finely
2 tbsp finely diced red pepper
2 tbsp tomato purée
125 ml/4 fl oz dry white wine
450 g/1 lb tagliatelle or spaghetti
350 g/12 oz raw peeled prawns, cut
    into 1 cm/1⁄2 inch pieces
125 ml/4 fl oz double cream
salt and pepper
3 tbsp chopped fresh flat-leaved
    parsley, to garnish

thai-style chicken salad

Bring 2 saucepans of water to the boil. Put the potatoes into one saucepan and cook for 15 minutes until tender. Put the corn cobs into the other saucepan and cook for 5 minutes until tender. Drain the potatoes and corn cobs well and leave to cool.

When the vegetables are cool, transfer them into a large serving dish. Add the beansprouts, spring onions, chicken, lemon grass and coriander and season with salt and pepper.

To make the dressing, put all the ingredients into a screw-top jar and shake well. Alternatively, put them into a bowl and mix together well.

Drizzle the dressing over the salad and garnish with lime wedges and coriander leaves. Serve at once.

ingredients

400 g/14 oz small new potatoes,
    scrubbed and halved lengthways
200 g/7 oz baby corn cobs, sliced
150 g/5½ oz beansprouts
3 spring onions, trimmed and sliced
4 cooked, skinless chicken
    breasts, sliced
1 tbsp chopped lemon grass
2 tbsp chopped fresh coriander
salt and pepper

DRESSING
6 tbsp chilli oil or sesame oil
2 tbsp lime juice
1 tbsp light soy sauce
1 tbsp chopped fresh coriander
1 small, red chilli, deseeded and
    finely chopped

TO GARNISH
wedges of lime
fresh coriander leaves

---

aubergines with tsatziki

Preheat the barbecue. To make the tsatziki, finely chop the cucumber. Place the yogurt in a bowl and beat well until smooth. Stir in the cucumber, spring onions, garlic and mint. Season to taste with salt and pepper. Transfer to a serving bowl, cover with clingfilm and leave to chill in the refrigerator until required.

Season the olive oil with salt and pepper, then brush the aubergine slices with the oil.

Cook the aubergines over hot coals for 5 minutes on each side, brushing with more oil, if necessary. Transfer to a large serving plate and serve immediately with the tsatziki, garnished with a mint sprig.

ingredients

2 tbsp olive oil
salt and pepper
2 aubergines, thinly sliced

TSATZIKI
½ cucumber
200 ml/7 fl oz natural Greek yogurt
4 spring onions, finely chopped
1 garlic clove, finely chopped
3 tbsp chopped fresh mint
salt and pepper
1 fresh mint sprig, to garnish

bircher muesli

Put the oats and apple juice into a mixing bowl and combine well. Cover and refrigerate overnight.

To serve, stir the apple and yogurt into the soaked oats and divide between 4 serving bowls. Top with the blackberries and plums and drizzle with the honey.

ingredients

150 g/5½ oz rolled oats
225 ml/8 fl oz apple juice
1 apple, grated
125 ml/4 fl oz natural yogurt
150 g/5½ oz blackberries
2 plums, stoned and sliced
2 tbsp clear honey

chilled chocolate dessert

Beat the mascarpone with the coffee and icing sugar until thoroughly combined.

Set aside 4 teaspoons of the grated chocolate and stir the remainder into the cheese mixture with 5 tablespoons of the unwhipped cream.

Whisk the remaining cream until it forms soft peaks. Stir 1 tablespoon of the mascarpone mixture into the cream to slacken it, then fold the cream into the remaining mascarpone mixture with a figure-of-eight action.

Spoon the mixture into a freezerproof container and place in the freezer for about 3 hours.

To serve, scoop the chocolate dessert into sundae glasses and drizzle with a little Marsala. Top with whipped cream and decorate with the reserved chocolate. Serve immediately.

ingredients

225 g/8 oz mascarpone cheese
2 tbsp finely ground coffee beans
25 g/1 oz icing sugar
85 g/3 oz plain chocolate, grated
   finely
350 ml/12 fl oz double cream, plus
   extra to decorate
Marsala, to serve

COOK'S TIP
Do not freeze the mixture
for too long or it will lose
its texture.

stuffed courgettes with walnuts & feta

Put the courgettes in a saucepan of boiling water, return to the boil and then boil for 3 minutes. Drain, rinse under cold water and drain again. Leave to cool.

When the courgettes are cool enough to handle, cut a thin strip off the top side of each one with a sharp knife and gently score around the inside edges to help scoop out the flesh. Using a teaspoon, scoop out the flesh, leaving a shell to hold the stuffing. Chop the courgette flesh.

Heat 2 tablespoons of the oil in a saucepan. Add the onion and garlic and fry for 5 minutes, until softened. Add the courgette flesh and fry for 5 minutes, until the onion is golden brown. Remove from the heat and leave to cool slightly. Stir in the cheese then the walnuts, breadcrumbs, egg, dill, salt and pepper. Use the stuffing to fill the courgette shells and place side by side in an ovenproof dish. Drizzle over the remaining oil.

Cover the dish with foil and bake in a preheated oven, 190°C/375°F/Gas Mark 5, for 30 minutes. Remove the foil and bake for a further 10–15 minutes or until golden brown. Serve hot.

ingredients

4 fat, medium courgettes

3 tbsp olive oil

1 onion, chopped finely

1 garlic clove, chopped finely

55 g/2 oz feta cheese, crumbled

25 g/1 oz walnut pieces, chopped

55 g/2 oz fresh white breadcrumbs

1 egg, beaten

1 tsp chopped fresh dill

salt and pepper

prawns wrapped in ham

First, make the dressing. Finely chop the prepared tomato flesh and put it in a bowl. Add the onion, parsley, capers and lemon rind and gently toss together. Combine the oil and vinegar and add to the other ingredients, then set aside until required.

Wrap a slice of ham around each prawn and rub with a little of the oil. Place the prawns in a heatproof dish large enough to hold them in a single layer. Bake in a preheated oven, 160°C/325°F/Gas Mark 3, for 10 minutes.

Transfer the prawns to a large serving platter and spoon the tomato-caper dressing over. Serve at once, or leave to cool to room temperature.

ingredients

2 tomatoes, peeled and deseeded

1 small red onion, chopped very finely

4 tbsp very finely chopped fresh parsley

1 tbsp capers in brine, drained, rinsed and chopped

finely grated rind of 1 large lemon

4 tbsp extra virgin olive oil

1 tbsp sherry vinegar

DRESSING

16 thin slices serrano ham or prosciutto

16 uncooked tiger prawns, peeled and deveined, tails left on

extra virgin olive oil

COOK'S TIP

To peel and deseed tomatoes, remove the stems and cut a small cross in the top of each one. Put the tomatoes into a heatproof bowl, pour over enough boiling water to cover, and leave for 30 seconds. Use a slotted spoon to transfer to a bowl of iced water. Working with 1 tomato at a time, peel off the skin, then cut in half and use a teaspoon to scoop out the cores and seeds.

CHAPTER

7

July

apple pancakes with maple syrup butter

Mix the flour, sugar and cinnamon together in a bowl and make a well in the centre. Beat the egg and milk together and pour into the well. Using a wooden spoon, gently incorporate the dry ingredients into the liquid until well combined, then stir in the grated apple.

Heat the butter in a large non-stick frying pan over low heat until melted and bubbling. Add three tablespoons of the pancake mixture to form 9 cm/3½ inch circles. Cook each pancake for about a minute, until it starts to bubble lightly on the top and looks set, then flip it over and cook the other side for 30 seconds, or until cooked through. The pancakes should be golden brown; if not, increase the heat a little. Remove from the pan and keep warm. Repeat the process until all of the pancake batter has been used up (it is not necessary to add extra butter).

To make the maple syrup butter, melt the butter with the maple syrup in a pan over low heat and stir until combined. To serve, place the pancakes on serving dishes and spoon over the flavoured butter. Serve warm.

ingredients

200 g/7 oz self-raising flour

100 g/3½ oz caster sugar

1 tsp ground cinnamon

1 egg

200 ml/7 fl oz milk

2 apples, peeled and grated

1 tsp butter

MAPLE SYRUP BUTTER

85 g/3 oz butter, softened

3 tbsp maple syrup

berry smoothie

Put the blueberries into a food processor or blender and process for 1 minute.
Add the raspberries, honey and yogurt and process for a further minute.

Add the ice and sesame seeds and process again for a further minute.
Pour into a tall glass and serve immediately.

SERVES 1

ingredients

25 g/1 oz blueberries

85 g/3 oz raspberries, thawed if
    frozen

1 tsp clear honey

200 ml/7 fl oz live or bio yogurt

about 1 heaped tbsp crushed ice

1 tbsp sesame seeds

SERVES 2 AS A
MAIN COURSE OR
4 AS A STARTER

mixed sushi rolls

Put the rice into a saucepan and cover with cold water. Bring
to the boil, then reduce the heat, cover and simmer for
15–20 minutes, or until the rice is tender and the water has
been absorbed. Drain if necessary and transfer to a bowl. Mix
the vinegar, sugar and salt together, then, using a spatula, stir
well into the rice. Cover with a damp cloth and leave to cool.

To make the rolls, lay a clean bamboo mat over a chopping
board. Lay a sheet of nori, shiny side-down, on the mat.
Spread a quarter of the rice mixture over the nori, using wet
fingers to press it down evenly, leaving a 1-cm/½-inch margin
at the top and bottom.

For smoked salmon and cucumber rolls, lay the salmon over
the rice and arrange the cucumber in a line across the centre.
For the prawn rolls, lay the prawns and avocado in a line
across the centre.

Carefully hold the nearest edge of the mat, then, using the
mat as a guide, roll up the nori tightly to make a neat tube of
rice enclosing the filling. Seal the uncovered edge with a little
water, then roll the sushi off the mat. Repeat to make 3 more
rolls – you need 2 salmon and cucumber and 2 prawn and
avocado in total.

Using a wet knife, cut each roll into 8 pieces and stand upright
on a platter. Wipe and rinse the knife between cuts to prevent
the rice from sticking. Serve the rolls with wasabi, tamari and
pickled ginger.

ingredients

250 g/9 oz sushi rice

2 tbsp rice vinegar

1 tsp caster sugar

½ tsp salt

4 sheets nori (seaweed) for rolling

FILLINGS

50 g/1¾ oz smoked salmon

4-cm/1½-inch piece cucumber,
    peeled, deseeded and cut into
    matchsticks

40 g/1½ oz cooked peeled prawns

1 small avocado, stoned, peeled,
    thinly sliced and tossed in
    lemon juice

TO SERVE

wasabi (Japanese horseradish
    sauce)

tamari (wheat-free soy sauce)

pink pickled ginger

the ultimate cheeseburger

Place the steak mince in a large bowl. Finely grate one onion and add to the steak mince in the bowl. Add the garlic, horseradish and pepper to the steak mixture in the bowl. Mix together, then shape into 4 equal-sized burgers. Wrap each burger in 2 rashers of bacon, then cover and leave to chill for 30 minutes.

Preheat the grill to medium-high. Slice the remaining onions. Heat the oil in a frying pan. Add the onions and cook over a medium heat for 8–10 minutes, stirring frequently, until the onions are golden brown. Drain on kitchen paper and keep warm.

Cook the burgers under the hot grill for 3–5 minutes on each side or until cooked to personal preference. Lightly toast the sesame seed baps and arrange the shredded lettuce on their bases. Add the burgers, some fried onion, a spoonful of relish and a cheese slice. Flash grill for 1–2 minutes. Add the lid and serve with extra relish.

JULY
4

SERVES 4

ingredients
450 g/1 lb best steak mince

4 onions

2–4 garlic cloves, crushed

2–3 tsp grated fresh horseradish or
1–1½ tbsp creamed horseradish

pepper

8 lean back bacon rashers

2 tbsp sunflower oil

TO SERVE

4 sesame seed baps

shredded Cos lettuce

4 slices cheese

VARIATION

For an extra spicy kick to this classic cheeseburger, place a good spoonful of English mustard on top of the cooked burger before adding the slice of cheese.

ingredients

2 tbsp vegetable oil

3 whole cloves

3 cardamom pods, cracked

1 onion, chopped

115 g/4 oz carrots, chopped

2–3 garlic cloves, crushed

1–2 fresh red chillies, deseeded and
    chopped

2.5-cm/1-inch piece fresh root
    ginger, grated

115 g/4 oz cauliflower, broken into
    small florets

175 g/6 oz broccoli, broken into
    small florets

115 g/4 oz French beans, chopped

400 g/14 oz canned chopped
    tomatoes

150 ml/5 fl oz vegetable stock

salt and pepper

115 g/4 oz okra, sliced

1 tbsp chopped fresh coriander, plus
    extra sprigs to garnish

115 g/4 oz brown basmati rice

few saffron strands (optional)

zested lime rind, to garnish

vegetable biryani

Heat the oil in a large saucepan over a low heat, add the spices, onion, carrots, garlic, chillies and ginger and cook, stirring frequently, for 5 minutes.

Add all the vegetables, except the okra, and cook, stirring frequently, for 5 minutes. Stir in the tomatoes, stock and salt and pepper to taste and bring to the boil. Reduce the heat, cover and simmer for 10 minutes.

Add the okra and cook for a further 8–10 minutes, or until the vegetables are tender. Stir in the coriander. Strain off any excess liquid and keep warm.

Meanwhile, cook the rice, with the saffron, if using, in a saucepan of lightly salted boiling water for 25 minutes, or until tender. Drain and keep warm.

Layer the vegetables and cooked rice in a deep dish or pudding basin, packing the layers down firmly. Leave for about 5 minutes, then invert on to a warmed serving dish and serve, garnished with zested lime rind and coriander sprigs, with the reserved liquid.

manhattan cheesecake

Preheat the oven to 190°C/375°F/Gas Mark 5. Brush a 20-cm/8-inch springform tin with oil. Melt the butter in a saucepan over a low heat. Stir in the biscuits, then spread in the tin. Place the cream cheese, eggs, 100 g/3½ oz of the sugar and ½ teaspoon of the vanilla essence in a food processor. Process until smooth. Pour over the biscuit base and smooth the top. Place on a baking tray and bake for 20 minutes, or until set. Remove from the oven and leave to stand for 20 minutes. Leave the oven switched on.

Mix the soured cream with the remaining sugar and vanilla essence in a bowl. Spoon over the cheesecake. Return it to the oven for 10 minutes, leave to cool, then chill in the refrigerator for 8 hours or overnight.

To make the topping, place the sugar in a saucepan with half the water over a low heat and stir until dissolved. Increase the heat, add the blueberries, cover and cook for a few minutes, or until they begin to soften. Remove from the heat. Mix the arrowroot and remaining water in a bowl, add to the fruit and stir until smooth. Return to a low heat. Cook until the juice thickens and turns translucent. Leave to cool. Remove the cheesecake from the tin 1 hour before serving. Spoon the fruit on top and chill until ready to serve.

ingredients

sunflower oil, for brushing
85 g/3 oz butter
200 g/7 oz digestive biscuits, crushed
400 g/14 oz cream cheese
2 large eggs
140 g/5 oz caster sugar
1½ tsp vanilla essence
450 ml/16 fl oz soured cream

BLUEBERRY TOPPING
55 g/2 oz caster sugar
4 tbsp water
250 g/9 oz fresh blueberries
1 tsp arrowroot

JULY

6

SERVES 4

VARIATION

As an alternative to blueberries, try raspberries, blackcurrants or cranberries for the topping.

pork with basil & lemon grass

Mix the lemon grass, fish sauce (if desired), basil and lime juice in a bowl. Stir in the pork and toss well to coat. Cover with clingfilm and refrigerate for 1–2 hours.

Heat 1 tablespoon of the oil in a frying pan or wok over a medium heat. Add the meat and the marinade and stir-fry until the pork is browned. Remove from the pan, set aside and keep warm.

Add the remaining 1 tablespoon of oil to the pan and heat. Add all the vegetables and the garlic and stir-fry for about 3 minutes.

Return the pork to the pan and add the chicken stock. Cook for 5 minutes until the stock is reduced.

Transfer the stir-fry to warm serving dishes and garnish with wedges of lime. Serve on a bed of basmati rice.

ingredients

MARINADE

1 stalk lemon grass, sliced finely

2 tbsp fish sauce (optional)

4 tbsp fresh basil, shredded

juice of 1 lime

STIR-FRY

350 g/12 oz pork tenderloin, cubed

2 tbsp sesame oil

280 g/10 oz mushrooms, sliced
   thinly

1 courgette, sliced thinly

2 carrots, sliced thinly

115 g/4 oz canned bamboo shoots

115 g/4 oz canned water chestnuts,
   sliced thinly

1 garlic clove, crushed

125 ml/4 fl oz chicken stock

wedges of lime, to garnish

freshly cooked basmati rice,
   to serve

aubergine and garlic dip

Preheat the oven to 190°C/370°F/Gas Mark 5. Prick the skins of the aubergines with a fork and put on a baking tray. Bake in the oven for 45 minutes, or until very soft. Leave to cool slightly then cut the aubergines in half lengthways and scoop out and reserve the flesh.

Heat the oil in a large, heavy-based frying pan, add the aubergine flesh and fry for 5 minutes. Transfer to a food processor, add the lemon juice and blend until smooth. Gradually add the yogurt, then the garlic and cumin. Season with salt and pepper.

Turn the mixture into a serving bowl and chill in the fridge for at least 1 hour. Garnish with chopped parsley and serve with pepper strips or sesame crackers.

ingredients

2 large aubergines

50 ml/2 fl oz extra virgin olive oil

juice of ½ lemon

150 ml/¼ pint Greek yogurt

2 garlic cloves, crushed

pinch of ground cumin

salt and pepper

chopped fresh flat-leaved parsley,
   to garnish

strips of red and green pepper or
   sesame crackers, to serve

ingredients

50 ml/2 fl oz olive oil

1 large onion, finely chopped

2 kg/4 lb 8 oz tiny clams, such as
   Venus, well scrubbed

125 ml/4 fl oz dry white wine

1 litre/1¾ pints fish stock

600 ml/1 pint water

3 garlic cloves, finely chopped

½ tsp crushed dried chilli

400 g/14 oz risotto rice

3 ripe plum tomatoes, peeled and
   roughly chopped

3 tbsp lemon juice

2 tbsp chopped fresh chervil or
   parsley

salt and pepper

risotto with clams

Heat 1–2 tablespoons of the oil in a large, heavy-based saucepan over a medium-high heat. Add the onion and cook, stirring constantly, for 1 minute. Add the clams and wine and cover tightly. Cook, shaking the pan frequently, for 2–3 minutes until the clams begin to open. Remove from the heat and discard any clams that do not open.

When cool enough to handle, remove the clams from their shells. Rinse in the cooking liquid. Cover the clams and set aside. Strain the cooking liquid through a coffee filter or a sieve lined with kitchen paper and reserve.

Bring the stock and water to the boil in a saucepan, then reduce the heat and keep simmering gently over a low heat while you are cooking the risotto.

Heat the remaining oil in a large, heavy-based saucepan over a medium heat. Add the garlic and chilli and cook gently for 1 minute.

Reduce the heat, add the rice and mix to coat in oil. Cook, stirring constantly, for 2–3 minutes, or until the grains are translucent.

Gradually add the hot stock mixture, a ladle at a time. Stir constantly and add more liquid as the rice absorbs each addition. Increase the heat to medium so that the liquid bubbles. Cook for 20 minutes, or until all the liquid is absorbed and the rice is creamy.

Stir in the tomatoes, reserved clams and their cooking liquid, the lemon juice and chervil. Heat through gently. Season to taste with salt and pepper. Spoon the risotto onto warmed plates and serve immediately.

nectarine crunch

Using a sharp knife, cut the nectarines in half, then remove and discard the stones. Chop the flesh into bite-sized pieces. Reserve a few pieces for decoration and place a few pieces in the bottom of 4 sundae glasses. Place a layer of oat cereal in each glass, then drizzle over a little yogurt.

Place the jam and peach nectar in a large jug and stir together to mix. Add a few more nectarine pieces to the glasses and drizzle over a little of the jam mixture. Continue building up the layers in this way, finishing with a layer of yogurt and a sprinkling of oat cereal. Decorate with the reserved nectarine pieces and serve.

ingredients

4 nectarines

175 g/6 oz raisin and nut crunchy oat cereal

300 ml/10 fl oz low-fat natural yogurt

2 tbsp peach jam

2 tbsp peach nectar

lemon posset

Mix the lemon rind, lemon juice, wine and sugar together in a bowl. Stir until the sugar has dissolved. Add the cream and beat with an electric mixer until soft peaks form.

Whisk the egg whites in a separate, spotlessly clean, greasefree bowl until stiff, then carefully fold them into the cream mixture.

Spoon the mixture into tall glasses and leave to chill in the refrigerator until required. Serve decorated with lemon slices and accompanied by the biscuits.

ingredients

grated rind and juice of 1 large lemon

4 tbsp dry white wine

55 g/2 oz caster sugar

300 ml/10 fl oz double cream

2 egg whites

lemon slices, to decorate

langues de chat biscuits, to serve

COOK'S TIP

Use only the very freshest eggs for this dish. It is not advisable to serve any dishes containing raw eggs to the very young or old, the infirm, or anyone whose immune system has been compromised.

cannelloni with ham & ricotta

Preheat the oven to 180°C/350°F/Gas Mark 4. Heat the olive oil in a large heavy-based frying pan. Add the onions and garlic and cook over a low heat, stirring occasionally, for 5 minutes, or until the onion is softened. Add the basil, chopped tomatoes and their can juices and tomato purée and season to taste with salt and pepper. Reduce the heat and simmer for 30 minutes, or until thickened.

Meanwhile, bring a large heavy-based saucepan of lightly salted water to the boil. Add the cannelloni tubes, return to the boil and cook for 8–10 minutes, or until tender but still firm to the bite. Using a slotted spoon, transfer the cannelloni tubes to a large plate and pat dry with kitchen paper.

Grease a large, shallow ovenproof dish with butter. Mix the ricotta, ham and egg together in a bowl and season to taste with salt and pepper. Using a teaspoon, fill the cannelloni tubes with the ricotta mixture and place in a single layer in the dish. Pour the tomato sauce over the cannelloni and sprinkle with the grated pecorino cheese. Bake in the preheated oven for 30 minutes, or until golden brown. Serve immediately.

ingredients

2 tbsp olive oil
2 onions, chopped
2 garlic cloves, finely chopped
1 tbsp shredded fresh basil
800 g/1 lb 12 oz canned chopped
   tomatoes
1 tbsp tomato purée
salt and pepper
350 g/12 oz cannelloni tubes
butter, for greasing
225 g/8 oz ricotta cheese
115 g/4 oz cooked ham, diced
1 egg
55 g/2 oz freshly grated pecorino
   cheese

JULY

12

SERVES 4

VARIATION

*Substitute the pecorino cheese with
the same amount of freshly grated
Parmesan cheese, if you prefer.*

basil dumplings

Pour the milk into a saucepan and bring to just below boiling point. Sprinkle in the semolina, stirring constantly. Lower the heat and simmer for 2 minutes until thick and smooth. Remove from the heat and stir in the basil, tomatoes, eggs, half the butter and half the Parmesan. Season with salt and pepper. Stir well, then pour into a shallow dish or baking tray and level the top. Cool, then chill for at least 1 hour until set.

To make the tomato sauce, heat the oil in a heavy-based saucepan. Add the onion, garlic and pepper and cook over a low heat, stirring occasionally, for 5 minutes, until softened. Add the tomatoes, tomato purée, sugar, basil and bay leaf and season with salt and pepper. Cover and simmer, stirring occasionally, for 30 minutes, until thickened.

Grease an ovenproof dish with butter. Using a lightly floured round cutter, stamp out rounds of the semolina mixture. Place the trimmings in the base of the dish and top with the rounds. Melt the remaining butter and brush over the rounds, then sprinkle with the remaining Parmesan. Bake in a preheated oven, 190°C/375°F/Gas Mark 5, for 30–35 minutes, until golden. Serve immediately with the tomato sauce.

ingredients

700 ml/1 ¼ pints milk

200 g/7 oz semolina

1 tbsp finely chopped fresh basil leaves

4 sun-dried tomatoes in oil, drained and chopped finely

2 eggs, beaten lightly

55 g/2 oz butter, plus extra for greasing

85 g/3 oz freshly grated Parmesan cheese

salt and pepper

TOMATO SAUCE

2 tbsp olive oil

1 small onion, chopped finely

1 garlic clove, chopped finely

1 red pepper, deseeded and chopped

225 g/8 oz plum tomatoes, peeled and chopped

1 tbsp tomato purée

1 tsp soft brown sugar

1 tbsp shredded fresh basil leaves

1 bay leaf

salt and pepper

apricot & yogurt cups

Line a 12-cup bun tin with small paper cake cases.

Spoon the yogurt into a mixing bowl, add the almond extract and honey and stir well.

Using a small, sharp knife, cut the almonds into very thin slivers and stir into the yogurt mixture.

Using a pair of kitchen scissors, cut the apricots into small pieces, then stir into the yogurt.

Spoon the mixture into the paper cases and freeze for 1½–2 hours, or until just frozen. Serve immediately.

JULY

14

MAKES 12 CUPS

ingredients

600 ml/1 pint natural yogurt

few drops of almond extract

2–3 tsp clear honey, warmed

55 g/2 oz whole blanched almonds

175 g/6 oz no-soak dried apricots

bouillabaisse

Heat the oil in a large pan over a medium heat. Add the garlic and onions and cook, stirring, for 3 minutes. Stir in the tomatoes, stock, wine, bay leaf, saffron and herbs. Bring to the boil, reduce the heat, cover and simmer for 30 minutes.

Meanwhile, soak the mussels in lightly salted water for 10 minutes. Scrub the shells under cold running water and pull off any beards. Discard any with broken shells. Tap the remaining mussels and discard any that refuse to close. Put the rest in a large pan with a little water, bring to the boil and cook over a high heat for 4 minutes. Remove from the heat and discard any closed ones.

When the tomato is cooked, rinse the fish, pat dry and cut into chunks. Add to the pan and simmer for 5 minutes. Add the mussels, prawns and scallops and season. Cook for 3 minutes, until the fish is cooked through. Discard the bay leaf, ladle into bowls and serve with a baguette.

JULY

15

SERVES 4

ingredients

100 ml/3½ fl oz olive oil

3 garlic cloves, chopped

2 onions, chopped

2 tomatoes, deseeded and chopped

700 ml/1¼ pints fish stock

400 ml/14 fl oz white wine

1 bay leaf

pinch of saffron threads

2 tbsp chopped fresh basil

2 tbsp chopped fresh parsley

200 g/7 oz live mussels

250 g/9 oz snapper or monkfish fillets

250 g/9 oz haddock fillets, skinned

200 g/7 oz prawns, peeled and deveined

100 g/3½ oz scallops

salt and pepper

baguette, to serve

ingredients

250 g/9 oz mixed salad leaves,
    such as lollo rosso, escarole and
    lamb's lettuce

6 tbsp lemon juice

4 globe artichokes

5 tbsp Calvados

1 shallot, very finely chopped

pinch of salt

1 tbsp red wine vinegar

3 tbsp walnut oil

TO GARNISH

55 g/2 oz shelled walnuts, chopped

1 tbsp finely chopped fresh parsley

COOK'S TIP

*This recipe also works well with
good quality canned or bottled
artichoke hearts. Drain and rinse
well before using.*

artichoke hearts
with a warm dressing

Place the salad leaves in a bowl and set aside. Fill another bowl with cold water and add 2 tablespoons of the lemon juice. Working on one artichoke at a time, twist off the stalks, cut the bases flat and pull off all the dark outer leaves. Slice the artichokes in half horizontally and discard the top parts. Trim around the bases to remove the outer dark green layer and place in the acidulated water. Bring a saucepan of water to the boil, add the remaining lemon juice and the artichokes, cover and cook for 30–40 minutes, or until tender. Drain, refresh under cold running water and drain again. Pull off and discard the remaining leaves, slice off and discard the chokes and set the hearts aside.

Pour the Calvados into a small saucepan, add the shallot and salt and bring to just below boiling point. Reduce the heat, carefully ignite the Calvados and continue to cook until the flames have died down. Stir in the vinegar and walnut oil and cook, stirring constantly, for 1 minute. Remove the saucepan from the heat.

Spoon half the dressing over the salad leaves and toss well to coat. Transfer the salad leaves to a large serving plate and top with the artichoke hearts. Spoon the remaining dressing over the artichoke hearts, garnish with the walnuts and chopped parsley and serve immediately.

strawberry rose meringues

Preheat the oven to 110°C/225°F/Gas Mark ¼. Line 2 large baking sheets with non-stick baking paper. Place the egg whites in a large, spotlessly clean, greasefree bowl and whisk until stiff peaks form. Whisk in half the sugar, then carefully fold in the remainder.

Spoon the meringue into a piping bag fitted with a large star nozzle. Pipe 24 x 7.5-cm/ 3-inch lengths on to the baking sheets. Bake in the oven for 1 hour, or until the meringues are dry and crisp. Cool on wire racks.

MAKES 24

To make the filling, place the strawberries in a blender or food processor and process to a purée. Sieve the purée into a bowl and stir in the icing sugar and rosewater. Place the cream in a separate bowl and whip until thick. Stir into the strawberry mixture and mix well together. Sandwich the meringues together with the strawberry cream. Cut 6 of the strawberries for the decoration in half and use to decorate the meringues. Scatter rose petals over the top and serve immediately with the remaining whole strawberries.

ingredients

2 egg whites

115 g/4 oz caster sugar

FILLING

55 g/2 oz strawberries

2 tsp icing sugar

3 tbsp rosewater

150 ml/5 fl oz double cream

TO DECORATE

12 fresh strawberries

rose petals

COOK'S TIP

When sugar is whisked into egg whites to make a meringue, it should gradually dissolve into the egg whites. Make sure the bowl is very clean, otherwise the meringue will not hold its shape.

VARIATION

You can substitute raspberries for the strawberries, or use a mixture of the 2 fruits, if you like.

SERVES 4

fried cheese sandwiches

First, make the sauce. Heat the olive oil in a medium, heavy-based saucepan. Add the onion and garlic and cook over a low heat, stirring occasionally, for 5 minutes, until softened. Add the red pepper and cook, stirring frequently, for a further 5 minutes. Stir in the tomatoes, tomato purée, lemon juice and water and season to taste with salt and pepper. Cover the saucepan and simmer for about 15 minutes, until pulpy.

Meanwhile, slice the mozzarella into 4 thick or 8 medium slices. Spread the bread slices with the butter and place the mozzarella on 4 of them. Top with the salami and sandwich together with the remaining slices of bread. Cut in half to make triangles, wrap in clingfilm and chill in the fridge.

Remove the sauce from the heat and set aside to cool slightly in the saucepan, then process in a food processor or blender until smooth. Return the sauce to a clean saucepan and reheat gently.

Heat the corn oil in a deep-fryer to 180–190°C/ 350–375°F or, if using a heavy-based saucepan, until a cube of day-old bread browns in 30 seconds. Meanwhile, beat the eggs with the milk in a shallow dish and season to taste with salt and pepper. Unwrap the sandwiches and dip them, in batches, into the egg mixture, allowing them to soak briefly. Add the sandwiches, in batches, to the hot oil and cook until golden brown on both sides. Remove with tongs, drain well on kitchen paper and keep warm while you cook the remaining triangles. Serve the sandwiches hot and hand round the sauce separately.

ingredients

200g /7 oz mozzarella di bufala
8 x 1-cm/½-inch thick slices day-old white bread, crusts removed
85 g/3 oz unsalted butter
4 slices Italian salami
corn oil, for deep-frying
3 eggs
3 tbsp milk
salt and pepper

SAUCE
3 tbsp olive oil
1 onion, chopped
2 garlic cloves, chopped finely
1 red pepper, deseeded and chopped
400 g/14 oz canned tomatoes, chopped
2 tbsp tomato purée
1 tbsp lemon juice
2 tbsp water
salt and pepper

strawberry rose meringues

Preheat the oven to 110°C/225°F/Gas Mark ¼. Line 2 large baking sheets with non-stick baking paper. Place the egg whites in a large, spotlessly clean, greasefree bowl and whisk until stiff peaks form. Whisk in half the sugar, then carefully fold in the remainder.

Spoon the meringue into a piping bag fitted with a large star nozzle. Pipe 24 x 7.5-cm/ 3-inch lengths on to the baking sheets. Bake in the oven for 1 hour, or until the meringues are dry and crisp. Cool on wire racks.

To make the filling, place the strawberries in a blender or food processor and process to a purée. Sieve the purée into a bowl and stir in the icing sugar and rosewater. Place the cream in a separate bowl and whip until thick. Stir into the strawberry mixture and mix well together. Sandwich the meringues together with the strawberry cream. Cut 6 of the strawberries for the decoration in half and use to decorate the meringues. Scatter rose petals over the top and serve immediately with the remaining whole strawberries.

ingredients

2 egg whites

115 g/4 oz caster sugar

FILLING

55 g/2 oz strawberries

2 tsp icing sugar

3 tbsp rosewater

150 ml/5 fl oz double cream

TO DECORATE

12 fresh strawberries

rose petals

COOK'S TIP

When sugar is whisked into egg whites to make a meringue, it should gradually dissolve into the egg whites. Make sure the bowl is very clean, otherwise the meringue will not hold its shape.

VARIATION

You can substitute raspberries for the strawberries, or use a mixture of the 2 fruits, if you like.

monkfish with lime and chilli sauce

Toss the fish in the flour, shaking off any excess. Heat the oil in a wok and fry the fish on all sides until browned and cooked through, taking care when turning not to break it up.

Lift the fish out of the wok and keep warm. Add the garlic and chillies and stir-fry for 1–2 minutes, until they have softened.

Add the sugar, the lime juice and rind and 2–3 tablespoons of water and bring to the boil. Simmer gently for 1–2 minutes, then spoon the mixture over the fish. Serve immediately with rice.

ingredients

4 x 115 g/4 oz monkfish fillets

25 g/1 oz rice flour or cornflour

6 tbsp vegetable or groundnut oil

4 garlic cloves, crushed

2 large fresh red chillies, deseeded
    and sliced

2 tsp palm sugar or soft, light brown
    sugar

juice of 2 limes

grated rind of 1 lime

boiled rice, to serve

spaghetti with garlicky tomato sauce

JULY

19

SERVES 4

Heat the oil in a large saucepan over a medium heat. Add the onion and fry gently for 5 minutes until soft. Add the tomatoes and garlic. Bring to the boil, then simmer over a medium–low heat for 25–30 minutes until the oil separates from the tomato. Season with salt and pepper.

Cook the pasta in plenty of boiling salted water until al dente. Drain and transfer to a warm serving dish.

Pour the sauce over the pasta. Add the basil and toss well to mix. Serve with Parmesan.

ingredients

5 tbsp extra-virgin olive oil

1 onion, chopped finely

800 g/1 lb 12 oz canned chopped tomatoes

4 garlic cloves, quartered

salt and pepper

450 g/1 lb dried spaghetti

large handful fresh basil leaves, shredded

freshly grated Parmesan, to serve

red mullet cooked in a parcel

JULY

20

SERVES 4

Cut 4 squares of greaseproof paper large enough to enclose the fish and brush with a little olive oil.

Rinse the fish inside and out under cold running water and pat dry with kitchen paper. Season. Using a sharp knife, cut 3 diagonal slits in both sides of each fish. Insert the garlic slices into the slits.

Combine the olive oil, tomatoes and rosemary in a bowl. Spoon a little of the mixture onto each of the greaseproof paper squares, then place the fish on top. Divide the remaining tomato mixture among the fish.

Fold up the paper around the fish, twisting it into tiny pleats to seal securely. Place the parcels on a baking sheet and bake in a preheated oven, 200°C/400°F/ Gas Mark 6, for 15 minutes.

Transfer the parcels to warmed plates and cut off the folded edges of the parcels. Serve with bread.

ingredients

4 tbsp extra virgin olive oil, plus extra for brushing

4 x 280 g/10 oz red mullet or red snapper, cleaned and scaled, heads on

salt and pepper

4 garlic cloves, sliced thinly lengthways

4 tomatoes, peeled, deseeded and diced

2 tsp finely chopped fresh rosemary

bread, to serve

JULY

21

SERVES 4

fried cheese sandwiches

First, make the sauce. Heat the olive oil in a medium, heavy-based saucepan. Add the onion and garlic and cook over a low heat, stirring occasionally, for 5 minutes, until softened. Add the red pepper and cook, stirring frequently, for a further 5 minutes. Stir in the tomatoes, tomato purée, lemon juice and water and season to taste with salt and pepper. Cover the saucepan and simmer for about 15 minutes, until pulpy.

Meanwhile, slice the mozzarella into 4 thick or 8 medium slices. Spread the bread slices with the butter and place the mozzarella on 4 of them. Top with the salami and sandwich together with the remaining slices of bread. Cut in half to make triangles, wrap in clingfilm and chill in the fridge.

Remove the sauce from the heat and set aside to cool slightly in the saucepan, then process in a food processor or blender until smooth. Return the sauce to a clean saucepan and reheat gently.

Heat the corn oil in a deep-fryer to 180–190°C/ 350–375°F or, if using a heavy-based saucepan, until a cube of day-old bread browns in 30 seconds. Meanwhile, beat the eggs with the milk in a shallow dish and season to taste with salt and pepper. Unwrap the sandwiches and dip them, in batches, into the egg mixture, allowing them to soak briefly. Add the sandwiches, in batches, to the hot oil and cook until golden brown on both sides. Remove with tongs, drain well on kitchen paper and keep warm while you cook the remaining triangles. Serve the sandwiches hot and hand round the sauce separately.

ingredients

200g /7 oz mozzarella di bufala

8 x 1-cm/½-inch thick slices day-old
   white bread, crusts removed

85 g/3 oz unsalted butter

4 slices Italian salami

corn oil, for deep-frying

3 eggs

3 tbsp milk

salt and pepper

SAUCE

3 tbsp olive oil

1 onion, chopped

2 garlic cloves, chopped finely

1 red pepper, deseeded and
   chopped

400 g/14 oz canned tomatoes,
   chopped

2 tbsp tomato purée

1 tbsp lemon juice

2 tbsp water

salt and pepper

walnut & cinnamon blondies

Preheat the oven to 180°C/350°F/Gas Mark 4. Grease and line the base of an 18-cm/ 7-inch square cake tin. Place the butter and sugar in a saucepan over a low heat and stir until the sugar has dissolved. Cook, stirring, for a further 1 minute. The mixture will bubble slightly, but do not let it boil. Leave to cool for 10 minutes.

MAKES 9

Stir the egg and egg yolk into the mixture. Sift in the flour and cinnamon, add the nuts and stir until just blended. Pour the cake mixture into the prepared tin, then bake in the preheated oven for 20–25 minutes, or until springy in the centre and a skewer inserted into the centre of the cake comes out clean.

Leave to cool in the tin for a few minutes, then run a knife around the edge of the cake to loosen it. Turn the cake out on to a wire rack and peel off the paper. Leave to cool completely. When cold, cut into squares.

ingredients

115 g/4 oz butter, plus extra for
  greasing
225 g/8 oz light muscovado sugar
1 egg
1 egg yolk
140 g/5 oz self-raising flour
1 tsp ground cinnamon
85 g/3 oz walnuts, roughly chopped

COOK'S TIP
Do not chop the walnuts too finely,
as the blondies should have a good
texture and a slight crunch to them.

mustard steaks with tomato relish

To make the tomato relish, place all the ingredients in a heavy-based saucepan. Bring to the boil, stirring until the sugar has completely dissolved. Reduce the heat and simmer, stirring occasionally, for 40 minutes, or until thickened. Transfer to a bowl, cover with clingfilm and leave to cool.

Preheat the barbecue or a griddle. Using a sharp knife, cut almost completely through each steak horizontally to make a pocket. Spread the mustard inside the pockets and rub the steaks all over with the garlic. Place them on a plate, cover with clingfilm and leave to stand for 30 minutes.

Cook the steaks over hot coals or in the hot griddle for 2½ minutes each side for rare, 4 minutes each side for medium or 6 minutes each side for well done. Transfer to serving plates, garnish with fresh tarragon sprigs and serve immediately with the tomato relish.

ingredients

4 sirloin or rump steaks

1 tbsp tarragon mustard

2 garlic cloves, crushed

fresh tarragon sprigs, to garnish

TOMATO RELISH

225 g/8 oz cherry tomatoes

55 g/2 oz muscovado sugar

50 ml/2 fl oz white wine vinegar

1 piece of stem ginger, chopped

½ lime, thinly sliced

salt, to taste

hot cajun seafood fusilli

Heat the cream in a large saucepan over a medium heat, stirring constantly. When almost boiling, reduce the heat and add the spring onions, parsley, thyme, pepper, chilli flakes and salt. Simmer for 7–8 minutes, stirring, until thickened. Remove from the heat.

Cook the pasta in plenty of boiling salted water until al dente. Drain and return to the pan. Add the cream mixture and the cheeses to the pasta. Toss over a low heat until the cheeses have melted. Transfer to a warm serving dish.

Heat the oil in a large frying pan over a medium–high heat. Add the prawns and scallops. Stir-fry for 2–3 minutes until the prawns have just turned pink.

Pour the seafood over the pasta and toss well to mix. Sprinkle with the basil. Serve immediately.

ingredients

500 ml/18 fl oz whipping cream

8 spring onions, sliced thinly

55 g/2 oz chopped fresh flat-leaved parsley

1 tbsp chopped fresh thyme

½ tbsp freshly ground black pepper

½–1 tsp dried chilli flakes

1 tsp salt

450 g/1 lb dried fusilli or tagliatelle

40 g/1½ oz freshly grated Gruyère

20 g/¾ oz freshly grated Parmesan

2 tbsp olive oil

225 g/8 oz raw peeled prawns

225 g/8 oz scallops, sliced

1 tbsp shredded fresh basil, to serve

crab cakes with salsa verde

Place the crabmeat, fish, red chilli, garlic, ginger, lemon grass, coriander and egg white in a food processor and process until thoroughly blended, then transfer to a bowl, cover with clingfilm and chill in the refrigerator for 30–60 minutes.

Meanwhile, make the salsa verde. Put the green chillies, spring onions, garlic and parsley in a food processor and process until finely chopped. Transfer to a small bowl and stir in the lime rind, lime and lemon juice, olive oil and green Tabasco sauce. Season to taste with salt and pepper, cover with clingfilm and leave to chill in the refrigerator until ready to serve.

Heat 2 tablespoons of the groundnut oil in a non-stick frying pan. Add spoonfuls of the crab mixture, flattening them gently with a spatula and keeping them spaced well apart. Cook for 4 minutes, then turn with a spatula and cook the other side for 3 minutes, or until golden brown. Remove from the frying pan and keep warm while you cook the remaining batches, adding more oil if necessary. Transfer the crab cakes to a large serving plate, garnish and serve with the salsa verde.

ingredients

250 g/9 oz crabmeat, thawed
    if frozen
250 g/9 oz white fish fillet, such as
    cod, skinned and roughly chopped
1 fresh red chilli, deseeded and
    roughly chopped
1 garlic clove, roughly chopped
2.5-cm/1-inch piece of fresh root
    ginger, roughly chopped
1 lemon grass stalk, roughly
    chopped
3 tbsp chopped fresh coriander
1 egg white
groundnut or sunflower oil, for frying

SALSA VERDE

2 fresh green chillies, deseeded and
    roughly chopped
8 spring onions, roughly chopped
2 garlic cloves, roughly chopped
1 bunch of fresh parsley
grated rind and juice of 1 lime
juice of 1 lemon
4 tbsp olive oil
1 tbsp green Tabasco sauce
salt and pepper

VARIATION

For an elegant presentation, garnish the crab cakes with fresh Chinese chives. If these are unavailable, use ordinary fresh chives instead.

ingredients

PASTRY

175 g/6 oz plain flour, plus extra
for dusting

3 tbsp caster sugar

salt

115 g/4 oz unsalted butter, chilled
and diced

1 egg yolk

FILLING

450 g/1 lb ricotta cheese

125 ml/4 fl oz double cream

2 eggs, plus 1 egg yolk

85 g/3 oz caster sugar

finely grated rind of 1 lemon

finely grated rind of 1 orange

ricotta cheesecake

To make the pastry, sift the flour with the sugar and a pinch of salt onto a work surface and make a well in the centre. Add the diced butter and egg yolk to the well and, using your fingertips, gradually work in the flour mixture until fully incorporated.

Gather up the dough and knead very lightly. Cut off about one-quarter, wrap in clingfilm and chill in the fridge. Press the remaining dough into the base of a 23-cm/9-inch, loose-based flan tin. Chill for 30 minutes.

To make the filling, beat the ricotta with the cream, eggs and extra egg yolk, sugar, lemon rind and orange rind. Cover with clingfilm and set aside in the fridge until required.

Prick the base of the pastry case all over with a fork. Line with foil, fill with baking beans and bake blind in a preheated oven, 190°C/375°F/Gas Mark 5, for 15 minutes.

Remove the pastry case from the oven and take out the foil and beans. Stand the tin on a wire rack and set aside to cool.

Spoon the ricotta mixture into the pastry case and smooth the surface. Roll out the reserved pastry on a lightly floured surface and cut it into strips. Arrange the strips over the filling in a lattice pattern, brushing the overlapping ends with water so that they stick.

Bake in the preheated oven, 190°C/375°F/Gas Mark 5, for 30–35 minutes, until the top of the cheesecake is golden and the filling has set. Cool on a wire rack before lifting off the side of the tin. Cut into wedges to serve.

light bacon and cottage cheese buns

Preheat the grill to high. Remove any visible fat and rind from the bacon and cut 4 of the tomatoes in half. Place the bacon and tomatoes, cut-side up, under the preheated grill and cook, turning the bacon over halfway through cooking, for 8–10 minutes, or until the bacon is crisp and the tomatoes are softened. Remove the tomatoes and bacon from the grill and drain the bacon on kitchen paper to help remove any excess fat. Keep the bacon and tomatoes warm.

Meanwhile, cut the remaining tomatoes into bite-sized pieces and combine with the cottage cheese in a bowl. Cut the bacon into bite-sized pieces and stir into the cottage cheese mixture. Season to taste with pepper.

Cut the bread rolls in half and divide the bacon filling evenly over each roll base. Sprinkle the spring onions over the filling and cover with the roll tops. Serve immediately with the grilled tomatoes.

ingredients

8 low-salt lean smoked back bacon
    rashers
6 tomatoes
250 g/9 oz low-fat natural cottage
    cheese
freshly ground black pepper
4 large seeded wholemeal or white
    bread rolls
2 spring onions, chopped

meringue and strawberries

Preheat the oven to 150°C/300°F/Gas Mark 2.

Whisk the egg whites in a mixing bowl using an electric mixer until thick and in soft peaks. Add the sugar gradually, whisking well with each addition. The meringue mixture should be glossy and firm.

Spoon the meringue onto a baking tray lined with baking paper and spread into a rough 30-cm/12-inch round. Cook for 45–50 minutes until the meringue is firm on the outside but still soft in the centre. Remove from the oven and allow to cool.

Check over the strawberries and hull them.

Place a third of the berries (choose the larger ones) in a liquidizer and purée with the icing sugar. Pour the purée into a bowl, add the liqueur, if using, and the remaining strawberries and turn in the sauce until well mixed.

Whip together the double and single cream until thick but still light and floppy.

Break the meringue into large pieces and place half in a large glass serving bowl. Spoon over half the fruit mixture and half the cream. Layer up the remaining ingredients and lightly fold the mixtures together so you have a streaky appearance.

Serve soon after mixing or the meringues will soften.

ingredients
3 egg whites
175 g/6 oz caster sugar
700 g/1 lb 9 oz strawberries
2 tbsp icing sugar
2 tbsp crème de fraise (strawberry)
    liqueur (optional)
300 ml/½ pint double cream
150 ml/¼ pint single cream

ingredients

1 litre/1¾pints chicken or vegetable
  stock
85 g/3 oz butter
3 shallots, chopped finely
115 g/4 oz pancetta or rindless
  streaky bacon, diced
280 g/10 oz arborio rice
150 ml/¼ pint dry white wine
225 g/8 oz petits pois, thawed if
  using frozen
salt and pepper
Parmesan cheese shavings, to
  garnish

SERVES 4

VARIATION

*You can substitute diced cooked
ham for the pancetta or bacon. Add
it towards the end of the cooking
time so that it heats through.*

JULY

29

rice and peas

Pour the stock into a large saucepan and bring to the boil. Lower the heat and simmer
gently. Melt 55 g/2 oz of the butter in another large, heavy-based saucepan. Add the
shallots and pancetta or bacon and cook over a low heat, stirring occasionally, for
5 minutes, until the shallots are softened. Add the rice and cook, stirring constantly, for
2–3 minutes, until all the grains are thoroughly coated and glistening.

Pour in the wine and cook, stirring constantly, until it has almost completely evaporated.
Add a ladleful of hot stock and cook, stirring constantly, until all the stock has been
absorbed. Continue cooking and adding the stock, a ladleful at a time, for about
10 minutes.

Add the peas, then continue adding the stock, a ladleful at a time, for about a further
10 minutes, or until the rice is tender and the liquid has been absorbed.

Stir in the remaining butter and season to taste with salt and pepper. Transfer the risotto
to a warmed serving dish, garnish with Parmesan shavings and serve immediately.

tomato salad with fried feta

Make the dressing by whisking together the extra virgin olive oil, the lemon juice, oregano, sugar and pepper in a small bowl. Set aside.

Prepare the salad by arranging the tomatoes, onion, rocket and olives on 4 individual plates.

Cut the feta cheese into cubes about 2.5 cm/1 inch square. Beat the egg in a dish and put the flour on a separate plate. Toss the cheese first in the egg, shake off the excess, and then toss in the flour.

Heat the olive oil in a large frying pan, add the cheese and fry over a medium heat, turning over the cubes of cheese until they are golden on all sides.

Scatter the fried feta over the salad. Whisk together the prepared dressing, spoon over the salad and serve warm.

ingredients

3 tbsp extra virgin olive oil

juice of ½ lemon

2 tsp chopped fresh oregano

pinch of sugar

pepper

DRESSING

12 plum tomatoes, sliced

1 very small red onion, sliced very thinly

15 g/½ oz rocket leaves

20 Greek black olives

200 g/7 oz feta cheese

1 egg

3 tbsp plain white flour

2 tbsp olive oil

blueberry dazzler

Pour the apple juice into a food processor. Add the yogurt and process until smooth.

Add the banana and half of the blueberries and process well, then add the remaining blueberries and process until smooth.

Pour the mixture into tall glasses and add straws.

Decorate with whole fresh blueberries and serve.

ingredients

175 ml/6 fl oz apple juice

125 ml/4 fl oz natural yogurt

1 banana, sliced and frozen

175 g/6 oz frozen blueberries

DECORATION

whole fresh blueberries

August

prosciutto with rocket

Separate the rocket leaves, wash in cold water and pat dry on kitchen paper. Place the leaves in a bowl.

Pour the lemon juice into a small bowl and season to taste with salt and pepper. Whisk in the olive oil, then pour the dressing over the rocket leaves and toss lightly so they are evenly coated.

Carefully drape the prosciutto in folds on individual serving plates, then add the rocket. Serve at room temperature.

ingredients

115 g/4 oz rocket

1 tbsp lemon juice

salt and pepper

3 tbsp extra virgin olive oil

225 g/8 oz prosciutto, sliced thinly

VARIATION

For a more substantial salad, add 1 thinly sliced fennel bulb and 2 thinly sliced oranges to the rocket in step 1. Substitute orange juice or balsamic vinegar for the lemon juice in step 2.

jerk chicken

Deseed and finely chop the red chillies, then place them in a small glass bowl with the oil, garlic, onion, spring onion, vinegar, lime juice, sugar, thyme, cinnamon, mixed spice and nutmeg. Season to taste with salt and pepper and mash thoroughly with a fork.

Using a sharp knife, make a series of diagonal slashes in the chicken pieces and place them in a large, shallow, non-metallic dish. Spoon the jerk seasoning over the chicken, rubbing it well into the slashes. Cover and leave to marinate in the refrigerator for up to 8 hours.

Preheat the barbecue or a griddle. Remove the chicken from the marinade, discarding the marinade, brush with oil and cook over medium hot coals, turning frequently, until cooked through. Transfer to plates and serve.

ingredients

2 fresh red chillies

2 tbsp corn oil, plus extra for brushing

2 garlic cloves, finely chopped

1 tbsp finely chopped onion

1 tbsp finely chopped spring onion

1 tbsp white wine vinegar

1 tbsp lime juice

2 tsp demerara sugar

1 tsp dried thyme

1 tsp ground cinnamon

1 tsp ground mixed spice

¼ tsp freshly grated nutmeg

salt and pepper

4 chicken quarters

AUGUST

2

SERVES 4

chilled pea soup

Bring the stock to the boil in a large saucepan over a medium heat. Reduce the heat, add the peas and spring onions and simmer for 5 minutes.

Leave to cool slightly, then sieve twice, making sure that you remove and discard any pieces of skin. Pour into a large bowl, season to taste with salt and pepper and stir in the yogurt. Cover the bowl with clingfilm and chill in the refrigerator for several hours.

To serve, mix the soup well and ladle into a large tureen or individual soup bowls or mugs. Garnish with chopped mint or snipped chives, spring onions and grated lemon rind.

ingredients

425 ml/15 fl oz vegetable stock
or water
450 g/1 lb frozen peas
55 g/2 oz spring onions, chopped,
plus extra to garnish
salt and pepper
300 ml/10 fl oz natural yogurt or
single cream

TO GARNISH
2 tbsp chopped fresh mint or
snipped fresh chives
grated lemon rind

easy mango ice cream

Mix the custard, cream and mango purée together in a bowl.

Taste for sweetness and, if desired, add icing sugar to taste, remembering that when frozen the mixture will taste less sweet.

Transfer to an ice cream maker and process for 15 minutes. Alternatively, transfer the mixture to a freezerproof container. Cover and freeze for 2–3 hours until just frozen. Spoon into a bowl and beat with a fork or whisk to break down any ice crystals. Return the mixture to the container and freeze for a further 2 hours. Beat the ice cream once more, then freeze for 2–3 hours until firm.

Transfer from the freezer to the refrigerator 20–30 minutes before serving, to soften. Serve with the passion fruit pulp.

ingredients
600 ml/1 pint ready-made
traditional custard
150 ml/5 fl oz whipping cream,
lightly whipped
flesh of 2 ripe mangoes, puréed
icing sugar, to taste (optional)
passion fruit pulp, to serve

tomato, courgette & basil filo tartlets

Preheat the oven to 190°C/375°F/Gas Mark 5. Lightly oil 4 x 12-cm/4½-inch individual loose-bottomed flan tins.

Working quickly so that the filo pastry does not dry out, cut each sheet into 6 equal-sized pieces measuring about 16 x 14 cm/6¼ x 5½ inches. Layer 3 pieces of pastry at a time in the 4 flan tins, lightly brushing between each layer with oil. Carefully press the pastry into the sides of the tins so that the corners of the pastry squares point upwards. Arrange the tins on a large baking sheet.

Sprinkle two-thirds of the torn basil leaves over the pastry bases and cover with overlapping slices of tomato and courgette. Beat the eggs with the milk in a bowl and season well with pepper. Divide the egg mixture evenly between the tins and sprinkle the remaining torn basil leaves over it.

Bake in the preheated oven for 20–25 minutes, or until the egg mixture has set and the pastry is crisp and golden. Serve warm or cold, garnished with basil leaves and with a selection of salads and boiled new potatoes.

ingredients

olive oil, for oiling and brushing

2 x 48- x 28-cm/19- x 11-inch sheets
   filo pastry

1 tbsp torn fresh basil leaves, plus
   extra leaves to garnish

7–8 cherry tomatoes, thinly sliced

1 courgette, thinly sliced

2 eggs, beaten

150 ml/5 fl oz skimmed or semi-
   skimmed milk

freshly ground black pepper

TO SERVE

selection of salads

boiled new potatoes

skate in mustard & caper sauce

Cut each skate wing in half and place in a large frying pan. Cover with salted water, bring to the boil then simmer for 10–15 minutes, until tender.

Meanwhile, make the mustard and caper sauce. Heat the oil in a saucepan, add the onion and garlic and cook for 5 minutes, until softened. Add the yogurt, lemon juice, parsley and capers and cook for 1–2 minutes, until heated through. (Do not boil or the sauce will curdle.) Stir in the mustard and season with salt and pepper.

Drain the skate and put on 4 warmed serving plates. Pour over the mustard and caper sauce and sprinkle with chopped parsley. Serve hot with lemon wedges.

ingredients
2 skate wings
2 tbsp olive oil
1 onion, chopped finely
1 garlic clove, chopped finely
150 ml/¼ pint Greek yogurt
1 tsp lemon juice
1 tbsp chopped fresh flat-leaved parsley
1 tbsp capers, chopped roughly
1 tbsp wholegrain mustard
salt and pepper
chopped fresh flat-leaved parsley, to garnish
lemon wedges, to serve

peach cobbler

Preheat the oven to 220°C/425°F/Gas Mark 7. Put the peaches in a 23-cm/9-inch square ovenproof dish that is also suitable for serving. Add the sugar, lemon juice, cornflour and almond essence and toss together. Bake the peaches in the oven for 20 minutes.

Meanwhile, to make the topping, sift the flour, all but 2 tablespoons of the sugar, the baking powder and salt into a bowl. Rub in the butter with the fingertips until the mixture resembles breadcrumbs. Mix the egg and 5 tablespoons of the milk in a jug, then mix into the dry ingredients with a fork until a soft, sticky dough forms. If the dough seems too dry, stir in the extra tablespoon of milk.

Reduce the oven temperature to 200°C/400°F/Gas Mark 6. Remove the peaches from the oven and drop spoonfuls of the topping over the surface, without smoothing. Sprinkle with the remaining sugar, return to the oven and bake for a further 15 minutes, or until the topping is golden brown and firm – the topping will spread as it cooks. Serve hot or at room temperature with ice cream.

ingredients
FILLING
6 peaches, peeled and sliced
4 tbsp caster sugar
½ tbsp lemon juice
1½ tsp cornflour
½ tsp almond or vanilla essence
vanilla or pecan ice cream, to serve

PIE TOPPING
175 g/6 oz plain flour
115 g/4 oz caster sugar
1½ tsp baking powder
½ tsp salt
85 g/3 oz butter, diced
1 egg
5–6 tbsp milk

speedy vegetable pilau

Rinse the basmati rice thoroughly in 2–3 changes of water, drain well and reserve until required.

Heat the sunflower oil in a large, heavy-based saucepan or flameproof casserole. Add the garlic, cinnamon stick, cardamom and cumin and cook, stirring constantly, for 1 minute. Add the tomato and mushrooms and cook, stirring constantly, for 3 minutes.

Stir in the rice and peas and cook for 1 minute, stirring to coat the grains, then add the vegetable stock and bring to the boil. Reduce the heat, cover and simmer for 10–15 minutes, or until the rice is tender and the liquid has been absorbed. Remove the cinnamon stick and serve the pilau immediately.

ingredients

450 g/1 lb basmati rice
2 tbsp sunflower oil
2 garlic cloves, finely chopped
½ cinnamon stick
2 cardamom pods
½ tsp black cumin seeds
1 tomato, sliced
55 g/2 oz baby button mushrooms
85 g/3 oz shelled peas
700 ml/1¼ pints vegetable stock

AUGUST

8

SERVES 4

COOK'S TIP
If you have time, soak the rice in a large bowl of cold water for 10 minutes before cooking to lighten the grain.

VARIATION
Use the same amount of sliced chestnut mushrooms instead of the button ones, and if shelled peas are not available, use frozen instead.

minted green risotto

Bring the stock to the boil in a saucepan, then reduce the heat and keep simmering over a low heat while you are cooking the risotto.

Heat half the butter in a deep frying pan over a medium-high heat until sizzling. Add the peas, spinach, mint leaves, basil and oregano and season with the nutmeg. Cook, stirring frequently, for 3 minutes, or until the spinach and mint leaves are wilted. Cool slightly.

Pour the spinach mixture into a food processor and process for 15 seconds. Add the mascarpone (or cream) and process again for 1 minute. Transfer to a bowl and set aside.

Heat the oil and remaining butter in a large, heavy-based saucepan over a medium heat. Add the onion, celery, garlic and thyme and cook, stirring occasionally, for 2 minutes, or until the vegetables are softened.

Reduce the heat, add the rice and mix to coat in oil and butter. Cook, stirring constantly, for 2–3 minutes, or until the grains are translucent.

Add the vermouth and cook, stirring constantly, until it has reduced. Gradually add the hot stock, a ladle at a time. Stir constantly and add more liquid as the rice absorbs each addition. Increase the heat to medium so that the liquid bubbles. Cook for 20 minutes, or until the liquid is absorbed and the rice is creamy.

Stir in the spinach-mascarpone mixture and the Parmesan. Transfer to warmed plates and serve immediately.

ingredients

1 litre/1¾ pints chicken or
   vegetable stock
25 g/1 oz butter
225 g/8 oz shelled fresh peas or
   thawed frozen peas
250 g/9 oz fresh young spinach
   leaves, washed and drained
1 bunch of fresh mint, leaves
   stripped from stalks
2 tbsp chopped fresh basil
2 tbsp chopped fresh oregano
pinch of freshly grated nutmeg
4 tbsp mascarpone cheese or
   double cream
2 tbsp vegetable oil
1 onion, finely chopped
2 celery sticks, including leaves,
   finely chopped
2 garlic cloves,finely chopped
½ tsp dried thyme
300 g/10½ oz risotto rice
50 ml/2 fl oz dry white vermouth
85 g/3 oz freshly grated Parmesan
   cheese

grilled steak with tomatoes & garlic

Place the oil, tomatoes, red pepper, onion, garlic, parsley, oregano and sugar in a heavy-based saucepan and season to taste with salt and pepper. Bring to the boil, lower the heat and simmer for 15 minutes.

Meanwhile, snip any fat around the outsides of the steaks. Season each generously with pepper (no salt) and brush with olive oil. Cook under a very hot preheated grill for 1 minute on each side. Lower the heat to medium and cook according to taste: 1½–2 minutes each side for rare; 2½–3 minutes each side for medium; 3–4 minutes on each side for well done.

Transfer the steaks to warmed individual plates and spoon the sauce over them. Serve immediately.

ingredients

3 tbsp olive oil, plus extra for
    brushing
700 g/1 lb 9 oz tomatoes, peeled
    and chopped
1 red pepper, deseeded and
    chopped
1 onion, chopped
2 garlic cloves, chopped finely
1 tbsp chopped fresh flat-leaved
    parsley
1 tsp dried oregano
1 tsp sugar
salt and pepper
4 x 175 g/6 oz entrecôte or rump
    steaks

prawns, peas & pasta

Place the saffron in a small bowl, add the wine and leave to soak. Heat the olive oil and butter in a large heavy-based frying pan. Add the shallot and cook over a low heat, stirring occasionally, for 5 minutes, or until softened. Add the peas and cooked prawns and cook, stirring occasionally, for 2–3 minutes.

Bring a large heavy-based saucepan of lightly salted water to the boil. Add the pasta, return to the boil and cook for 8–10 minutes, or until tender but still firm to the bite.

Meanwhile, stir the saffron and wine mixture into the frying pan. Increase the heat and cook until the liquid is reduced by about half. Season to taste with salt and pepper. Drain the pasta and add to the frying pan. Cook for 1–2 minutes, or until it is well coated with the sauce. Transfer to a warmed serving dish, sprinkle with dill and serve immediately.

ingredients

pinch of saffron threads
225 ml/8 fl oz dry white wine
3 tbsp olive oil
25 g/1 oz unsalted butter
1 shallot, chopped
225 g/8 oz peas
350 g/12 oz cooked peeled prawns
350 g/12 oz dried fusilli bucati or
    ditali
salt and pepper
2 tbsp snipped fresh dill, to garnish

COOK'S TIP

If you are using frozen prawns and/or frozen peas, make sure that they are thoroughly thawed before you begin.

hot & spicy ribs

Preheat the barbecue or griddle. Put the onion, garlic, ginger, chilli and soy sauce into a food processor and process to a paste. Transfer to a jug and stir in the lime juice, sugar and oil and season to taste with salt and pepper.

Place the spare ribs in a preheated wok or large, heavy-based saucepan and pour in the soy sauce mixture. Place on the hob and bring to the boil, then simmer over a low heat, stirring frequently, for 30 minutes. If the mixture appears to be drying out, add a little water.

Remove the spare ribs, reserving the sauce. Cook the ribs over medium hot coals or in the pan, turning and basting frequently with the sauce, for 20–30 minutes. Transfer to a large serving plate and serve immediately.

ingredients

1 onion, chopped

2 garlic cloves, chopped

2.5-cm/1-inch piece fresh root
    ginger, sliced

1 fresh red chilli, deseeded and
    chopped

5 tbsp dark soy sauce

3 tbsp lime juice

1 tbsp palm or muscovado sugar

2 tbsp groundnut oil

salt and pepper

1 kg/2 lb 4 oz pork spare ribs,
    separated

COOK'S TIP

*Groundnut oil is used extensively
in South-east Asian markets, but if
you cannot find it, then use
sunflower oil instead.*

italian pesto chicken

Preheat the oven to 180°C/350°F/Gas Mark 4. To make the pesto, put all the ingredients into a food processor. Blend for a few seconds until smooth.

Halve each chicken breast and pound lightly to flatten each piece. Spread on one side only with pesto, then top with the Parma ham. Add a tablespoon of sun-dried tomatoes to each, then roll them up and secure with cocktail sticks.

Pour the olive oil into a large roasting tin. Arrange the chicken in the tin, then pour over the wine. Add the chopped tomatoes and bake in the preheated oven for 30 minutes.

Stir any remaining pesto into the cooked pasta and arrange on 4 serving plates. Remove the chicken from the oven, discard the cocktail stick and slice the chicken breasts in half, widthways. Divide between the plates. Pour over some of the cooking sauce, garnish with halved black olives and sprigs of basil and serve.

ingredients

4 skinless chicken breasts

8 slices Parma ham

75 g/2¾ oz sun-dried tomatoes in olive oil, drained and chopped

2 tbsp extra-virgin olive oil

125 ml/4 fl oz white wine

200 g/7 oz canned chopped tomatoes

PESTO

25 g/1 oz fresh basil, stalks removed

150 g/5½ oz pine kernels

3 garlic cloves, roughly chopped

100 ml/3½ fl oz extra-virgin olive oil

75 g/2¾ oz Parmesan cheese, freshly grated

salt and pepper, to taste

GARNISH

black olives, stoned and halved

sprigs of fresh basil

freshly cooked linguine, to serve

blueberry frozen yogurt

Put the blueberries and orange juice into a food processor or blender and process to a purée. Strain through a nylon sieve into a bowl or jug.

Stir the maple syrup and yogurt together in a large mixing bowl, then fold in the fruit purée.

Churn the mixture in an ice cream machine, following the manufacturer's instructions, then freeze for 5–6 hours. If you don't have an ice cream machine, transfer the mixture to a freezerproof container and freeze for 2 hours. Remove from the freezer, turn out into a bowl and beat until smooth. Return to the freezer and freeze until firm.

ingredients

175 g/6 oz fresh blueberries

finely grated rind and juice of 1 orange

3 tbsp maple syrup

500 g/1 lb 2 oz natural low-fat yogurt

aubergine tagine with polenta

Preheat the grill to medium. Toss the aubergine in 1 tablespoon of the oil and arrange in the grill pan. Cook under the preheated grill for 20 minutes, turning occasionally, until softened and beginning to blacken around the edges – brush with more oil if the aubergine becomes too dry.

Heat the remaining oil in a large, heavy-based saucepan over a medium heat. Add the onion and fry, stirring occasionally, for 8 minutes, or until soft and golden. Add the carrot, garlic and mushrooms and cook for 5 minutes. Add the spices and cook, stirring constantly, for a further minute.

Add the tomatoes and stock, stir well, then add the tomato purée. Bring to the boil, then reduce the heat and simmer for 10 minutes, or until the sauce begins to thicken and reduce.

Add the aubergine, apricots and chickpeas, partially cover and cook for a further 10 minutes, stirring occasionally.

Meanwhile, to make the polenta, pour the hot stock into a non-stick saucepan and bring to the boil. Pour in the polenta in a steady stream, stirring constantly with a wooden spoon. Reduce the heat to low and cook for 1–2 minutes, or until the polenta thickens to a mashed potato-like consistency. Serve the tagine with the polenta, sprinkled with the fresh coriander.

ingredients

1 aubergine, cut into 1-cm/½-inch cubes
3 tbsp olive oil
1 large onion, thinly sliced
1 carrot, diced
2 garlic cloves, chopped
115 g/4 oz brown-cap mushrooms, sliced
2 tsp ground coriander
2 tsp cumin seeds
1 tsp chilli powder
1 tsp ground turmeric
600 ml/1 pint canned chopped tomatoes
300 ml/10 fl oz vegetable stock
1 tbsp tomato purée
75 g/2¾ oz no-soak dried apricots, roughly chopped
400 g/14 oz canned chickpeas, drained and rinsed
2 tbsp fresh coriander, to garnish

POLENTA
1.2 litres/2 pints hot vegetable stock
200 g/7 oz instant polenta
salt and pepper

pasta with sun-dried tomato sauce

Put the tomatoes and boiling water in a bowl and leave to stand for 5 minutes. Using a perforated spoon, remove one-third of the tomatoes from the bowl. Cut into bite-sized pieces. Put the remaining tomatoes and water into a blender and purée.

Heat the oil in a large frying pan over a medium heat. Add the onion and gently fry for 5 minutes until soft. Add the garlic and fry until just beginning to colour. Add the puréed tomato and the reserved tomato pieces to the pan. Bring to the boil, then simmer over a medium–low heat for 10 minutes. Stir in the herbs and season with salt and pepper. Simmer for 1 minute, then remove from the heat.

Cook the pasta in plenty of boiling salted water until al dente. Drain and transfer to a warm serving dish. Briefly reheat the sauce. Pour over the pasta, add the basil and toss well to mix. Sprinkle with the Parmesan and serve immediately.

ingredients

85 g/3 oz sun-dried tomatoes
 (not in oil)
700 ml/1¼ pints boiling water
2 tbsp olive oil
1 onion, chopped finely
2 large garlic cloves, sliced finely
2 tbsp chopped fresh flat-leaved
 parsley
2 tsp chopped fresh oregano
1 tsp chopped fresh rosemary
salt and pepper
350 g/12 oz dried spaghetti or fusilli
10 fresh basil leaves, shredded
3 tbsp freshly grated Parmesan, to
 serve

lime-drizzled prawns

Grate the rind and squeeze out the juice from 2 of the limes. Cut the remaining 2 limes into wedges and reserve for later.

To prepare the prawns, remove the legs, leaving the shells and tails intact. Using a sharp knife, make a shallow slit along the underside of each prawn, then pull out the dark vein and discard. Rinse the prawns under cold water and dry well on kitchen paper.

Heat the olive oil in a large, heavy-based frying pan, then add the garlic and fry for 30 seconds. Add the prawns and fry for 5 minutes, stirring from time to time, or until they turn pink and beginning to curl. Mix in the lime rind, juice and a splash of sherry to moisten, then stir well together.

Transfer the cooked prawns to a serving dish, season to taste with salt and pepper and sprinkle over the parsley. Serve piping hot, accompanied by the reserved lime wedges for squeezing over the prawns.

ingredients

4 limes

12 raw king prawns, in their shells

3 tbsp Spanish olive oil

2 garlic cloves, finely chopped

splash of dry sherry

salt and pepper

4 tbsp chopped fresh
   flat-leaved parsley

AUGUST

17

SERVES 6

gazpacho

Reserve some of the tomatoes, cucumber and pepper for a garnish. Place the bread in a food processor and process until crumbs form. Add the remaining tomatoes, cucumber and pepper. Add the onion, garlic, vinegar and oil and process until smooth.

The tomatoes should have sufficient juice in them to make enough liquid but add a little water if the soup is too thick. Season to taste with salt.

Divide the soup between 4 serving bowls and add a few ice cubes to make sure that the soup is served chilled. Garnish with the reserved tomatoes, cucumber and pepper. Add a few sprigs of basil and serve with fresh crusty bread.

ingredients

1 kg/2lb 4 oz ripe tomatoes, pealed,
   deseeded and roughly chopped

½ cucumber, peeled, deseeded and
   roughly chopped

1 green pepper, deseeded and
   roughly chopped

115 g/4 oz fresh bread, crusts
   removed

1 small onion, roughly chopped

1 garlic clove, chopped

1 tbsp white wine vinegar

125 ml/4 fl oz olive oil

salt, to taste

ice cubes

few fresh basil sprigs, to garnish

fresh, crusty bread, to serve

AUGUST

18

SERVES 4

AUGUST

19

MAKES 20

ingredients

200 g/7 oz ready-made puff pastry

plain flour, for dusting

3 tbsp pesto

20 cherry tomatoes, each cut into
   3 slices

115 g/4 oz goat's cheese

salt and pepper

fresh basil sprigs, to garnish

COOK'S TIP

These tartlets are even quicker
to make if you use the ready-rolled
variety of ready-made puff pastry,
which is available in most of the
large supermarkets.

instant pesto & goat's cheese tartlets

Preheat the oven to 200°C/400°F/Gas Mark 6, then lightly flour a baking sheet. Roll out
the pastry on a floured work surface to 3 mm/⅛ inch thick. Cut out 20 rounds with a
5-cm/2-inch plain cutter and arrange the pastry rounds on the floured baking sheet.

Spread a little pesto on each round, leaving a margin around the edges, then arrange
3 tomato slices on top of each one. Crumble the goat's cheese over and season to taste
with salt and pepper. Bake in the preheated oven for 10 minutes, or until the pastry is
puffed up, crisp and golden. Garnish with basil sprigs and serve warm.

cajun chicken salad

Make 3 diagonal slashes across each chicken breast. Put the chicken into a shallow dish and sprinkle all over with the Cajun seasoning. Cover and refrigerate for at least 30 minutes.

When ready to cook, brush a griddle with the sunflower oil, if using. Heat over a high heat until very hot and a few drops of water sprinkled on to it sizzle immediately. Add the chicken and cook for 7–8 minutes on each side, or until thoroughly cooked. If still slightly pink in the centre, cook a little longer. Remove the chicken and reserve.

Add the mango slices to the pan and cook for 2 minutes on each side. Remove and reserve.

Meanwhile, arrange the salad leaves in a salad bowl and scatter over the onion, beetroot, radishes and walnut halves.

Put the walnut oil, mustard, lemon juice and salt and pepper to taste in a screw-top jar and shake until well blended. Pour over the salad and sprinkle with the sesame seeds.

Arrange the mango and the salad on a serving plate and top with the chicken breast and a few of the salad leaves.

ingredients

4 skinless, boneless chicken
    breasts, about 140 g/5 oz each
4 tsp Cajun seasoning
2 tsp sunflower oil (optional)
1 ripe mango, peeled, stoned and
    cut into thick slices
200 g/7 oz mixed salad leaves
1 red onion, thinly sliced and cut
    in half
175 g/6 oz cooked beetroot, diced
85 g/3 oz radishes, sliced
55 g/2 oz walnut halves
4 tbsp walnut oil
1–2 tsp Dijon mustard
1 tbsp lemon juice
salt and pepper
2 tbsp sesame seeds

lemonade

Put the pared lemon rind, the sugar, water and cinnamon in a saucepan. Bring to the boil, stirring until the sugar has dissolved and then simmer for 5 minutes, without allowing the syrup to colour. Leave to cool.

When cool, strain the syrup then strain in the lemon juice. Pour into a clean bottle and seal well. Label the lemonade and store in the fridge for up to 2 weeks if desired.

To serve, pour the lemonade into a glass, add ice cubes and dilute with still or sparkling water, allowing 1 part lemonade to 3 parts water or according to taste.

ingredients

pared rind and juice of 3 large
   lemons
450 g/1 lb white granulated sugar
150 ml/¼ pint water
1 cinnamon stick

TO SERVE
still or sparkling water
ice cubes

good coleslaw

Finely shred the cabbage. Grate the carrots and core and slice the apples. Finely chop the celery and spring onions. Put in a large bowl.

Mix the mayonnaise and yogurt together in a small bowl. Whisk in the mustard and lemon juice and season well with salt and pepper.

Add the raisins and walnuts to the salad vegetables, if using. Pour over the dressing and mix well. Serve at once.

ingredients
½ hard white cabbage
2 carrots
2 eating apples
2 celery sticks
3 spring onions
150 ml/5 fl oz mayonnaise
150 ml/5 fl oz natural yogurt
1 tsp French mustard
2 tbsp lemon juice
40 g/1½ oz raisins (optional)
40 g/1½ oz walnuts (optional)

chargrilled devils

Preheat the barbecue or a griddle. Open the oysters, catching the juice from the shells in a bowl. Cut the oysters from the bottom shells, reserve and tip any remaining juice into the bowl. To make the sauce, add the red chilli, garlic, shallot, parsley and lemon juice to the bowl, then season to taste with salt and pepper and mix well. Cover the bowl with clingfilm and leave to chill in the refrigerator until required.

Cut each bacon rasher in half across the centre. Season the oysters with paprika and cayenne, then roll each oyster up inside half a bacon rasher. Thread 9 wrapped oysters on to 4 presoaked wooden skewers or cocktail sticks.

SERVES 4

Cook over hot coals, turning frequently, for 5 minutes, or until the bacon is well browned and crispy. Transfer to a large serving plate and serve immediately with the sauce.

ingredients

36 fresh oysters

18 streaky bacon rashers, rinded

1 tbsp mild paprika

1 tsp cayenne pepper

SAUCE

1 fresh red chilli, deseeded and
   finely chopped

1 garlic clove, finely chopped

1 shallot, finely chopped

2 tbsp finely chopped fresh parsley

2 tbsp lemon juice

salt and pepper

COOK'S TIP

*To shuck an oyster, wrap a tea
towel around one hand and grasp
the oyster, flat shell uppermost.
Prise open with a strong knife, then
run the blade around the inside of
the shell to sever the muscle.*

VARIATION

*You can replace the shallot with
a small, finely chopped onion and
the fresh parsley with the same
amount of snipped fresh chives,
if you prefer.*

spicy indian vegetarian stir-fry

In a large frying pan or wok, heat 2 tablespoons of the oil and add the turmeric and a pinch of salt. Carefully add the potatoes, stirring continuously to coat in the turmeric. Stir-fry for 5 minutes, remove from the pan and set aside.

Heat the remaining tablespoon of oil and stir-fry the shallots for 1–2 minutes. Mix in the bay leaf, cumin, ginger and chilli powder, then add the tomatoes and stir-fry for 2 minutes.

Add the spinach, mixing well to combine all the flavours. Cover and simmer for 2–3 minutes. Return the potatoes to the pan and add the peas and lemon juice. Cook for 5 minutes or until the potatoes are tender.

Remove the pan from the heat, discard the bay leaf and season with salt and pepper. Serve with cooked basmati rice.

ingredients

3 tbsp vegetable oil

½ tsp turmeric

salt and pepper

225 g/8 oz potatoes, cut into
    1 cm/½ inch cubes

3 shallots, chopped finely

1 bay leaf

½ tsp ground cumin

1 tsp finely grated fresh root ginger

¼ tsp chilli powder

4 tomatoes, chopped roughly

300 g/10½ oz spinach (de-stalked),
    chopped roughly

125 g/4½ oz fresh or frozen peas

1 tbsp lemon juice

freshly cooked basmati rice,
    to serve

stuffed aubergines

Preheat the oven to 200°C/400°F/Gas Mark 6. Put the aubergines on a roasting tin and cook in the preheated oven for 8–10 minutes until just softened. Cut in half and scoop out the flesh, reserving the shells.

Heat the oil in a preheated wok or large frying pan, add the shallots, garlic and chillies and stir-fry for 2–3 minutes. Add the courgette, aubergine flesh, coconut, herbs and soy sauce and simmer, stirring frequently, for 3–4 minutes.

Divide the mixture between the aubergine shells. Return to the oven for 5–10 minutes until heated through and serve at once, accompanied by rice with spring onions and sweet chilli sauce.

ingredients
8 small aubergines
2 tbsp vegetable or groundnut oil
4 shallots, finely chopped
2 garlic cloves, crushed
2 fresh red chillies, deseeded and chopped
1 courgette, roughly chopped
115 g/4 oz creamed coconut, chopped
few fresh Thai basil leaves, chopped
small handful of fresh coriander, chopped
4 tbsp Thai soy sauce

TO SERVE
rice with chopped spring onions
sweet chilli sauce

COOK'S TIP
If you can only find large aubergines, 1 half per person would probably be enough.

smooth nectarine shake

Pour the milk into a food processor, add half of the lemon sorbet and process gently until combined. Add the remaining sorbet and process until smooth.

When the mixture is thoroughly blended, gradually add the mango and nectarines and process until smooth. Pour the mixture into glasses, add straws and serve.

ingredients
250 ml/9 fl oz milk
350 g/12 oz lemon sorbet
1 ripe mango, stoned and diced
2 ripe nectarines, stoned and diced

27

SERVES 4

pasta salad with chargrilled peppers

Put the whole peppers on a baking sheet and place under a preheated grill, turning frequently, for 15 minutes, until charred all over. Remove with tongs and place in a bowl. Cover with crumpled kitchen paper and set aside.

Meanwhile, bring a large saucepan of lightly salted water to the boil. Add the pasta, bring back to the boil and cook for 8–10 minutes, until tender, but still firm to the bite.

Combine the olive oil, lemon juice, pesto and garlic in a bowl, whisking well to mix. Drain the pasta, add it to the pesto mixture while still hot and toss well. Set aside.

When the peppers are cool enough to handle, peel off the skins, then cut open and remove all the seeds. Chop the flesh coarsely and add to the pasta with the basil. Season to taste with salt and pepper and toss together. Serve at room temperature.

ingredients

1 red pepper

1 orange pepper

280 g/10 oz dried conchiglie

5 tbsp extra virgin olive oil

2 tbsp lemon juice

2 tbsp pesto

1 garlic clove

3 tbsp shredded fresh basil leaves

salt and pepper

VARIATION

A more traditional salad, without the pasta, can be made in the same way. When the peppers have been under the grill for 10 minutes, add 4 tomatoes and grill for a further 5 minutes. Cover the peppers with kitchen paper, then peel and chop as in step 4. Peel and coarsely chop the tomatoes. Combine them with the dressing and garnish with black olives.

turkish kebabs

Place the lamb cubes in a large, shallow, non-metallic dish. Mix the olive oil, wine, mint, garlic, orange rind, paprika and sugar together in a jug and season to taste with salt and pepper. Pour the mixture over the lamb, turning to coat, then cover with clingfilm and leave to marinate in the refrigerator for 2 hours, turning occasionally.

Preheat the barbecue or a griddle. To make the tahini cream, put the tahini paste, garlic, oil and lemon juice into a food processor and process briefly to mix. With the motor still running, gradually add the water through the feeder tube until smooth. Transfer to a bowl, cover with clingfilm and leave to chill in the refrigerator until required.

Drain the lamb, reserving the marinade, and thread it on to several long metal skewers. Cook over medium hot coals or medium heat, turning and brushing frequently with the marinade, for 10–15 minutes. Serve with the tahini cream.

ingredients
500 g/1 lb 2 oz boned shoulder
  of lamb, cut into 2.5-cm/1-inch
  cubes
1 tbsp olive oil
2 tbsp dry white wine
2 tbsp finely chopped fresh mint
4 garlic cloves, finely chopped
2 tsp grated orange rind
1 tbsp paprika
1 tsp sugar
salt and pepper

TAHINI CREAM
225 g/8 oz tahini paste
2 garlic cloves, finely chopped
2 tbsp extra virgin olive oil
2 tbsp lemon juice
125 ml/4 fl oz water

COOK'S TIP
Tahini or sesame seed paste is available from most supermarkets and specialist food shops. It is made from ground, pulped sesame seeds.

AUGUST
28

SERVES 4

SERVES 2

carrot & ginger energiser

Put the carrot juice, tomatoes and lemon juice into a food processor and process gently until combined.

Add the parsley to the food processor along with the ginger and ice cubes. Process until well combined, then pour in the water and process until smooth.

Pour the mixture into tall glasses and garnish with chopped fresh parsley. Serve at once.

ingredients

250 ml/9 fl oz carrot juice

4 tomatoes, skinned, deseeded
 and roughly chopped

1 tbsp lemon juice

25 g/1 oz fresh parsley

1 tbsp grated fresh root ginger

6 ice cubes

125 ml/4 fl oz water

chopped fresh parsley, to garnish

raspberry shortcake

Preheat the oven to190°C/375°F/Gas Mark 5. Lightly grease 2 baking trays with butter.

To make the shortcake, sift the flour into a large bowl. Add the butter and rub into the flour with your fingertips until the mixture resembles breadcrumbs.

Stir the sugar, egg yolk and rosewater into the mixture and mix together with your fingers to form a soft dough. Divide the dough in half.

Roll each piece of dough to a 20-cm/8-inch round on a floured work surface. Carefully lift each one with the rolling pin on to a prepared baking tray. Crimp the edges of the dough.

Bake in the preheated oven for 15 minutes, or until lightly golden. Transfer the shortcakes to a wire rack and leave to cool completely.

Mix the whipped cream with the raspberries and spoon the mixture on top of one of the shortcakes, spreading it out evenly. Top with the other shortcake round, dust with a little icing sugar and decorate with the extra raspberries. Put in the refrigerator to chill for 3–4 hours.

ingredients

100 g/3½ oz butter, cut into cubes,
  plus extra for greasing
175 g/6 oz self raising flour
75 g/2¾ oz caster sugar
1 egg yolk
1 tbsp rosewater
plain flour, for dusting
600 ml/1 pint whipping cream,
  lightly whipped
225 g/8 oz raspberries, plus a few
  extra to decorate

TO DECORATE

icing sugar

AUGUST

30

SERVES 4

31

SERVES 4

teriyaki chicken with sesame noodles

Using a sharp knife, score each chicken breast diagonally across 3 times and rub all over with some of the teriyaki sauce. Set aside to marinate for at least 10 minutes, or cover and chill all day.

When you are ready to cook the chicken, preheat the grill to high. Bring a saucepan of water to the boil, add the buckwheat noodles and boil for 3 minutes, until soft. Alternatively, cook according to packet instructions. Drain and rinse well in cold water to stop the cooking and remove excess starch, then drain again.

Lightly brush the grill rack with oil. Add the chicken breasts, skin-side up, and brush again with a little extra teriyaki sauce. Grill the chicken breasts about 10 cm/4 in from the heat, brushing occasionally with extra teriyaki sauce, for 15 minutes, or until cooked through and the juices run clear.

Meanwhile, heat a wok or large frying pan over a high heat. Add the sesame oil and heat until it shimmers. Add the noodles and stir around to heat through, then stir in the sesame seeds and parsley. Finally, add salt and pepper to taste.

Transfer the chicken breasts to plates and serve with a portion of noodles each.

COOK'S TIP
These noodles also go well with grilled cod, salmon, tuna or mackerel, but leave the fish to marinate for 30 minutes at the most. Grill the fish, brushing with the sauce, until the flesh flakes easily.

ingredients

4 boneless chicken breasts, about 175 g/6 oz each, with or without skin, as you wish
about 4 tbsp teriyaki sauce
groundnut or sunflower oil
cucumber fans, to garnish

SESAME NOODLES

250 g/9 oz dried thin buckwheat noodles
1 tbsp toasted sesame oil
2 tbsp toasted sesame seeds
2 tbsp finely chopped fresh parsley
salt and pepper

CHAPTER

9

September

tabasco steaks with watercress butter

Preheat the barbecue or a griddle. Using a sharp knife, finely chop enough watercress to fill 4 tablespoons. Reserve a few watercress leaves for the garnish. Place the butter in a small bowl and beat in the chopped watercress with a fork until fully incorporated. Cover with clingfilm and leave to chill in the refrigerator until required.

SERVES 4

Sprinkle each steak with 1 teaspoon of the Tabasco sauce, rubbing it in well. Season to taste with salt and pepper.

Cook the steaks in the pan or over hot coals for 2½ minutes each side for rare, 4 minutes each side for medium and 6 minutes each side for well done. Transfer to serving plates, garnish with the reserved watercress leaves and serve immediately, topped with the watercress butter.

ingredients

1 bunch of watercress

85 g/3 oz unsalted butter, softened

4 sirloin steaks, about
    225 g/8 oz each

4 tsp Tabasco sauce

salt and pepper

VARIATION

If you like, substitute the same amount of fresh parsley for the watercress. Alternatively, serve the steaks with some pesto.

traditional greek salad

Make the dressing by whisking together the oil, lemon juice, garlic, sugar, salt and pepper in a small bowl. Set aside.

Cut the feta cheese into cubes about 2.5 cm/1 inch square. Put the lettuce, tomatoes and cucumber in a salad bowl. Scatter over the cheese and toss together.

Just before serving, whisk the dressing, pour over the salad leaves and toss together. Scatter over the olives and chopped herbs and serve.

ingredients
6 tbsp extra virgin olive oil
2 tbsp fresh lemon juice
1 garlic clove, crushed
pinch of sugar
salt and pepper
200 g/7 oz feta cheese
½ head of iceberg lettuce or
   1 lettuce such as Cos or
   escarole, shredded or sliced
4 tomatoes, quartered
½ cucumber, sliced
12 Greek black olives
2 tbsp chopped fresh herbs such
   as oregano, flat-leaved parsley,
   mint or basil

SEPTEMBER
2

SERVES 4

corn on the cob with creamy blue cheese dressing

Preheat the barbecue or grill. Crumble the Danish Blue cheese, then place in a bowl. Beat with a wooden spoon until creamy. Beat in the curd cheese until thoroughly blended. Gradually beat in the yogurt and season to taste with salt and pepper. Cover with clingfilm and leave to chill in the refrigerator until required.

Fold back the husks on each corn cob and remove the silks. Smooth the husks back into place. Cut out 6 rectangles of foil, each large enough to enclose a corn cob. Wrap the corn cobs in the foil.

Cook the corn cobs under the grill or over hot coals, turning frequently, for 15–20 minutes. Unwrap the corn cobs and discard the foil. Peel back the husk on one side of each and trim off with a sharp knife or kitchen scissors. Serve immediately with the blue cheese dressing.

ingredients
140 g/5 oz Danish Blue cheese
140 g/5 oz curd cheese
125 ml/4 fl oz natural Greek yogurt
salt and pepper
6 corn cobs in their husks

SEPTEMBER
3

SERVES 6

traditional apple pie

To make the pastry, sift the flour and salt into a mixing bowl. Add the butter and fat and rub in with the fingertips until the mixture resembles fine breadcrumbs. Add the water and gather the mixture together into a dough. Wrap the dough and chill in the refrigerator for 30 minutes.

Preheat the oven to 220°C/425°F/Gas Mark 7. Roll out almost two-thirds of the pastry thinly and use to line a deep 23-cm/9-inch pie plate or pie tin.

Mix the apples with the sugar and spice and pack into the pastry case; the filling can come up above the rim. Add the water if needed, particularly if the apples are not very juicy.

Roll out the remaining pastry to form a lid. Dampen the edges of the pie rim with water and position the lid, pressing the edges firmly together. Trim and crimp the edges.

Use the trimmings to cut out leaves or other shapes to decorate the top of the pie, dampen and attach. Glaze the top of the pie with beaten egg or milk, make 1–2 slits in the top and place the pie on a baking sheet.

Bake in the preheated oven for 20 minutes, then reduce the temperature to 180°C/350°F/Gas Mark 4 and bake for a further 30 minutes, or until the pastry is a light golden brown. Serve hot or cold, sprinkled with sugar.

ingredients

PASTRY

350 g/12 oz plain flour

pinch of salt

85 g/3 oz butter or margarine, cut into small pieces

85 g/3 oz lard or white vegetable fat, cut into small pieces

about 6 tbsp cold water

beaten egg or milk, for glazing

FILLING

750 g–1 kg/1 lb 10 oz–2 lb 4 oz cooking apples, peeled, cored and sliced

125 g/4½ oz soft light brown or caster sugar, plus extra for sprinkling

1/2–1 tsp ground cinnamon, mixed spice or ground ginger

1–2 tbsp water (optional)

macaroni with roasted vegetables

Preheat the oven to 240°C/475°F/Gas Mark 9. Spread out the onions, courgettes, red and yellow peppers, aubergine and tomatoes in a single layer in a large roasting tin. Sprinkle with the garlic, drizzle with the olive oil and season to taste with salt and pepper. Stir well until all the vegetables are coated. Roast in the preheated oven for 15 minutes, then remove from the oven and stir well. Return to the oven for a further 15 minutes.

Bring a large heavy-based saucepan of lightly salted water to the boil. Add the pasta, return to the boil and cook for 8–10 minutes, or until tender but still firm to the bite.

Meanwhile, transfer the roasted vegetables to a large heavy-based saucepan and add the passata and olives. Heat through gently, stirring occasionally. Drain the pasta and transfer to a warmed serving dish. Add the roasted vegetable sauce and toss well. Garnish with the fresh basil and parsley and serve immediately.

ingredients

2 red onions, cut into wedges

2 courgettes, cut into chunks

1 red pepper, deseeded and cut
    into chunks

1 yellow pepper, deseeded and cut
    into chunks

1 aubergine cut into chunks

450 g/1 lb plum tomatoes, quartered
    and deseeded

3 garlic cloves, chopped

4 tbsp olive oil

salt and pepper

350 g/12 oz dried short-cut macaroni

300 ml/10 fl oz passata

85 g/3 oz black olives, stoned and
    halved

TO GARNISH

fresh basil sprigs

fresh flat-leaved parsley sprigs

SERVES 4

COOK'S TIP

*When buying fresh tomatoes,
always choose ones that are firm
and bright red. Ripe tomatoes can
be stored in the refrigerator for up to
2 days, and underripe ones should
be kept at room temperature.*

VARIATION

*Other vegetables would work well
in this dish, such as bite-sized
pieces of butternut squash and
cherry tomato halves.*

SEPTEMBER

6

SERVES 4

COOK'S TIP

Fresh dill goes particularly well with fish, especially salmon, as it has a delicate aniseed flavour. It cannot withstand high temperatures, so is best used at the end of cooking or as a garnish.

VARIATION

If watercress is unavailable, then replace with the same amount of rocket or baby spinach leaves.

salmon with watercress cream

Pour the crème fraîche into a large, heavy-based saucepan and heat gently to simmering point. Remove the saucepan from the heat, stir in the dill and reserve until required.

Melt the butter and oil in a heavy-based frying pan. Add the salmon and cook over a medium heat for 4–5 minutes on each side, or until cooked through. Remove, cover and keep warm.

Add the garlic to the pan and cook, stirring, for 1 minute. Pour in the wine, bring to the boil and cook until reduced. Stir the crème fraîche mixture into the pan and cook for 2–3 minutes, or until thickened. Stir in the watercress and cook until just wilted. Season to taste with salt and pepper.

Place the salmon fillets on warm plates, spoon the watercress sauce over them and serve immediately.

ingredients

300 ml/10 fl oz crème fraîche
2 tbsp snipped fresh dill
25 g/1 oz unsalted butter
1 tbsp sunflower oil
4 salmon fillets, about 175 g/6 oz
   each, skinned
1 garlic clove, finely chopped
100 ml/3½ fl oz dry white wine
1 bunch of watercress, finely
   chopped
salt and pepper

individual chocolate puddings

To make the puddings, put the sugar and eggs into a heatproof bowl and place over a saucepan of simmering water. Whisk for about 10 minutes until frothy. Remove the bowl from the heat and fold in the flour and cocoa powder. Fold in the butter, then the chocolate. Mix well.

Grease 4 small pudding basins with butter. Spoon the mixture into the basins and cover with greaseproof paper. Top with foil and secure with string. Place the puddings in a large saucepan filled with enough simmering water to reach halfway up the sides of the basins. Steam for about 40 minutes, or until cooked through.

About 2–3 minutes before the end of the cooking time, make the sauce. Put the butter, chocolate, water and sugar into a small saucepan and warm over a low heat, stirring constantly, until melted together. Stir in the liqueur.

Remove the puddings from the heat, turn out into serving dishes and pour over the sauce. Decorate with coffee beans and serve.

ingredients

PUDDINGS

100 g/3½ oz caster sugar

3 eggs

75 g/2¾ oz plain flour, sifted

50 g/1¾ oz cocoa powder, sifted

100 g/3½ oz unsalted butter, melted, plus extra for greasing

100 g/3½ oz plain chocolate, melted

CHOCOLATE SAUCE

2 tbsp unsalted butter

100 g/3½ oz plain chocolate

5 tbsp water

1 tbsp caster sugar

1 tbsp coffee-flavoured liqueur, such as Kahlua

coffee beans, to decorate

chicken, cheese & rocket salad

Wash the rocket leaves, pat dry with kitchen paper and put them into a large salad bowl. Add the celery, cucumber, spring onions, parsley and walnuts and mix together well. Transfer onto a large serving platter. Arrange the chicken slices over the salad, then scatter over the cheese. Add the red grapes, if using. Season well with salt and pepper.

To make the dressing, put all the ingredients into a screw-top jar and shake well. Alternatively, put them into a bowl and mix together well. Drizzle the dressing over the salad and serve.

ingredients

150 g/5½ oz rocket leaves

2 celery sticks, trimmed and sliced

½ cucumber, sliced

2 spring onions, trimmed and sliced

2 tbsp chopped fresh parsley

25 g/1 oz walnut pieces

350 g/12 oz boneless roast chicken, sliced

125 g/4½ oz Stilton cheese, cubed

handful of seedless red grapes, halved (optional)

salt and pepper

DRESSING

2 tbsp olive oil

1 tbsp sherry vinegar

1 tsp Dijon mustard

1 tbsp chopped mixed herbs

sage & onion drumsticks

Preheat the oven to 200°C/400°F/Gas Mark 6. Melt the butter in a frying pan over a medium heat. Add the onion and garlic and cook, stirring, for 3 minutes. Remove from the heat and stir in the breadcrumbs, sage and lemon juice. Season well with salt and pepper. Transfer to a large bowl.

Rinse the drumsticks and pat dry with kitchen paper. Turn the drumsticks in the beaten egg, then cover in the sage and onion mixture by pressing it around them. Arrange them in a shallow roasting tin, drizzle over the oil, then roast in the oven for 50 minutes until golden, crispy and cooked right through. If they start to brown too quickly, cover the tin with foil.

Remove from the oven and pile onto a serving platter. Garnish with the lemon wedges and parsley and serve with a fresh green salad. Alternatively, to serve cold, leave to cool, cover with clingfilm and refrigerate until required.

ingredients

6 tbsp butter

1 onion, finely chopped

1 garlic clove, finely chopped

125 g/4½ oz fresh white or wholemeal breadcrumbs

2 tbsp finely chopped fresh sage

1 tbsp lemon juice

salt and pepper

8 large chicken drumsticks

2 eggs, beaten

3 tbsp vegetable oil

fresh green salad, to serve

GARNISH

wedges of lemon

sprigs of fresh flat-leaved parsley

sausage & rosemary risotto

Strip the long thin leaves from the rosemary sprigs and chop finely, then set aside.

Bring the stock to the boil in a saucepan, then reduce the heat and keep simmering gently over a low heat while you are cooking the risotto.

Heat the oil and half the butter in a deep saucepan over a medium heat. Add the onion and celery and cook, stirring occasionally, for 2 minutes. Stir in the garlic, thyme, sausage and rosemary. Cook, stirring frequently, for 5 minutes, or until the sausage begins to brown. Transfer the sausage to a plate.

Reduce the heat, add the rice and mix to coat in oil and butter. Cook, stirring constantly, for 2–3 minutes, or until the grains are translucent.

Add the wine and cook, stirring constantly, for 1 minute until it has reduced.

Gradually add the hot stock, a ladle at a time. Stir constantly and add more liquid as the rice absorbs each addition. Increase the heat to medium so that the liquid bubbles. Cook for 20 minutes, or until all the liquid is absorbed and the rice is creamy.

Towards the end of cooking, return the sausage pieces to the risotto and heat through. Season to taste with salt and pepper.

Remove from the heat and add the remaining butter. Mix well, then stir in the Parmesan until it melts. Spoon the risotto onto warmed plates, garnish with rosemary sprigs and serve.

ingredients

2 long fresh rosemary sprigs, plus
    extra to garnish

1.3 litres/2¼ pints chicken stock

2 tbsp olive oil

55 g/2 oz butter

1 large onion, finely chopped

1 celery stick, finely chopped

2 garlic cloves, finely chopped

½ tsp dried thyme leaves

450 g/1 lb pork sausage, such as
    Italian luganega or Cumberland,
    cut into 1-cm/½-inch pieces

350 g/12 oz risotto rice

125 ml/4 fl oz fruity red wine

85 g/3 oz freshly grated Parmesan
    cheese

salt and pepper

lemon meringue pie

Grease a 25-cm/10-inch fluted flan tin. On a lightly floured work surface, roll out the pastry into a circle 5 cm/2 inches larger than the flan tin. Ease the pastry into the tin without stretching and press down lightly into the corners. Roll off the excess pastry to neaten the pastry case. Prick the base of the flan base and chill, uncovered, in the refrigerator for 20–30 minutes.

Preheat the oven to 200°C/400°F/Gas Mark 6. Line the pastry case with baking paper and fill with baking beans. Bake on a heated baking tray for 15 minutes. Remove the beans and paper and return to the oven for 10 minutes until the pastry is dry and just colouring. Remove from the oven and reduce the temperature to 150°C/300°F/Gas Mark 2.

Put the cornflour, sugar and lemon rind into a saucepan. Pour in a little of the water and blend to a smooth paste. Gradually add the remaining water and the lemon juice. Place the saucepan over a medium heat and bring the mixture to the boil, stirring continuously. Simmer gently for 1 minute until smooth and glossy. Remove the saucepan from the heat and beat in the egg yolks, one at a time, then beat in the butter. Place the saucepan in a bowl of cold water to cool the filling. When cool, spoon the mixture into the pastry case.

To make the meringue, whisk the egg whites using an electric mixer until thick and in soft peaks. Add the caster sugar gradually, whisking well with each addition. The mixture should be glossy and firm. Spoon the meringue over the filling to cover it completely and make a seal with the pastry shell. Swirl the meringue into peaks and sprinkle with the granulated sugar.

Bake for 20–30 minutes until the meringue is crispy and pale gold (the centre should still be soft). Allow to cool slightly before serving.

ingredients

butter, for greasing
plain flour, for dusting
250 g/9 oz ready-rolled pastry, thawed if frozen
3 tbsp cornflour
85 g/3 oz caster sugar
grated rind of 3 lemons
300 ml/½ pint cold water
150 ml/¼ pint lemon juice
3 egg yolks
55 g/2 oz unsalted butter, cut into small cubes

MERINGUE

3 egg whites
175 g/6 oz caster sugar
1 tsp golden granulated sugar

ingredients

600 g/1 lb 5 oz new potatoes

3 red onions, cut into wedges

2 courgettes, cut into chunks

8 garlic cloves, peeled but left whole

2 lemons, cut into wedges

1 fresh rosemary sprigs

4 tbsp olive oil

350 g/12 oz unpeeled raw prawns

2 small raw squid, cut into rings

4 tomatoes, quartered

COOK'S TIP

Most vegetables are suitable for roasting in the oven. Try adding 450 g/1 lb pumpkin, squash or aubergine, if you like.

roasted seafood

Preheat the oven to 200°C/400°F/Gas Mark 6.

Scrub the potatoes to remove any dirt. Cut any large potatoes in half. Parboil the potatoes in a saucepan of boiling water for 10–15 minutes. Place the potatoes in a large roasting tin together with the onions, courgettes, garlic, lemons and rosemary sprigs.

Pour over the oil and toss to coat all the vegetables in it. Roast in the oven for 30 minutes, turning occasionally, until the potatoes are tender.

Once the potatoes are tender, add the prawns, squid and tomatoes, tossing to coat them in the oil, and roast for 10 minutes. All the vegetables should be cooked through and slightly charred for full flavour.

Transfer the roasted seafood and vegetables to warmed serving plates and serve hot.

charred pepper salad

Preheat the grill. Cook the peppers under the grill, turning frequently, until the skins are charred all over. Put the peppers in a bowl, cover with a damp tea towel and leave until cold.

When the peppers are cold, hold them over a clean bowl to collect the juices and peel off the skin. Remove the stem, core and seeds and cut the peppers into thin strips. Arrange the pepper strips on a flat serving plate.

If using cumin seeds, dry-toast them in a dry frying pan until they turn brown and begin to pop. Shake the frying pan continuously to prevent them from burning and do not allow them to smoke. Lightly crush the toasted seeds with a pestle and mortar.

Add the toasted cumin seeds or marjoram, the olive oil, lemon juice, garlic, sugar, salt and pepper to the pepper juices and whisk together.

Pour the dressing over the peppers and chill in the fridge for 3–4 hours or overnight. Serve at room temperature, garnished with Greek olives.

ingredients

2 green peppers

2 red peppers

2 yellow peppers

½ tsp cumin seeds or 2 tbsp chopped fresh marjoram

5 tbsp extra virgin olive oil

2 tbsp lemon juice

2 garlic cloves, crushed

pinch of sugar

salt and pepper

Greek olives, to garnish

warm fruit nests

Preheat the oven to 180°C/350°F/Gas Mark 4. Brush 4 small tartlet tins with oil. Cut the filo pastry into 16 squares measuring about 12 cm/4½ inches across. Brush each square with oil and use to line the tartlet tins. Place 4 sheets in each tin, staggering them so that the overhanging corners make a decorative star shape. Transfer the tins to a baking sheet and bake in the preheated oven for 7–8 minutes until golden. Remove from the oven and reserve.

Meanwhile, warm the fruit in a saucepan with the caster sugar and mixed spice over a medium heat until simmering. Lower the heat and continue simmering, stirring, for 10 minutes. Remove from the heat and drain. Using a slotted spoon, divide the warm fruit between the pastry shells. Garnish with sprigs of fresh mint and serve warm with double cream.

ingredients

2–3 tbsp lemon oil

8 sheets of frozen filo pastry, defrosted

250 g/9 oz blueberries

250 g/9 oz raspberries

250 g/9 oz blackberries

3 tbsp caster sugar

1 tsp ground mixed spice

sprigs of fresh mint, to decorate

double cream, to serve

chicken with smoked ham and parmesan

SERVES 4

Cut each chicken breast lengthways to open them out, then place the pieces between 2 sheets of plastic wrap and pound with the flat end of a meat mallet or the side of a rolling pin until they are as thin as possible. Spread out the flour on a shallow plate and season with salt and pepper. Coat the chicken pieces in the seasoned flour, shaking off any excess.

Melt half the butter in a large, heavy-bottom skillet. Add the chicken pieces, in batches if necessary, and cook over medium heat, turning frequently, for 10–15 minutes, until golden brown all over and cooked through.

Meanwhile, melt the remaining butter in a small pan. Remove the skillet containing the chicken from the heat. Place a slice of ham on each piece of chicken and sprinkle with the cheese. Pour the melted butter over the chicken and return the skillet to the heat for 3–4 minutes, until the cheese has melted. Serve immediately, garnished with basil sprigs.

ingredients

4 skinned, boned chicken breasts

2 tbsp all-purpose flour

salt and pepper

2 oz/55 g unsalted butter

8 thin slices smoked ham, trimmed

2 oz/55 g freshly grated Parmesan
  cheese

fresh basil sprigs, to garnish

VARIATION

A similar dish is made in the Valle d'Aosta, but instead of the chicken breasts being cut and opened out, they are slit to make a pocket. The pockets are then filled with slices of smoked ham or prosciutto and fontina cheese before cooking.

basque scrambled eggs

Heat 2 tablespoons of oil in a large, heavy-based frying pan over a medium-high heat. Add the onion and peppers and cook for about 5 minutes, or until the vegetables are soft, but not brown. Add the tomatoes and heat through. Transfer to a plate and keep warm in a preheated low oven.

Add another tablespoon of oil to the frying pan. Add the chorizo and cook for 30 seconds, just to warm through and flavour the oil. Add the sausage to the reserved vegetables.

There should be about 2 tablespoons of oil in the frying pan, add a little extra but if less, to make up the amount. Add the butter and allow to melt. Season the eggs with salt and pepper to taste, then add to the frying pan and scramble until cooked to the desired degree of firmness. Return the vegetables to the frying pan and stir through. Serve at once with hot toast.

ingredients

olive oil

1 large onion, chopped finely

1 large red pepper, cored, deseeded and chopped

1 large green pepper, cored, deseeded and chopped

2 large tomatoes, peeled, deseeded and chopped

55 g/2 oz chorizo sausage, sliced thinly, casings removed, if preferred

35 g/1¼ oz butter

10 large eggs, beaten lightly

salt and pepper

4–6 thick slices country-style bread, toasted, to serve

ingredients

1 large head radicchio, outer
damaged leaves removed

1.5 litres/2¾ pints chicken or
vegetable stock

2 tbsp sunflower or other
vegetable oil

25 g/1 oz butter

115 g/4 oz pancetta or thick-cut
smoked bacon, diced

1 large onion, finely chopped

1 garlic clove, finely chopped

400 g/14 oz risotto rice

50 ml/2 fl oz double cream

55 g/2 oz freshly grated Parmesan
cheese

3–4 tbsp chopped fresh flat-leaved
parsley

salt and pepper

SEPTEMBER

17

SERVES 6–8

radicchio risotto

Cut the radicchio head in half lengthways and remove the triangular core. Place the halves cut-side down and shred finely. Set aside.

Bring the stock to the boil in a saucepan, then reduce the heat and keep simmering gently over a low heat while you are cooking the risotto.

Heat the oil and butter in a large, heavy-based saucepan over a medium heat. Add the pancetta and cook, stirring occasionally, for 3–4 minutes until it begins to colour. Add the onion and garlic and cook for 1 minute.

Reduce the heat, add the rice and mix to coat in oil and butter. Cook, stirring constantly, for 2–3 minutes or until the grains are translucent. Add the radicchio and cook, stirring for 1 minute until it just begins to wilt.

Gradually add the hot stock, a ladle at a time. Stir constantly and add more liquid as the rice absorbs each addition. Increase the heat to medium so that the liquid bubbles. Cook for 20 minutes, or until all the liquid is absorbed and the rice is creamy.

Stir in the cream, Parmesan and parsley and season to taste with salt and pepper. Remove the saucepan from the heat and spoon the risotto onto warmed plates. Serve immediately.

sweetcorn & smoked chilli soup

Heat the oil in a large, heavy-based saucepan. Add the onion and cook over a low heat, stirring occasionally, for 5 minutes, or until softened. Stir in the sweetcorn, cover and cook for a further 3 minutes.

Add the stock, half the milk, the chillies and garlic and season with salt. Bring to the boil, reduce the heat, then cover and simmer for 15–20 minutes.

Stir in the remaining milk. Reserve about 175 ml/6 fl oz of the soup solids, draining off as much liquid as possible. Transfer the remaining soup to a food processor or blender and process to a coarse purée.

Return the soup to the saucepan and stir in the reserved soup solids, the chorizo, lime juice and coriander. Reheat to simmering point, stirring constantly. Ladle into warmed bowls and serve immediately.

ingredients

1 tbsp corn oil

2 onions, chopped

550 g/1 lb 4 oz frozen sweetcorn
    kernels, thawed

600 ml/1 pint chicken stock

425 ml/15 fl oz milk

4 chipotle chillies, deseeded and
    finely chopped

2 garlic cloves, finely chopped

salt

55 g/2 oz thinly sliced chorizo
    sausage

2 tbsp lime juice

2 tbsp chopped fresh coriander

fruit & nut squares

Preheat the oven to 180°C/350°F/Gas Mark 4. Lightly grease an 18-cm/7-inch shallow, square baking tin with butter. Beat the remaining butter with the honey in a bowl until creamy, then beat in the egg with the almonds.

Add the remaining ingredients and mix together. Press into the prepared tin, ensuring that the mixture is firmly packed. Smooth the top.

Bake in the preheated oven for 20–25 minutes, or until firm to the touch and golden brown.

Remove from the oven and leave for 10 minutes before marking into squares. Leave until cold before removing from the tin. Store in an airtight container.

MAKES 9 SQUARES

ingredients

115 g/4 oz unsalted butter, plus
    extra for greasing
2 tbsp clear honey
1 egg, beaten
85 g/3 oz ground almonds
115 g/4 oz no-soak dried apricots,
    finely chopped
55 g/2 oz dried cherries
55 g/2 oz toasted chopped hazelnuts
25 g/1 oz sesame seeds
85 g/3 oz jumbo porridge oats

20

SERVES 4

ingredients

4 tbsp olive oil

5 tbsp butter

3 garlic cloves, chopped very finely

450 g/1 lb boneless, skinless
    chicken breasts, diced

¼ tsp dried chilli flakes

salt and pepper

450 g/1 lb small broccoli florets

300 g/10½ oz dried farfalle or fusilli

175 g/6 oz bottled roasted red
    peppers, drained and diced

250 ml/9 fl oz chicken stock

freshly grated Parmesan cheese,
    to serve

farfalle with chicken, broccoli & roasted red pepper

Bring a large pan of salted water to the boil. Meanwhile, heat the olive oil, butter and garlic in a large frying pan over a medium-low heat. Cook the garlic until just beginning to colour.

Add the diced chicken, raise the heat to medium and stir-fry for 4–5 minutes until the chicken is no longer pink. Add the chilli flakes and season with salt and pepper. Remove from the heat.

Plunge the broccoli into the boiling water and cook for 2 minutes until tender-crisp. Remove with a perforated spoon and set aside. Bring the water back to the boil. Add the pasta and cook until al dente. Drain and add to the chicken mixture in the pan.

Add the broccoli and roasted peppers. Pour in the stock. Simmer briskly over a medium-high heat, stirring frequently, until most of the liquid has been absorbed. Sprinkle with the Parmesan and serve.

lamb with aubergine and black olive sauce

SERVES 4

Cut the aubergine into 2-cm/¾-inch cubes, put in a colander, standing over a large plate, and sprinkle each layer with salt. Cover with a plate and place a heavy weight on top. Leave for 30 minutes to degorge.

Preheat the grill. Rinse the aubergine slices under cold running water, then pat dry with kitchen paper. Season the lamb chops with pepper.

Place the lamb chops on the grill pan and cook under a medium heat for 10-15 minutes until tender, turning once during the cooking time.

Meanwhile, heat the olive oil in a saucepan, add the aubergine, onion and garlic and fry for 10 minutes, until softened and starting to brown. Add the tomatoes and their juice, the sugar, olives, chopped herbs, salt and pepper and simmer for 5-10 minutes.

To serve, spoon the sauce onto 4 warmed serving plates and top with the lamb chops.

ingredients

1 aubergine

salt and pepper

4-8 lamb chops

3 tbsp olive oil

1 onion, chopped roughly

1 garlic clove, chopped finely

400 g/14 oz canned chopped
   tomatoes in juice

pinch of sugar

16 black olives, preferably Kalamáta,
   stoned and chopped roughly

1 tsp chopped fresh herbs such as
   basil, flat-leaved parsley or
   oregano

steak and potato pies

22

MAKES 4

To make the pastry, sift the flour and salt into a bowl and gently rub in the lard and butter until the mixture resembles breadcrumbs. Add the water, a spoonful at a time, and stir the mixture with a knife until it holds together.

Turn out onto a lightly floured surface and gently press together until smooth. Wrap in clingfilm and allow to chill for 1 hour.

Meanwhile, to prepare the filling, mix the meat and vegetables together and season well with salt and pepper.

Divide the pastry into 4 even-sized pieces and roll one out until just larger than the size of a 20-cm/8-inch plate. Place the plate on top of the pastry and cut round it to give a neat edge. Repeat with the other pieces.

Arrange the meat and vegetable mixture across the 4 rounds of pastry, making sure the filling goes to the edge.

Brush the edges of the pastry with water, then bring the edges up over the filling and press together to form a ridge. You can flute the edges of the pasties with your fingers or fold over the pastry to form a cord-like seal. Tuck in the ends.

Allow to chill for 1 hour, then glaze with the egg.

Preheat the oven to 190ºC/375ºF/ Gas Mark 5.

Place on a greased baking tray and cook in the centre of the oven for 50–60 minutes. The pasties should be crisp and golden in colour. Cover with foil and reduce the temperature if the pastry is getting too brown.

ingredients

250 g/9 oz chuck steak, trimmed
and cut into 1-cm/½-inch dice
175 g/6 oz swede, peeled and cut
into 1-cm/½-inch dice
350 g/12 oz potatoes, peeled and
cut into 1-cm/½-inch dice
1 onion, finely chopped
salt and pepper
1 egg, beaten

SHORTCRUST PASTRY
450 g/1 lb plain flour, plus extra
for dusting
pinch of salt
115 g/4 oz lard
115 g/4 oz butter
175 ml/6 fl oz cold water

spaghetti with anchovies, olives, capers & tomatoes

Heat the oil with the anchovies in a large frying pan over a low heat. Stir until the anchovies dissolve. Add the garlic and cook for a few seconds until just beginning to colour. Add the tomatoes, oregano and chilli flakes, then season with salt and pepper. Bring to the boil, then simmer over a medium-low heat for 30 minutes until the oil begins to separate from the tomatoes.

Cook the pasta in plenty of boiling salted water until al dente. Drain and transfer to a warm serving dish. Add the olives and capers to the sauce. Pour over the pasta and toss well to mix. Serve immediately.

ingredients

6 tbsp olive oil

4 anchovy fillets, chopped

2 garlic cloves, chopped very finely

800 g/1 lb 12 oz canned chopped
    tomatoes

1 tsp dried oregano

¼ tsp dried chilli flakes

salt and pepper

350 g/12 oz dried spaghetti

10-12 black olives, pitted and sliced

2 tbsp capers, drained

ingredients

450 g/1 lb green cabbage

1 onion, thinly sliced

4 tbsp olive oil

salt and pepper

MASHED POTATO

450 g/1 lb floury potatoes, such
    as King Edwards, Maris Piper
    or Desirée, peeled and cut
    into chunks

salt and pepper

55 g/2 oz butter

3 tbsp hot milk

potato and cabbage cake

To make the mashed potato, cook the potatoes in a large saucepan of boiling salted water for 15–20 minutes. Drain well and mash with a potato masher until smooth. Season with salt and pepper, add the butter and milk and stir well.

Cut the cabbage into quarters, remove the centre stalk and shred finely.

In a large frying pan, fry the onion in half the oil until soft. Add the cabbage to the pan and stir-fry for 2–3 minutes until softened. Season with salt and pepper, add the mashed potato and mix together well.

Press the mixture firmly into the frying pan and allow to cook over a high heat for 4–5 minutes so that the base is crispy. Place a plate over the frying pan and invert the pan so that the potato cake falls onto the plate. Add the remaining oil to the pan, reheat and slip the cake back into the pan with the uncooked side down.

Continue to cook for a further 5 minutes until the bottom is crispy too. Turn out onto a hot plate and cut into wedges for serving. Serve at once.

orange & fennel salad

Finely grate the rind of the oranges into a bowl and set aside. Working over a bowl to catch the juice, use a small serrated knife to remove all the white pith from the oranges. Cut the oranges horizontally into thin slices.

Toss the orange slices with the fennel and onion slices in a large bowl. Whisk the oil into the reserved orange juice, then spoon over the oranges. Scatter the olive slices over the top, add the chilli, if using, then sprinkle with the orange rind and parsley. Serve with French bread.

ingredients
4 large, juicy oranges

1 large fennel bulb, very thinly sliced

1 mild white onion, finely sliced

2 tbsp extra virgin olive oil

12 plump black olives, stoned and thinly sliced

1 fresh red chilli, deseeded and very thinly sliced (optional)

finely chopped fresh parsley

French bread, to serve

SERVES 4

stir-fried japanese noodles

Place the noodles in a large bowl, pour over enough boiling water to cover and leave to soak for 10 minutes. Heat the oil in a large, preheated wok.

Add the red onion and garlic to the wok and stir-fry for 2–3 minutes, or until softened. Add the mushrooms to the wok and stir-fry for 5 minutes, or until soft. Drain the noodles and add to the wok.

Add the pak choi, sweet sherry and soy sauce to the wok and toss to mix well. Stir-fry for 2–3 minutes, or until the liquid is just bubbling. Transfer the noodle mixture to warmed serving bowls, sprinkle with sliced spring onions and toasted sesame seeds and serve immediately.

ingredients
225 g/8 oz Japanese egg noodles

2 tbsp sunflower oil

1 red onion, sliced

1 garlic clove, crushed

500 g/1 lb 2 oz mixed mushrooms, such as shiitake, oyster and brown cap

350 g/12 oz pak choi

2 tbsp sweet sherry

6 tbsp soy sauce

4 spring onions, sliced

1 tbsp sesame seeds, toasted

SERVES 4

chocolate brownie roulade

Grease a 30 x 20 cm/12 x 8 inch Swiss roll tin, line with baking parchment and grease the parchment.

Place the chocolate, with the water, in a small saucepan over a low heat, stirring until the chocolate has just melted. Leave to cool a little.

SERVES 8

In a bowl, whisk the sugar and egg yolks for 2–3 minutes with an electric whisk until thick and pale. Fold in the cooled chocolate, raisins and pecan nuts.

In a separate bowl, whisk the egg whites with the salt. Fold a quarter of the egg whites into the chocolate mixture, then fold in the rest of the whites, working lightly and quickly.

Transfer the mixture to the prepared tin and bake in a preheated oven, 180°C/350°F/ Gas Mark 4, for 25 minutes, until risen and just firm to the touch. Leave to cool before covering with a sheet of non-stick baking parchment and a damp, clean tea towel. Leave to stand until completely cold.

Turn the roulade on to another piece of baking parchment dusted with icing sugar. Remove the lining parchment.

Spread the whipped cream over the roulade. Starting from a short end, roll the sponge away from you, using the paper to guide you. Trim the ends of the roulade to make a neat finish and transfer to a serving plate. Leave the roulade to chill in the refrigerator until ready to serve. Dust with a little more icing sugar.

ingredients

2 tsp melted butter, for greasing

150 g/5½ oz dark chocolate, broken into pieces

3 tbsp water

175 g/6 oz caster sugar

5 eggs, separated

25 g/1 oz raisins, chopped

25 g/1 oz pecan nuts, chopped

pinch of salt

icing sugar, for dusting

300 ml/10 fl oz double cream, whipped lightly

crisp noodle & vegetable stir-fry

Half-fill a preheated wok or deep, heavy-based frying pan with oil. Heat to 180-190°C/350-375°F, or until a cube of bread browns in 30 seconds. Add the noodles, in batches, and cook for 1½–2 minutes, or until crisp and puffed up. Remove and drain on kitchen paper. Pour off all but 2 tablespoons of oil from the wok.

Heat the remaining oil over a high heat, add the beans and stir-fry for 2 minutes. Add the carrot, courgette, mushroom and ginger and stir-fry for 2 minutes. Add the Chinese leaves, spring onion and beansprouts and stir-fry for 1 minute. Add the soy sauce, rice wine and sugar and stir for 1 minute. Add the noodles and coriander and toss well. Serve immediately.

ingredients

oil, for deep-frying
115 g/4 oz rice vermicelli, broken into 7.5 cm/3 inch lengths
115 g/4 oz green beans, cut into short lengths
2 carrots, cut into thin batons
2 courgettes, cut into thin batons
115 g/4 oz shiitake mushrooms, sliced
2.5-cm/1-inch piece fresh root ginger, shredded
½ small head Chinese leaves, shredded
4 spring onions, shredded
85 g/3 oz beansprouts
2 tbsp dark soy sauce
2 tbsp Chinese rice wine
large pinch of sugar
2 tbsp roughly chopped fresh coriander

pork chops with peppers & sweetcorn

Heat the oil in a large, flameproof casserole. Add the pork chops in batches and cook over a medium heat, turning occasionally, for 5 minutes, or until browned. Transfer the chops to a plate with a slotted spoon.

Add the onion to the casserole and cook, stirring occasionally, for 5 minutes, or until softened. Add the garlic and peppers and cook, stirring occasionally for a further 5 minutes. Stir in the sweetcorn kernels and their juices, the parsley and salt and pepper to taste.

Return the chops to the casserole, spooning the vegetable mixture over them. Cover and simmer for 30 minutes, or until tender. Serve immediately with mashed potato.

ingredients

1 tbsp sunflower oil
4 pork chops, trimmed of visible fat
1 onion, chopped
1 garlic clove, finely chopped
1 green pepper, deseeded and sliced
1 red pepper, deseeded and sliced
325 g/11½ oz canned sweetcorn kernels
1 tbsp chopped fresh parsley
salt and pepper
mashed potato, to serve

30

SERVES 4

ingredients

4 tbsp butter

2 garlic cloves, chopped

3 onions, sliced

450 g/1 lb mixed white and chestnut
  mushrooms, sliced

100 g/3½ oz fresh ceps or porcini
  mushrooms, sliced

3 tbsp chopped fresh parsley

500 ml/18 fl oz vegetable stock

salt and pepper

3 tbsp plain flour

125 ml/4 fl oz milk

2 tbsp sherry

125 ml/4 fl oz soured cream

soured cream and chopped fresh
  parsley, to garnish

fresh crusty rolls, to serve

mushroom & sherry soup

Melt the butter in a large saucepan over a low heat. Add the garlic and onions and cook, stirring, for 3 minutes, until slightly softened. Add the mushrooms and cook for a further 5 minutes, stirring. Add the chopped parsley, pour in the stock and season with salt and pepper. Bring to the boil, then reduce the heat, cover the pan and simmer for 20 minutes.

Put the flour into a bowl, mix in enough milk to make a smooth paste, then stir it into the soup. Cook, stirring, for 5 minutes. Stir in the remaining milk and the sherry and cook for a further 5 minutes. Remove from the heat and stir in the soured cream. Return the pan to the heat and warm gently.

Remove from the heat and ladle into serving bowls. Garnish with soured cream and chopped fresh parsley, and serve with fresh crusty rolls.

CHAPTER

10

October

1

SERVES 4

mixed vegetable curry
with chickpea pancakes

To make the pancakes, sift the flour, salt and bicarbonate of soda into a large mixing bowl. Make a well in the centre and add the water. Using a balloon whisk, gradually mix the flour into the water until you have a smooth batter. Leave to stand for 15 minutes.

Heat enough oil to cover the base of a frying pan over a medium heat. To make small pancakes, pour a small quantity of batter into the pan, or, if you prefer to make larger pancakes, swirl the pan to spread the batter mixture. Cook one side for 3 minutes, then, using a palette knife, turn over and cook the other side until golden. Keep warm while you repeat with the remaining batter to make 8 pancakes.

Meanwhile, to make the curry, put the carrots and potatoes into a steamer and steam until just tender but still retaining some bite.

Heat the oil in a large, heavy-based saucepan over a medium heat and add the cumin seeds, cardamom seeds and mustard seeds. When they begin to darken and sizzle, add the onions, partially cover and cook over a medium-low heat, stirring frequently, for 10 minutes, or until soft and golden.

Add the turmeric, coriander, bay leaf, chilli powder, ginger and garlic and cook, stirring constantly, for 1 minute. Add the passata, stock, potatoes and carrots, partially cover and cook for 10–15 minutes, or until the vegetables are tender. Add the peas and spinach, then cook for a further 2–3 minutes. Season to taste with salt before serving with the warm chickpea pancakes.

ingredients

VEGETABLE CURRY

200 g/7 oz carrots, cut into chunks

300 g/10½ oz potatoes, quartered

2 tbsp vegetable oil

1½ tsp cumin seeds

seeds from 5 green cardamom pods

1½ tsp mustard seeds

2 onions, grated

1 tsp ground turmeric

1 tsp ground coriander

1 bay leaf

1½ tsp chilli powder

1 tbsp grated fresh root ginger

2 large garlic cloves, crushed

250 ml/9 fl oz passata

200 ml/7 fl oz vegetable stock

115 g/4 oz frozen peas

115 g/4 oz frozen spinach leaves

salt

CHICKPEA PANCAKES

225 g/8 oz gram or chickpea flour

1 tsp salt

½ tsp bicarbonate of soda

400 ml/14 fl oz water

vegetable oil, for frying

wild mushroom omelettes

To make the wild mushroom filling, heat the butter in a large, heavy-based frying pan. Add the mushrooms and cook over a low heat, stirring occasionally, for 5 minutes. Stir in the crème fraîche and season to taste with salt and pepper. Keep warm.

To make the omelettes, melt half the butter in an omelette pan or small frying pan over a medium-high heat. Season the eggs to taste with salt and pepper, add half to the omelette pan and stir with a fork. As the egg sets, draw it towards the centre and tilt the omelette pan so that the uncooked egg runs underneath. Cook until the underside of the omelette is golden and set, but the top is still moist.

Remove the omelette pan from the heat. Spoon half the mushroom mixture along a line just to one side of the centre of the omelette. Flip the other side over and slide the omelette on to a plate. Keep warm. Melt the remaining butter and cook a second omelette in the same way. Serve immediately.

ingredients
25 g/1 oz butter
6 eggs, lightly beaten
salt and pepper
WILD MUSHROOM FILLING
25 g/1 oz butter
150 g/5½ oz wild mushrooms,
    sliced
2 tbsp crème fraîche

COOK'S TIP
Use whatever wild mushrooms are available, such as morels, chanterelles and flat or field mushrooms. To clean, rinse morels and chanterelles in cold water and shake dry. Wipe field mushrooms with a damp cloth.

ingredients

4 skinless chicken breasts

salt and pepper

75 g/2¾ oz plain flour

2 tbsp olive oil

2 large garlic cloves, chopped

1 bay leaf

1 tbsp grated fresh root ginger

1 tbsp chopped fresh lemon grass

4 tbsp sherry vinegar

5 tbsp rice wine or sherry

1 tbsp clear honey

1 tsp chilli powder

125 ml/4 fl oz orange juice

4 tbsp lime juice

toasted flaked almonds and wedges
    of lime, to garnish

freshly cooked noodles, to serve

sweet & sour chicken

Season the chicken breasts on both sides with salt and pepper, then roll them in the flour until coated. Heat the olive oil in a large frying pan. Add the garlic and cook, stirring, over a medium heat for 1 minute. Add the chicken, bay leaf, ginger and lemon grass and cook for 2 minutes on each side.

Add the vinegar, rice wine and honey, bring to the boil, then lower the heat and simmer, stirring occasionally, for 10 minutes. Add the chilli powder, then stir in the orange juice and lime juice. Simmer for a further 10 minutes. Using a slotted spoon, lift out the chicken and reserve. Strain and reserve the liquid and discard the bay leaf, then return the liquid to the pan with the chicken. Simmer for a further 15–20 minutes.

Remove from the heat and transfer to individual serving plates. Garnish with toasted flaked almonds and lime wedges and serve with noodles.

watercress soup

Remove the leaves from the stalks of the watercress and set aside. Roughly chop the stalks.

Melt the butter in a large saucepan over a medium heat, add the onion and cook for 4–5 minutes until soft. Do not brown.

Add the potato to the saucepan and mix well with the onion. Add the watercress stalks and the stock.

Bring to the boil, then reduce the heat, cover and simmer for 15–20 minutes until the potato is soft.

Add the watercress leaves and stir in to heat through. Remove from the heat and use a hand-held stick blender to process the soup until smooth. Alternatively, liquidize the soup in a blender and return to the rinsed-out saucepan. Reheat and season with salt and pepper to taste, adding a good grating of nutmeg, if using.

Serve in warm bowls with the crème fraîche spooned on top.

ingredients

2 bunches of watercress (approx 200 g/7 oz), thoroughly cleaned
40 g/1½ oz butter
2 onions, chopped
225 g/8 oz potatoes, peeled and roughly chopped
1.2 litres/2 pints vegetable stock or water
salt and pepper
whole nutmeg, for grating (optional)
125 ml/4 fl oz crème fraîche

OCTOBER
4

SERVES 4

---

buttery cabbage and potato mash

OCTOBER
5

To make the mashed potato, cook the potatoes in a large saucepan of boiling salted water for 15–20 minutes. Drain well and mash with a potato masher until smooth. Season with salt and pepper, add the butter and cream and stir well. The potato should be very soft.

Cut the cabbage into quarters, remove the centre stalk and shred finely.

Cook the cabbage in a large saucepan of boiling salted water for just 1–2 minutes until it is soft. Drain thoroughly.

Mix the potato and cabbage together and stir in the spring onion. Season well with salt and pepper.

Serve in individual bowls and top with a good piece of butter.

ingredients

225 g/8 oz green or white cabbage
6 spring onions, cut into 5-mm/¼-inch pieces
salt and pepper
55 g/2 oz butter, cut into 4 pieces

MASHED POTATO

450 g/1 lb floury potatoes, such as King Edwards, Maris Piper or Desirée, peeled and cut into chunks
salt and pepper
55 g/2 oz butter
150 ml/5 fl oz single cream

SERVES 4

fettuccine with scallops & porcini

Put the porcini and hot water in a bowl. Leave to soak for 20 minutes. Strain the mushrooms, reserving the soaking water, and chop roughly. Line a sieve with 2 pieces of kitchen paper and strain the mushroom water into a bowl.

Heat the oil and butter in a large frying pan over a medium heat. Add the scallops and cook for 2 minutes until just golden. Add the garlic and mushrooms, then stir-fry for another minute.

Stir in the lemon juice, cream and 125 ml/4 fl oz of the mushroom water. Bring to the boil, then simmer over a medium heat for 2–3 minutes, stirring constantly, until the liquid is reduced by half. Season with salt and pepper. Remove from the heat.

Cook the pasta in plenty of boiling salted water until al dente. Drain and transfer to a warm serving dish. Briefly reheat the sauce and pour over the pasta. Sprinkle with the parsley and toss well to mix. Serve immediately.

ingredients

25 g/1 oz dried porcini mushrooms
500 ml/18 fl oz hot water
3 tbsp olive oil
3 tbsp butter
350 g/12 oz scallops, sliced
2 garlic cloves, chopped very finely
2 tbsp lemon juice
250 ml/9 fl oz double cream
salt and pepper
350 g/12 oz dried fettuccine or
    pappardelle
2 tbsp chopped fresh flat-leaved
    parsley, to serve

carrot and pumpkin curry

Pour the stock into a large saucepan and bring to the boil. Add the galangal, half the garlic, the lemon grass and chillies and simmer for 5 minutes. Add the carrots and pumpkin and simmer for 5–6 minutes, until tender.

To make the curry paste, put all the ingredients into a food processor or blender and process to a thick paste, scraping down the sides occasionally and making sure they are well combined.

Meanwhile, heat the oil in a wok or frying pan and stir-fry the shallots and the remaining garlic for 2–3 minutes. Add the curry paste and stir-fry for 1–2 minutes.

Stir the shallot mixture into the saucepan and add the coconut milk and basil. Simmer for 2–3 minutes. Serve hot, sprinkled with the toasted pumpkin seeds.

ingredients

150 ml/¼ pint vegetable stock

2.5-cm/1-inch piece fresh galangal, sliced

2 garlic cloves, chopped

1 lemon grass stalk (white part only), chopped finely

2 fresh red chillies, deseeded and chopped

4 carrots, peeled and cut into chunks

225 g/8 oz pumpkin, peeled, deseeded and cut into cubes

2 tbsp vegetable or groundnut oil

2 shallots, chopped finely

3 tbsp Yellow Curry Paste

400 ml/14 fl oz coconut milk

4-6 sprigs fresh Thai basil

25 g/1 oz toasted pumpkin seeds, to garnish

YELLOW CURRY PASTE

3 small fresh orange or yellow chillies, chopped coarsely

3 large garlic cloves, chopped coarsely

4 shallots, chopped coarsely

3 tsp ground turmeric

1 tsp salt

12–15 black peppercorns

1 lemon grass stalk (white part only), chopped coarsely

2.5-cm/1-inch piece fresh root ginger, chopped

SERVES 4

braised pork with fennel

Crush the fennel seeds and mix together with the lemon rind, salt and pepper. Spread the mixture over both sides of the pork chops and leave to marinate for about 1 hour.

Dust the pork chops with the flour. Heat the oil in a flameproof casserole, add the pork and fry until browned on both sides. Remove from the casserole. Add the onions, garlic and fennel to the casserole and fry for 5–10 minutes until softened and beginning to brown. Return the chops to the casserole.

Pour in the wine, stirring in any glazed bits from the bottom of the casserole, and bring to the boil. Reduce the heat and add the bay leaf. Cover the casserole with a lid and simmer for 45 minutes, until the pork chops are tender. Serve sprinkled with the reserved snipped fennel fronds.

ingredients

1 tsp fennel seeds
grated rind of 1 lemon
salt and pepper
4 pork chops
1 tbsp plain white flour
2 tbsp olive oil
2 bunches spring onions, sliced
　thinly
1 garlic clove, chopped finely
2 fennel bulbs, sliced thinly with
　fronds reserved
250 ml/9 fl oz dry white wine
1 bay leaf

cinnamon lamb casserole

Put the flour and some pepper in a polythene bag, add the lamb and shake well to coat each piece. Heat the oil in a large, flameproof casserole. Add the onions and chopped garlic and fry for 5 minutes, until soft. Add the lamb to the casserole and fry for about 5 minutes, stirring frequently, until browned.

Pour in the wine, vinegar and tomatoes, stirring in any glazed bits from the bottom of the casserole, and bring to the boil. Reduce the heat and add the raisins, cinnamon, sugar and bay leaf. Season with salt and pepper.

Cover the casserole with a lid and simmer gently for 2 hours, until the lamb is tender.

Meanwhile, make the topping. Put the yogurt into a small serving bowl, stir in the garlic and season with salt and pepper. Chill in the fridge until ready to serve.

Serve the casserole hot, topped with a spoonful of the garlic yogurt, and dust with paprika.

ingredients

2 tbsp plain white flour
salt and pepper
1 kg/2 lb 4 oz lean boned lamb,
　cubed
2 tbsp olive oil
2 large onions, sliced
1 garlic clove, chopped finely
300 ml/½ pint full-bodied red wine
2 tbsp red wine vinegar
400 g/14 oz canned chopped
　tomatoes in juice
55 g/2 oz seedless raisins
1 tbsp ground cinnamon
pinch of sugar
1 bay leaf
150 ml/¼ pint Greek yogurt
2 garlic cloves, crushed
paprika, to garnish

ingredients

4 large eggs

2 tbsp water

1 tbsp Thai soy sauce

6 spring onions, chopped finely

1 fresh red chilli, deseeded and
chopped finely

1 tbsp vegetable or groundnut oil

1 tbsp green curry paste

bunch of fresh coriander, chopped

SERVES 4

omelette rolls

Put the eggs, water and Thai soy sauce in a bowl. Set aside. Mix together the spring
onions and chopped chilli to form a paste.

Heat half the oil in a 20-cm/8-inch frying pan and pour in half the egg mixture. Tilt to coat
the base of the frying pan evenly and cook until set. Lift out and set aside. Heat the
remaining oil and make a second omelette in the same way.

Spread the spring onion, chilli paste, and the curry paste, in a thin layer over each
omelette and sprinkle the coriander on top. Roll up tightly. Cut each in half and then cut
each piece on the diagonal in half again. Serve immediately, while still warm.

pappardelle with pumpkin sauce

Melt the butter in a large, heavy-based saucepan. Add the shallots, sprinkle with a little salt, cover and cook over a very low heat, stirring occasionally, for 30 minutes.

Add the pumpkin pieces and season to taste with nutmeg. Cover and cook over a very low heat, stirring occasionally, for 40 minutes, or until the pumpkin is pulpy. Stir in the cream, Parmesan cheese and parsley and remove the saucepan from the heat.

Meanwhile, bring a large, heavy-based saucepan of lightly salted water to the boil. Add the pasta, return to the boil and cook for 8–10 minutes, or until tender but still firm to the bite. Drain, reserving 2–3 tablespoons of the cooking water.

Add the pasta to the pumpkin mixture and stir in the reserved cooking water if the mixture seems too thick. Cook, stirring, for 1 minute, then transfer to a warmed serving dish and serve immediately with extra grated Parmesan cheese.

ingredients

55 g/2 oz butter

6 shallots, very finely chopped

salt

800 g/1 lb 12 oz pumpkin, peeled, deseeded and cut into pieces

pinch of freshly grated nutmeg

200 ml/7 fl oz single cream

4 tbsp freshly grated Parmesan cheese, plus extra to serve

2 tbsp chopped fresh flat-leaved parsley

350 g/12 oz dried pappardelle

ingredients

55 g/2 oz butter, plus extra for
 greasing

115 g/4 oz plain chocolate, broken
 into pieces

175 g/6 oz dark muscovado sugar

2 eggs

2 tbsp strong coffee, cooled

85 g/3 oz plain flour

½ tsp baking powder

pinch of salt

55 g/2 oz shelled walnuts, chopped

ICING

115 g/4 oz plain chocolate, broken
 into pieces

150 ml/5 fl oz soured cream

COOK'S TIP

Do not leave the brownies to set in
the refrigerator but leave them in
the cake tin in a cool place. Store
any un-iced brownies in an airtight
container for up to 3 days.

mocha brownies with soured cream icing

Preheat the oven to 180°C/350°F/Gas Mark 4. Grease a 20-cm/8-inch square cake tin with butter and line with baking paper. Place the chocolate and butter in a small heatproof bowl and set over a saucepan of gently simmering water until melted. Stir until smooth. Remove from the heat and leave to cool.

Beat the sugar and eggs together until pale and thick. Fold in the chocolate mixture and coffee. Mix well. Sift the flour, baking powder and salt into the mixture and fold in. Fold in the walnuts. Pour the mixture into the tin and bake in the oven for 20–25 minutes, or until set. Leave in the tin to cool.

To make the icing, melt the chocolate in a heatproof bowl over a saucepan of simmering water. Stir in the soured cream and beat until evenly blended. Spoon the topping over the brownies and make a swirling pattern with a palette knife. Leave in a cool place to set. Cut into squares, then remove from the tin and serve.

smoked cheddar & cider fondue

OCTOBER

13

SERVES 4

Put the lime juice and all but 2 tablespoons of the cider into a large saucepan and bring to a gentle simmer over a low heat. Add a small handful of the cheese and stir until melted. Add the remaining cheese gradually, stirring constantly after each addition.

In a bowl, mix the cornflour with the remaining cider, then stir into the saucepan. Continue to stir for 3–4 minutes, until thickened and bubbling. Stir in the mixed spice and add salt and pepper to taste.

Pour the mixture into a fondue pot and, using protective gloves, transfer to a lit tabletop burner. To serve, allow your guests to spear pieces of apple, bread, pineapple and ham on to fondue forks and dip them into the fondue.

ingredients

2 tbsp lime juice

475 ml/17 fl oz dry cider

700 g/1 lb 9 oz smoked Cheddar cheese, grated

2 tbsp cornflour

pinch of ground mixed spice

salt and pepper

DIPPERS

4 apples, cored and cut into bite-sized cubes, then brushed with lemon juice

fresh crusty bread, cut into bite-sized cubes

canned pineapple chunks, drained

lean cooked ham, cut into bite-sized cubes

bacon-wrapped trout

OCTOBER

14

SERVES 4

Preheat the barbecue or a griddle. Rinse the trout inside and out under cold running water and pat dry with kitchen paper. Stretch the bacon using the back of a heavy, flat-bladed knife.

Season the flour with salt and pepper and spread it out on a large, flat plate. Gently roll each trout in the seasoned flour until thoroughly coated. Beginning just below the head, wrap a rasher of bacon in a spiral along the length of each fish.

Brush the trout with olive oil and cook over medium hot coals or on the griddle for 5–8 minutes on each side. Transfer to 4 large serving plates and drizzle with the lemon juice. Garnish with parsley and lemon wedges and serve with lamb's lettuce.

ingredients

4 trout, gutted

4 smoked streaky bacon rashers, rinded

4 tbsp plain flour

salt and pepper

2 tbsp olive oil

2 tbsp lemon juice

fresh parsley sprigs, to garnish

lemon wedges, to garnish

lamb's lettuce, to serve

ingredients

115 g/4 oz unsalted peanuts

325 g/11½ oz canned sweetcorn,
    drained

1 onion, finely chopped

115 g/4 oz plain flour

1 tsp ground coriander

½ tsp sambal ulek or chilli sauce

salt

1–2 tbsp warm water (optional)

groundnut oil, for deep-frying

SERVES 3–4

COOK'S TIP

Sambal ulek is a fiery hot chilli sauce
available from Asian food shops and
supermarkets. If you cannot find it,
then use chilli sauce instead.

indonesian sweetcorn balls

Place the peanuts in a food processor and process briefly until coarsely ground. Alternatively, grind them in a mortar with a pestle. Transfer to a bowl and stir in the sweetcorn, onion, flour, coriander and sambal ulek. Season to taste with salt. Knead to a dough, adding a little warm water, if necessary, to make the dough workable.

Heat the oil in a deep-fryer or large, heavy-based saucepan. Using your hands, form tablespoonfuls of the dough into balls, then drop the sweetcorn balls into the hot oil, in batches, and cook until golden and crisp.

Remove the sweetcorn balls with a slotted spoon, drain on kitchen paper and keep warm while you cook the remaining batches. Serve immediately or leave to cool first.

ingredients

2½ tbsp plain flour

1 tsp salt

¼ tsp pepper

1 rolled brisket joint, weighing
1.6 kg/3 lb 8 oz

2 tbsp vegetable oil

2 tbsp butter

1 onion, finely chopped

2 celery sticks, diced

2 carrots, peeled and diced

1 tsp dill seed

1 tsp dried thyme or oregano

350 ml/12 fl oz red wine

150–225 ml/5–8 fl oz beef stock

4–5 potatoes, cut into large chunks
and boiled until just tender

2 tbsp chopped fresh dill, to serve

beef pot roast with potatoes & dill

Preheat the oven to 140°C/275°F/Gas Mark 1.

Mix 2 tablespoons of the flour with the salt and pepper in a shallow dish. Dip the meat to coat. Heat the oil in a flameproof casserole and brown the meat all over. Transfer to a plate.

Add half the butter to the casserole and cook the onion, celery, carrots, dill seed and thyme for 5 minutes. Return the meat and juices to the casserole.

Pour in the wine and enough stock to reach one-third of the way up the meat. Bring to the boil, cover and cook in the oven for 3 hours, turning the meat every 30 minutes. After it has been cooking for 2 hours, add the potatoes and more stock if necessary.

When ready, transfer the meat and vegetables to a warmed serving dish. Strain the cooking liquid into a saucepan.

Mix the remaining butter and flour to a paste. Bring the cooking liquid to the boil. Whisk in small pieces of the flour and butter paste, whisking constantly until the sauce is smooth. Pour the sauce over the meat and vegetables. Sprinkle with the fresh dill to serve.

COOK'S TIP
When using a flour and butter paste, also known as beurre manié, to thicken a sauce or gravy, whisk it into the sauce in small pieces, making sure each piece has been blended in before adding the next.

cod with spiced noodles

Preheat the grill to high. While the grill is heating, put the noodles in a saucepan of boiling water and boil for 3 minutes, until soft. Alternatively, cook according to the packet instructions. Drain, rinse with cold water to stop the cooking and drain again, then set aside. (If you want to cook the noodles in advance, toss them with a teaspoon or so of sesame oil and set aside.)

To cook the fish, mix 1 tablespoon of the oil with the lemon juice and brush over one side of each fish steak. Sprinkle with the lemon rind and a dusting of paprika and add a little salt and pepper. Lightly brush the grill rack with oil, then grill the fish, about 10 cm/4 inches from the heat, for 8–10 minutes until the flesh flakes easily.

Meanwhile, heat a wok or large frying pan over a high heat. Add 1 tablespoon oil and heat until it shimmers. Add the garlic and ginger and stir-fry for about 30 seconds. Add the coriander and kecap manis and stir around. Add the noodles and give a good stir so they are coated in the kecap manis. Stir in the chopped chilli and nam pla.

Serve each grilled fish steak on top of a bed of noodles.

ingredients

1 tbsp groundnut or sunflower oil

finely grated rind and juice of
   1 large lemon

4 cod or haddock steaks, about
   140 g/5 oz each, skinned

paprika, to taste

salt and pepper

SPICED NOODLES

250 g/9 oz dried medium Chinese
   egg noodles

1 tbsp groundnut or sunflower oil

2 garlic cloves, chopped

2.5-cm/1-inch piece fresh root
   ginger, peeled and finely chopped

2 tbsp very finely chopped fresh
   coriander roots

1 tbsp kecap manis (sweet soy
   sauce)

1 bird's eye chilli, deseeded and
   finely chopped

1 tbsp nam pla (Thai fish sauce)

OCTOBER

17

SERVES 4

grilled chicken with lemon

Prick the skin of the chicken quarters all over with a fork. Put the chicken pieces in a dish, add the lemon juice, oil, garlic, thyme, salt and pepper and mix well. Cover and leave to marinate in the fridge for at least 2 hours.

To cook the chicken, preheat the grill or barbecue. Put the chicken in a grill pan or on the barbecue grid and baste with the marinade. Cook for 30–40 minutes, basting and turning occasionally, until the chicken is tender. (To test if the chicken is cooked, pierce the thickest part of the chicken pieces with a skewer. If the juices run clear, they are ready.)

Serve hot, garnished with the grated lemon rind.

ingredients

4 chicken quarters

grated rind and juice of 2 lemons

4 tbsp olive oil

2 garlic cloves, crushed

2 sprigs fresh thyme

salt and pepper

onion soup with croûtons

Melt the butter in a large saucepan over a medium heat. Add the garlic, onions and sugar and cook, stirring, for about 25 minutes, until the onions have caramelised.

In a bowl, mix the flour with enough wine to make a smooth paste, then stir it into the onion mixture. Cook for 2 minutes, then stir in the remaining wine and the stock. Season with salt and pepper. Bring to the boil, then reduce the heat, cover the pan and simmer for 30 minutes.

Meanwhile, to make the croûtons, heat the oil in a frying pan until hot. Cut the bread into small cubes and cook over a high heat, stirring, for about 2 minutes, until crisp and golden. Remove from the heat, drain the croûtons on kitchen paper and reserve.

When the soup is cooked, remove from the heat and ladle into bowls. Scatter over some croûtons and serve with bread.

ingredients

100 g/3½ oz butter

2 garlic cloves, crushed

3 large onions, thinly sliced

1 tsp sugar

2 tbsp plain flour

225 ml/8 fl oz dry white wine

1.5 litres/2¾ pints vegetable stock

salt and pepper

CROUTONS

2 tbsp olive oil

2 slices day-old white bread,
   crusts removed

bread, to serve

ingredients

175 g/6 oz blanched almonds

300 ml/½ pint double cream

¼ tsp almond essence

150 ml/¼ pint single cream

55 g/2 oz icing sugar

HOT CHOCOLATE SAUCE

100 g/3½ oz plain chocolate, broken
  into pieces

3 tbsp golden syrup

4 tbsp water

25 g/1 oz unsalted butter, diced

¼ tsp vanilla essence

OCTOBER

20

SERVES 4–6

frozen almond cream
with hot chocolate sauce

Place the almonds on a baking sheet and toast in a preheated oven, 200°C/400°F/Gas Mark 6, for 8–10 minutes, stirring occasionally, until golden brown with a toasted aroma: watch carefully because they burn quickly. Immediately pour onto a chopping board and leave to cool. Coarsely chop 55 g/2 oz by hand, and finely grind the remainder. Set both aside separately.

Whip the double cream with the almond essence until soft peaks form. Stir in the single cream and continue whipping, sifting in the icing sugar in 3 batches. Transfer to an ice cream maker and freeze following the manufacturer's instructions. If you don't have an ice cream maker, put the mixture in a freezerproof container and freeze for 2 hours, or until it is starting to thicken and set around the edge. Beat well and return to the freezer until almost frozen. When the cream is almost frozen, transfer to a bowl, and stir in the chopped almonds. Put in a 450-g/ 1-lb loaf tin and smooth the top. Wrap tightly in foil and put in the freezer for at least 3 hours.

To make the sauce, place a heatproof bowl over a pan of simmering water. Add the chocolate, syrup and water and stir until the chocolate melts. Stir in the butter and vanilla until smooth.

To serve, unwrap the tin and dip the base in a sink of boiling water for a couple of seconds. Invert onto a freezerproof tray, giving a sharp shake until the frozen cream drops out. Using a palette knife, coat the top and sides with the finely chopped almonds; return to the freezer unless serving at once. Use a warm knife to slice into 8–12 slices. Arrange 2 slices on each plate and spoon the hot chocolate sauce around.

COOK'S TIP
You can make the sauce
and the dessert in advance.
Remove the dessert from
the freezer 15 minutes
before serving, and reheat
the sauce gently.

almost instant toffee pudding

Using a fork, beat the eggs with 6 tablespoons of the milk and the cinnamon in a large, shallow dish. Cut the bread into triangles and place in the dish, in batches if necessary, to soak for 2–3 minutes.

Melt half the butter with half the oil in a heavy-based frying pan. Add the bread, in batches, and cook for 2 minutes on each side, or until golden brown, adding a little more butter and oil as necessary. Remove with a fish slice, drain on kitchen paper, transfer to serving plates and keep warm.

Add the remaining butter and milk to the frying pan with the sugar and golden syrup and cook, stirring constantly, until hot and bubbling. Pour the toffee sauce over the bread triangles and serve.

ingredients

2 eggs
100 ml/3½ fl oz milk
pinch of ground cinnamon
6 slices of white bread, crusts removed
115 g/4 oz unsalted butter
1 tbsp sunflower oil
55 g/2 oz muscovado sugar
4 tbsp golden syrup

creamy chicken & shiitake pasta

Put the dried mushrooms in a bowl with the hot water. Leave to soak for 30 minutes until softened. Remove, squeezing excess water back into the bowl. Strain the liquid in a fine-meshed sieve and reserve. Slice the soaked mushrooms, discarding the stems.

Heat the oil in a large frying pan over a medium heat. Add the bacon and chicken, then stir-fry for about 3 minutes. Add the dried and fresh mushrooms, the onion and oregano. Stir-fry for 5–7 minutes until soft. Pour in the stock and the mushroom liquid. Bring to the boil, stirring. Simmer briskly for about 10 minutes, continuing to stir, until reduced. Add the cream and simmer for 5 minutes, stirring, until beginning to thicken. Season with salt and pepper. Remove the pan from the heat and set aside.

Cook the pasta until al dente. Drain and transfer to a serving dish. Pour the sauce over the pasta. Add half the Parmesan and mix together well. Sprinkle with parsley and serve with the remaining Parmesan.

ingredients

25 g/1 oz dried shiitake mushrooms
350 ml/12 fl oz hot water
1 tbsp olive oil
6 bacon rashers, chopped
3 boneless, skinless chicken breasts, sliced into strips
115 g/4 oz fresh shiitake mushrooms, sliced
1 small onion, chopped finely
1 tsp fresh oregano or marjoram, chopped finely
250 ml/9 fl oz chicken stock
300 ml/10 fl oz whipping cream
salt and pepper
450 g/1 lb dried tagliatelle
55 g/2 oz freshly grated Parmesan
chopped fresh flat-leaved parsley, to garnish

ingredients

2 tbsp plain flour

salt and pepper

4 x 225 g/8 oz swordfish steaks

100 ml/3½ fl oz olive oil

2 garlic cloves, halved

1 onion, chopped

4 anchovy fillets, drained and
   chopped

4 tomatoes, peeled, deseeded
   and chopped

12 green olives, stoned and sliced

1 tbsp capers, rinsed

fresh rosemary leaves, to garnish

OCTOBER

23

SERVES 4

swordfish with olives & capers

Spread out the flour on a plate and season with salt and pepper. Coat the fish in the seasoned flour, shaking off any excess.

Gently heat the olive oil in a large, heavy-based frying pan. Add the garlic and cook over a low heat for 2–3 minutes, until just golden. Do not allow it to turn brown or burn. Remove the garlic and discard.

Add the fish to the frying pan and cook over a medium heat for about 4 minutes on each side, until cooked through and golden brown. Remove the steaks from the frying pan and set aside.

Add the onion and anchovies to the frying pan and cook, mashing the anchovies with a wooden spoon until they have turned to a purée and the onion is golden. Add the tomatoes and cook over a low heat, stirring occasionally, for about 20 minutes, until the mixture has thickened.

Stir in the olives and capers and taste and adjust the seasoning. Return the steaks to the frying pan and heat through gently. Serve garnished with rosemary.

ingredients

100 g/3½ oz caster sugar

115 g/4 oz whole almonds, blanched
     or unblanched

12 ripe figs

350 g/12 oz blue cheese, crumbled

extra virgin olive oil

COOK'S TIP

*Store the nuts in an airtight jar for up
to 3 days until required; any longer
and they become soft.*

VARIATION

*Walnut halves can also be
caramelized and used in this recipe.*

figs with blue cheese

First make the caramelized almonds. Put the sugar in a saucepan over a medium-high heat
and stir until the sugar melts and turns golden brown and bubbles: do not stir once the
mixture starts to bubble. Remove from the heat and add the almonds one at a time and
quickly turn with a fork until coated; if the caramel hardens, return the saucepan to the
heat. Transfer each almond to a lightly buttered baking sheet once it is coated. Leave until
cool and firm.

To serve, slice the figs in half and arrange 4 halves on each plate. Coarsely chop the
almonds by hand. Place a mound of blue cheese on each plate and sprinkle with chopped
almonds. Drizzle the figs very lightly with the oil.

risotto with chargrilled chicken

Place the chicken breasts in a shallow, non-metallic dish and season. Mix the lemon rind and juice, 4 tablespoons of the olive oil, the garlic and thyme together in a bowl. Spoon the mixture over the chicken and rub in. Cover with clingfilm and marinate in the refrigerator for 4–6 hours.

Remove the chicken from the refrigerator and return to room temperature. Preheat a griddle over a high heat. Put the chicken, skin-side down, on the griddle and cook for 10 minutes, or until the skin is crisp and starting to brown. Turn over and brown the underside. Reduce the heat and cook for a further 10–15 minutes, or until the juices run clear when pierced with a skewer.

Meanwhile, bring the stock to the boil in a saucepan, then reduce the heat and keep simmering gently over a low heat while you are cooking the risotto.

Heat the remaining oil with 25 g/1 oz of the butter in a deep saucepan over a medium heat until the butter has melted. Add the onion and cook, stirring occasionally, for 5 minutes, or until soft and starting to turn golden. Do not brown.

Reduce the heat, add the rice and mix to coat in oil and butter. Cook, stirring constantly, for 2–3 minutes, or until the grains are translucent.

Add the wine and cook, stirring constantly, for 1 minute until reduced. Gradually add the hot stock, a ladle at a time. Stir constantly and add more liquid as the rice absorbs each addition. Increase the heat to medium so that the liquid bubbles. Cook for 20 minutes, or until all the liquid is absorbed and the rice is creamy. Season to taste.

Transfer the cooked chicken to a carving board. Leave to rest for 5 minutes, then cut into thick slices. Remove the risotto from the heat and add the remaining butter. Mix well, then stir in the Parmesan until it melts. Put a scoop of risotto on each plate and add the chicken slices. Garnish with lemon wedges and thyme sprigs and serve immediately.

ingredients

4 boneless chicken breasts, about
    115 g/4 oz each
grated rind and juice of 1 lemon
5 tbsp olive oil
1 garlic clove, crushed
8 fresh thyme sprigs, finely chopped
1 litre/1¾ pints chicken stock
40 g/1½ oz butter
1 small onion, finely chopped
280 g/10 oz risotto rice
150 ml/5 fl oz dry white wine
85 g/3 oz freshly grated Parmesan
    or Grana Padano cheese
salt and pepper

TO GARNISH
lemon wedges
fresh thyme sprigs

26

SERVES 2

leek & sausage tortilla

Slice the sausage. Heat the oil in a large frying pan. Add the leeks and cook over a medium heat, stirring occasionally, for 5 minutes, or until softened. Add the pepper and sausage slices and cook for 5 minutes.

Beat the eggs in a bowl and season to taste with salt and pepper. Pour the eggs into the frying pan and cook for a few seconds. Loosen any egg that has set at the edge of the pan with a palette knife and tilt the pan to let the uncooked egg run underneath. Continue cooking until the underside has set.

Remove the frying pan from the heat, place an upside-down plate on top and, holding the 2 together, invert the tortilla on to the plate. Slide it back into the frying pan and cook for a further 2 minutes, until the second side has set. Slide the tortilla out of the frying pan and cut into wedges to serve.

ingredients
115 g/4 oz chorizo sausage

2 tbsp olive oil

4 leeks, thinly sliced

½ red pepper, deseeded and
  chopped

6 eggs

salt and pepper

27

SERVES 4

chicken with vegetables & coriander rice

Heat the oil in a wok or large frying pan and fry the onion, garlic and ginger together for 1–2 minutes.

Add the chicken and mushrooms and fry over a high heat until browned. Add the coconut milk, sugar snap peas and sauces and bring to the boil. Simmer gently for 4–5 minutes until tender.

Heat the oil for the rice in a separate wok or large frying pan and fry the onion until softened but not browned. Add the cooked rice, pak choy and fresh coriander and heat gently until the leaves have wilted and the rice is hot. Sprinkle over the soy sauce and serve immediately with the chicken.

ingredients
2 tbsp vegetable or groundnut oil

1 red onion, chopped

2 garlic cloves, chopped

2.5-cm/1-inch piece root ginger,
  peeled and chopped

2 skinned, boned chicken breasts,
  cut into strips

115 g/4 oz button mushrooms

400 g/14 oz canned coconut milk

50 g/2 oz sugar snap peas, trimmed
  and halved lengthways

2 tbsp soy sauce

1 tbsp fish sauce

RICE

1 tbsp vegetable or groundnut oil

1 red onion, sliced

350 g/12 oz rice, cooked and cooled

250 g/8 oz pak choy, torn into large
  pieces

handful of fresh coriander, chopped

2 tbsp Thai soy sauce

apple fritters

Pour the oil into a deep fryer or large, heavy-based saucepan and heat to 180–190°C/ 350–375°F, or until a cube of bread browns in 30 seconds. Meanwhile, using an electric mixer, beat the egg and salt together until frothy, then quickly whisk in the water and flour. Do not overbeat the batter – it doesn't matter if it isn't completely smooth.

Mix the cinnamon and sugar together in a shallow dish and reserve.

SERVES 4

Slice the apples into 5-mm/¼-inch thick rings. Spear with a fork, 1 slice at a time, and dip in the batter to coat. Add to the hot oil, in batches, and cook for 1 minute on each side, or until golden and puffed up. Remove with a slotted spoon and drain on kitchen paper. Keep warm while you cook the remaining batches. Transfer to a large serving plate, sprinkle with the cinnamon sugar and serve.

ingredients

sunflower oil, for deep-frying

1 large egg

pinch of salt

175 ml/6 fl oz water

55 g/2 oz plain flour

2 tsp ground cinnamon

55 g/2 oz caster sugar

4 eating apples, peeled and cored

VARIATION

Replace the apple with 1 small pineapple, peeled and cut into rings. Banana fritters would also be delicious. Use 4 bananas instead of apples.

COOK'S TIP

The best and easiest way to core an apple is to use an apple corer. Push the corer into the stalk end of the apple and twist to cut around the core, then pull it out and discard.

pork with sweet peppers

Place the pork in a non-metallic bowl. Pour over the wine and add 4 of the garlic cloves. Cover with clingfilm and leave to marinate in the refrigerator for at least 8 hours.

Put the chillies in a heatproof bowl and pour over enough boiling water to cover. Leave for 20 minutes to soften, then deseed and chop. Set them aside.

Preheat the oven to 160°C/325°F/Gas Mark 3.

Heat 4 tablespoons of oil in a large, heavy-based flameproof casserole over a medium-high heat. Add the onions and fry for 3 minutes, then add the remaining garlic, chopped chillies, pepper slices and paprika and fry for a further 2 minutes until the onions are soft, but not brown. Use a slotted spoon to transfer the mixture to a plate, leaving as much oil as possible in the base of the casserole.

Drain the pork, reserving the marinade, and pat dry. Add the pork to the casserole, and fry until brown on both sides.

Return the onion mixture to the casserole with the pork and stir in the reserved marinade, tomatoes and their can juices, the herbs and salt and pepper to taste. Bring to the boil, scraping any glazed bits from the base of the pan. Cover, transfer the casserole to the oven and cook for 1 hour, or until the pork is tender. If the juices are too thin, remove the pork from the casserole and keep warm. Put the casserole over a high heat and let the juices bubble until reduced.

Taste and adjust the seasoning. Cut the pork into pieces and serve with the peppers and sauce from the casserole.

ingredients

1 piece of pork shoulder, weighing 900 g/2 lb, boned and trimmed, but left in 1 piece

225 ml/8 fl oz dry white wine

6 garlic cloves, crushed

2 dried ancho or pasilla chillies

about 4 tbsp olive oil

2 large onions, chopped

4 red or green peppers, or a mixture, grilled, peeled, deseeded and sliced

½ tsp hot paprika

800 g/1 lb 12 oz canned chopped tomatoes

2 fresh thyme sprigs

2 fresh parsley sprigs

salt and pepper

ingredients

8 tbsp olive oil

12 garlic cloves, very finely chopped

350 g/12 oz chickpeas, soaked
    overnight in cold water and
    drained

2.5 litres/4½ pints water

1 tsp ground cumin

1 tsp ground coriander

2 carrots, very finely chopped

2 onions, very finely chopped

6 celery sticks, very finely chopped

juice of 1 lemon

salt and pepper

4 tbsp chopped fresh coriander

SERVES 4

tunisian garlic & chickpea soup

Heat half the oil in a large, heavy-based saucepan. Add the garlic and cook over a low heat, stirring frequently, for 2 minutes. Add the chickpeas to the saucepan with the measured water, cumin and ground coriander. Bring to the boil, then reduce the heat and simmer for 2½ hours, or until tender.

Meanwhile, heat the remaining oil in a separate saucepan. Add the carrots, onions and celery, cover and cook over a medium-low heat, stirring occasionally, for 20 minutes.

Stir the vegetable mixture into the saucepan of chickpeas. Transfer about half the soup to a food processor or blender and process until smooth. Return the purée to the saucepan, add about half the lemon juice and stir. Taste and add more lemon juice as required. Season to taste with salt and pepper. Ladle into warmed bowls, sprinkle with the fresh coriander and serve.

pumpkin chestnut risotto

Bring the stock to the boil, then reduce the heat and keep simmering gently over a low heat while you are cooking the risotto.

Heat the oil with 25 g/1 oz of the butter in a deep saucepan over a medium heat until the butter has melted. Stir in the onion and pumpkin and cook, stirring occasionally, for 5 minutes, or until the onion is soft and starting to turn golden and the pumpkin begins to colour. Roughly chop the chestnuts and add to the mixture. Stir thoroughly to coat.

Reduce the heat, add the rice and mix to coat in oil and butter. Cook, stirring constantly, for 2–3 minutes, or until the grains are translucent. Add the wine and cook, stirring constantly, for 1 minute until it has reduced.

If using the saffron threads, dissolve them in 4 tablespoons of the hot stock and add the liquid to the rice after the wine has been absorbed. Cook, stirring constantly, until the liquid has been absorbed.

Gradually add the hot stock, a ladle at a time. Stir constantly and add more liquid as the rice absorbs each addition. Increase the heat to medium so that the liquid bubbles. Cook for 20 minutes, or until all the liquid is absorbed and the rice is creamy. Season to taste.

Remove the risotto from the heat and add the remaining butter. Mix well, then stir in the Parmesan until it melts. Adjust the seasoning if necessary, spoon the risotto onto 4 warmed plates and serve immediately.

ingredients

1 litre/1¾ pints vegetable or chicken stock
1 tbsp olive oil
40 g/1½ oz butter
1 small onion, finely chopped
225 g/8 oz pumpkin, diced
225 g/8 oz chestnuts, cooked and shelled
280 g/10 oz risotto rice
150 ml/5 fl oz dry white wine
1 tsp crumbled saffron threads (optional)
85 g/3 oz freshly grated Parmesan or Grana Padano cheese
salt and pepper

November

ingredients

100 g/3½ oz butter, slightly
     softened

1 tbsp chopped fresh thyme

1 tbsp chopped fresh parsley

2 oven-ready young pheasants

salt and pepper

4 tbsp vegetable oil

125 ml/4 fl oz red wine

TO SERVE

honey-glazed parsnips

sautéed potatoes

freshly cooked Brussels sprouts

COOK'S TIP

*Only young birds are suitable for
roasting, as older pheasants are
fairly tough and need a slower
cooking method. Even so, the meat
on the legs tends to be quite tough
and sinewy, whereas the lighter
breasts are more delicate and
tender. It is quite usual to serve only
the breasts. Keep the leg meat for
making a minced pasta sauce or
using in a pie. You can also make
delicious stock with the carcasses.*

roast pheasant with red wine & herbs

Preheat the oven to 190°C/375°F/Gas Mark 5.

Put the butter in a small bowl and mix in the chopped herbs. Lift the skins away from the breasts, taking care not to tear them, and push the herb butter under the skins. Season to taste with salt and pepper. Pour the oil into a roasting tin, add the pheasants and cook in the oven for 45 minutes, basting occasionally.

Remove from the oven, pour over the wine, then return to the oven and cook for a further 15 minutes, or until cooked through. Check that each bird is cooked by inserting a knife between the legs and body. If the juices run clear, they are cooked.

Remove the pheasants from the oven, cover with foil and leave to stand for 15 minutes. Divide between individual serving plates, and serve with honey-glazed parsnips, sautéed potatoes and freshly cooked Brussels sprouts.

steamed syrup sponge pudding

Butter a 1.2-litre/2-pint pudding basin and put the syrup into the bottom.

Beat together the butter and sugar until soft and creamy, then beat in the eggs, a little at a time.

Fold in the flour and stir in the milk to make a soft dropping consistency. Add the lemon rind. Turn the mixture into the pudding basin.

SERVES 6

Cover the surface with a circle of greaseproof or baking paper and top with a pleated sheet of foil. Secure with some string or crimp the edges of the foil to ensure a tight fit around the basin.

Place the pudding in a large saucepan half-filled with boiling water. Cover the saucepan and bring back to the boil over a medium heat. Reduce the heat to a slow simmer and steam for 1½ hours until risen and firm. Keep checking the water level and top up with boiling water as necessary.

Remove the pan from the heat and lift out the pudding basin. Remove the cover and loosen the pudding from the sides of the basin using a knife.

Turn out into a warmed dish and heat a little more syrup to serve with the pudding.

ingredients

butter, for greasing

2 tbsp golden syrup, plus extra
    to serve

115 g/4 oz butter

115 g/4 oz caster sugar

2 eggs, lightly beaten

175 g/6 oz self-raising flour

2 tbsp milk

grated rind of 1 lemon

chicken fried rice

ingredients

½ tbsp sesame oil

6 shallots, peeled and quartered

450g/1 lb cooked, cubed chicken
meat

3 tbsp soy sauce

2 carrots, diced

1 stalk celery, diced

1 red pepper, diced

175g/6 oz fresh peas

100 g/3½ oz canned sweetcorn

275 g/9½ oz cooked long-grain rice

2 large eggs, scrambled

Heat the oil in a large frying pan over a medium heat. Add the shallots and fry until soft, then add the chicken and 2 tablespoons of the soy sauce and stir-fry for 5–6 minutes.

Stir in the carrots, celery, red pepper, peas and sweetcorn and stir-fry for another 5 minutes. Add the rice and stir thoroughly.

Finally, stir in the scrambled eggs and the remaining tablespoon of soy sauce. Serve immediately.

toffee bananas

Sift the flour into a bowl. Make a well in the centre, add the egg and 5 tablespoons of iced water and beat from the centre outwards, until combined into a smooth batter. Peel the bananas and cut into 5-cm/2-inch pieces. Gently shape them into balls with your hands. Brush with lemon juice to prevent discoloration, then roll them in rice flour until coated. Pour oil into a deep-fryer to a depth of 6 cm/2½ inches and preheat to 190°C/375°F/Gas Mark 5. Coat the balls in the batter and deep-fry in batches for about 2 minutes, until golden. Lift them out and drain on kitchen paper.

To make the caramel, put the sugar into a small saucepan over a low heat. Add 4 tablespoons of iced water and heat, stirring, until the sugar dissolves. Simmer for 5 minutes, remove from the heat and stir in the sesame seeds. Toss the banana balls in the caramel, scoop them out and drop into the bowl of iced water to set. Lift them out and divide among individual serving bowls. Serve hot.

ingredients

70 g/2½ oz self-raising flour

1 egg, beaten

5 tbsp iced water

4 large, ripe bananas

3 tbsp lemon juice

2 tbsp rice flour

vegetable oil, for deep-frying

CARAMEL

115 g/4 oz caster sugar

4 tbsp iced water, plus an extra
bowl of iced water for setting

2 tbsp sesame seeds

ingredients

4 x 350 g/12 oz lamb shanks

6 garlic cloves

2 tbsp virgin olive oil

1 tbsp very finely chopped
   fresh rosemary

pepper

4 red onions

salt

350 g/12 oz carrots, cut
   into thin batons

4 tbsp water

lamb shanks with roasted onions

Trim off any excess fat from the lamb. Using a small, sharp knife, make 6 incisions in each shank. Cut the garlic cloves lengthways into 4 slices. Insert 6 garlic slices in the incisions in each lamb shank.

Place the lamb in a single layer in a roasting tin, drizzle with the olive oil, sprinkle with the rosemary and season with pepper. Roast in a preheated oven, 180°C/350°F/Gas Mark 4, for 45 minutes.

Wrap each of the onions in a square of foil. Remove the roasting tin from the oven and season the lamb shanks with salt. Return the tin to the oven and place the wrapped onions on the shelf next to it. Roast for a further 1–1¼ hours, until the lamb is very tender.

Meanwhile, bring a large saucepan of water to the boil. Add the carrot batons and blanch for 1 minute. Drain and refresh under cold water.

Remove the roasting tin from the oven when the lamb is meltingly tender and transfer it to a warmed serving dish. Skim off any fat from the roasting tin and place it over a medium heat. Add the carrots and cook for 2 minutes, then add the water, bring to the boil and simmer, stirring constantly and scraping up the glazed bits from the base of the roasting tin.

Transfer the carrots and sauce to the serving dish. Remove the onions from the oven and unwrap. Cut off and discard about 1 cm/½ inch of the tops and add the onions to the dish. Serve immediately.

ingredients

400 g/14 oz ready-made puff pastry

2 tbsp plain flour, for dusting

55 g/2 oz butter, softened

55 g/2 oz soft brown sugar

85 g/3 oz currants

25 g/1 oz mixed peel, chopped

½ tsp ground mixed spice (optional)

1 egg white, lightly beaten

1 tsp caster sugar

currant puffs

Preheat the oven to 220°C/425°F/Gas Mark 7.

Roll out the pastry thinly, using the flour to dust the work surface and the rolling pin.

Cut into rounds using a 9-cm/3½-inch cutter. Fold the trimmings carefully, re-roll and repeat the cuttings to give a total of 10–12 rounds.

In a basin, mix together the butter and soft brown sugar until creamy, then add the dried fruit and mixed spice, if using.

Put a teaspoon of the filling in the centre of each pastry round. Draw the edges of the circles together and pinch the edges over the filling. Reshape each cake into a round.

Turn the cakes over and lightly roll them with the rolling pin until the currants just show through. Score with a knife into a lattice pattern.

Place the cakes on a greased baking tray and allow to rest for 10–15 minutes.

Brush the cakes with the egg white, sprinkle with the caster sugar and bake at the top of the oven for about 15 minutes until golden brown and crisp.

Transfer to a wire rack and sprinkle with a little more sugar if desired. Delicious straight from the oven, they also keep well in an airtight tin for a week and can be reheated before serving.

parmesan pumpkin

Preheat the oven to 180°C/ 350°F/Gas Mark 4. Heat the olive oil in a large saucepan, add the onion and garlic and cook over a low heat for 5 minutes, until softened. Stir in the passata, basil, parsley and sugar and season to taste with salt and pepper. Simmer for 10–15 minutes, until thickened.

Meanwhile, put the beaten eggs in a shallow dish and spread out the breadcrumbs in another shallow dish. Dip the slices of pumpkin first in the egg, then in the breadcrumbs to coat, shaking off any excess.

Grease a large ovenproof dish with butter. Melt the butter in a large, heavy-based frying pan. Add the pumpkin slices, in batches, and cook until browned all over. Transfer the slices to the dish. Pour the sauce over them and sprinkle with the Parmesan.

Bake in the preheated oven for 30 minutes, until the cheese is bubbling and golden. Serve immediately.

ingredients
2 tbsp virgin olive oil
1 onion, chopped finely
1 garlic clove, chopped finely
400 ml/14 fl oz passata
10 fresh basil leaves, shredded
2 tbsp chopped fresh flat-leaved
  parsley
1 tsp sugar
salt and pepper
2 eggs, beaten lightly
55 g/2 oz dried, uncoloured
  breadcrumbs
1.6 kg/3½ lb pumpkin, peeled,
  deseeded and sliced
55 g/2 oz butter, plus extra for
  greasing
55 g/2 oz freshly grated Parmesan
  cheese

NOVEMBER

7

SERVES 6

greek sausages

Put all the ingredients in a bowl and mix well together. Cover and leave to marinate in the fridge overnight or for about 12 hours.

Preheat the grill. Stir the mixture and then, with damp hands, form the mixture into about 24 small sausage shapes, about 5 cm/2 inches long, and place on a grill pan.

Cook the sausages under the grill for about 15 minutes, turning several times, until brown on all sides. Serve hot, with lemon wedges.

ingredients
350 g/12 oz minced pork
115 g/4 oz minced beef
1 garlic clove, crushed
½ tsp ground cinnamon
¼ tsp dried savory or thyme
grated rind of 1 small orange
8 black peppercorns, crushed
100 ml/3½ fl oz dry red wine
lemon wedges, to garnish

NOVEMBER

8

MAKES ABOUT 24

risotto with sole & tomatoes

Bring the stock to the boil in a saucepan, then reduce the heat and keep simmering gently over a low heat while you are cooking the risotto.

Heat 1 tablespoon of the oil with 25 g/1 oz of the butter in a deep saucepan over a medium heat until the butter has melted. Stir in the onion and cook, stirring occasionally, for 5 minutes, or until soft and starting to turn golden. Do not brown.

Reduce the heat, add the rice and mix to coat in oil and butter. Cook, stirring constantly, for 2–3 minutes, or until the grains are translucent.

Gradually add the hot stock, a ladle at a time. Stir constantly and add more liquid as the rice absorbs each addition. Increase the heat to medium so that the liquid bubbles. Cook for 20 minutes, or until all the liquid is absorbed and the rice is creamy. Season to taste.

While the risotto is cooking, heat the remaining oil in a large, heavy-based frying pan. Add the fresh and dried tomatoes. Stir well and cook over a medium heat for 10–15 minutes, or until soft and slushy.

Stir in the tomato purée and wine. Bring the sauce to the boil, then reduce the heat until it is just simmering.

Cut the fish into strips and add to the sauce. Stir gently. Cook for 5 minutes, or until the fish flakes when checked with a fork. Most of the liquid should be absorbed, but if it isn't, remove the fish and then increase the heat to reduce the sauce.

Remove the risotto from the heat when all the liquid has been absorbed and add the remaining butter. Mix well, then stir in the Parmesan until it melts.

Place the risotto on serving plates and arrange the fish and tomato sauce on top. Garnish with fresh coriander and serve immediately.

ingredients

1.2 litres/2 pints fish or
   chicken stock
3 tbsp olive oil
40 g/1½ oz butter
1 small onion, finely chopped
280 g/10 oz risotto rice
450 g/1 lb tomatoes, peeled,
   deseeded and cut into strips
6 sun-dried tomatoes in olive oil,
   drained and thinly sliced
3 tbsp tomato purée
50 ml/2 fl oz red wine
450 g/1 lb sole or plaice fillets,
   skinned
115 g/4 oz freshly grated Parmesan
   or Grana Padano cheese
salt and pepper
2 tbsp finely chopped fresh
   coriander, to garnish

pad thai (thai fried noodles)

Soak the noodles in a bowl of warm water for about
20 minutes, or until soft. Drain thoroughly in a colander and
set aside. In a small bowl, combine the peanuts, lime juice,
sugar, fish sauce and hot chilli sauce and set aside.

Rinse the tofu in cold water, place between layers of kitchen
paper and pat dry. Heat the oil for deep-frying in a large
frying pan or wok. Deep-fry the tofu over a medium heat for
2 minutes until light brown and crisp. Remove from the heat,
lift the tofu out with a slotted spoon and set aside on kitchen
paper to drain.

Heat a large frying pan or wok and add the peanut oil, garlic,
onion, red pepper and chicken strips. Cook for 2–3 minutes.

Stir in the beansprouts and mangetouts and cook for
1 minute. Then add the prawns, noodles, eggs and tofu and
stir-fry for 4–5 minutes. Finally, add the peanut and lime juice
mixture and cook for 3–4 minutes. Transfer to warm dishes,
garnish and serve.

ingredients

225 g/9 oz rice noodles

90 g/3¼ oz peanuts, chopped
  roughly

2 tbsp lime juice

1 tbsp caster sugar

6 tbsp fish sauce

1 tsp hot chilli sauce, or to taste

250 g/9 oz firm tofu, cubed

vegetable oil, for deep frying

3 tbsp peanut oil

1 garlic clove, crushed

1 onion, sliced finely

1 red pepper, sliced thinly

250 g/9 oz chicken breast, cut into
  thin strips

90 g/3 oz beansprouts

125 g/4½ oz mangetouts

175 g/6 oz prawns, peeled, cut in
  half lengthways

3 eggs, beaten

TO GARNISH

1 lemon, cut into wedges

4 spring onions, chopped finely

2 tbsp chopped peanuts

1 tbsp chopped fresh basil

potato, fontina & rosemary tart

Preheat the oven to 190°C/375°F/Gas Mark 5. Roll out the dough on a lightly floured work surface into a round about 25 cm/10 inches in diameter and put on a baking tray.

Peel the potatoes and slice as thinly as possible so that they are almost transparent – use a mandolin if you have one. Arrange the potato slices in a spiral, overlapping the slices to cover the pastry, leaving a 2-cm/¾-inch margin around the edge.

Arrange the cheese and onion over the potatoes, scatter with the rosemary and drizzle over the oil. Season to taste with salt and pepper and brush the edges with the egg yolk to glaze.

Bake in the preheated oven for 25 minutes, or until the potatoes are tender and the pastry is brown and crisp.

ingredients

400 g/14 oz ready-made puff pastry
plain flour, for dusting

FILLING

3–4 waxy potatoes
300 g/10½ oz fontina cheese,
    cut into cubes
1 red onion, thinly sliced
3 large fresh rosemary sprigs
2 tbsp olive oil
1 egg yolk
salt and pepper

cold weather vegetable casserole

Melt the butter in a large, heavy-based saucepan over a low heat. Add the leeks, carrots, potatoes, swede, courgettes and fennel and cook, stirring occasionally, for 10 minutes. Stir in the flour and cook, stirring constantly, for 1 minute. Stir in the can juice from the beans, the stock, tomato purée, thyme and bay leaves and season to taste with salt and pepper. Bring to the boil, stirring constantly, then cover and simmer for 10 minutes.

Meanwhile, make the dumplings. Sift the flour and salt into a bowl. Stir in the suet and parsley, then add enough water to bind to a soft dough. Divide the dough into 8 pieces and roll into balls.

Add the butter beans and dumplings to the saucepan, cover and simmer for a further 30 minutes. Remove and discard the bay leaf before serving.

ingredients

55 g/2 oz butter

2 leeks, sliced

2 carrots, sliced

2 potatoes, cut into bite-sized pieces

1 swede, cut into bite-sized pieces

2 courgettes, sliced

1 fennel bulb, halved and sliced

2 tbsp plain flour

425 g/15 oz canned butter beans

600 ml/1 pint vegetable stock

2 tbsp tomato purée

1 tsp dried thyme

2 bay leaves

salt and pepper

DUMPLINGS

115 g/4 oz self-raising flour

pinch of salt

55 g/2 oz suet or vegetarian suet

2 tbsp chopped fresh parsley

about 4 tbsp water

SERVES 4

VARIATION

If you like, you could replace the swede with 2 parsnips, sliced, and the butter beans with canned kidney beans.

COOK'S TIP

If the juices seem too thin, put the casserole on the hob and use a slotted spoon to remove the meat and chickpeas; keep warm. Bring the juices to the boil and boil until reduced; then return the other ingredients.

lamb stew with chickpeas

Preheat the oven to 160°C/325°F/Gas Mark 3. Heat 4 tablespoons of oil in a large, heavy-based flameproof casserole over a medium-high heat. Reduce the heat, add the chorizo and fry for 1 minute; set aside. Add the onions to the casserole and fry for 2 minutes, then add the garlic and continue frying for 3 minutes, or until the onions are soft, but not brown. Remove from the casserole and set aside.

Heat a further 2 tablespoons of oil in the casserole. Add the lamb in a single layer, without overcrowding the casserole, and fry until browned. Work in batches, if necessary.

Return the onion mixture to the casserole with all the lamb. Stir in the stock, wine, vinegar, tomatoes with their juices and salt and pepper to taste. Bring to the boil, scraping any glazed bits from the base of the casserole. Reduce the heat and stir in the thyme, bay leaves and paprika.

Transfer to the oven and cook, covered, for 40–45 minutes until the lamb is tender. Stir in the chickpeas and return to the oven, uncovered, for 10 minutes, or until they are heated through and the juices are reduced. Taste and adjust the seasoning. Garnish with thyme and serve.

ingredients

olive oil

225 g/8 oz chorizo sausage, cut into 5-mm/¼-inch thick slices, casings removed

2 large onions, chopped

6 large garlic cloves, crushed

900 g/2 lb boned leg of lamb, cut into 5-cm/2-inch chunks

250 ml/9 fl oz lamb stock or water

125 ml/4 fl oz red wine, such as Rioja or Tempranillo

2 tbsp sherry vinegar

800 g/1 lb 12 oz canned chopped tomatoes

salt and pepper

4 sprigs fresh thyme

2 bay leaves

½ tsp sweet Spanish paprika

800 g/1 lb 12 oz canned chickpeas, rinsed and drained

sprigs fresh thyme, to garnish

spiced banana milkshake

Pour the milk into a food processor and add the mixed spice. Add half of the banana ice cream and process gently until combined, then add the remaining ice cream and process until well blended.

When the mixture is well combined, add the bananas and process until smooth. Pour the mixture into tall glasses, add straws and serve at once.

ingredients

300 ml/10 fl oz milk

½ tsp mixed spice

150 g/5½ oz banana ice cream

2 bananas, sliced and frozen

SERVES 2

ginger chicken with noodles

Heat the oil in a wok and stir-fry the onion, garlic, ginger and carrots for 1–2 minutes, until softened. Add the chicken and stir-fry for 3–4 minutes, until the chicken is cooked through and lightly browned.

Add the stock, soy sauce and bamboo shoots and gradually bring to the boil. Simmer for 2–3 minutes. Meanwhile, soak the noodles in boiling water for 6–8 minutes. Drain well. Garnish with the spring onions and coriander and serve immediately, with the chicken stir-fry.

ingredients

2 tbsp vegetable or groundnut oil

1 onion, sliced

2 garlic cloves, chopped finely

5-cm/2-inch piece fresh root ginger, sliced thinly

2 carrots, sliced thinly

4 skinned, boned chicken breasts, cut into cubes

300 ml/½ pint chicken stock

4 tbsp Thai soy sauce

225 g/8 oz canned bamboo shoots, drained and rinsed

75 g/2¾ oz flat rice noodles

TO GARNISH

4 spring onions, chopped

4 tbsp chopped fresh coriander

SERVES 4

16

SERVES 6–8

ingredients

700 g/1 lb 9 oz neck of lamb

1.7 litres/3 pints water

55 g/2 oz pearl barley

2 onions, chopped

1 garlic clove, finely chopped

3 small turnips, cut into small dice

3 carrots, peeled and finely sliced

2 celery sticks, sliced

2 leeks, sliced

salt and pepper

2 tbsp chopped fresh parsley, to
   garnish

lamb and barley soup

Cut the meat into small pieces, removing as much fat as possible. Put into a large saucepan and cover with the water. Bring to the boil over a medium heat and skim off any scum that appears.

Add the pearl barley, reduce the heat and cook gently, covered, for 1 hour.

Add the prepared vegetables and season well with salt and pepper. Continue to cook for a further hour. Remove from the heat and allow to cool slightly.

Remove the meat from the saucepan using a slotted spoon and strip the meat from the bones. Discard the bones and any remaining fat or gristle. Place the meat back in the saucepan and leave to cool thoroughly, then refrigerate overnight.

Scrape the solidified fat off the surface of the soup. Reheat, season with salt and pepper to taste and serve piping hot, garnished with the parsley scattered over the top.

pesto palmiers

Preheat the oven to 200°C/400°F/Gas Mark 6, then grease a baking sheet. On a floured work surface, roll out the pastry to a 35 x 15-cm/14 x 6-inch rectangle and trim the edges with a sharp knife. Spread the pesto evenly over the pastry. Roll up the ends tightly to meet in the middle of the pastry.

Wrap in clingfilm and chill in the refrigerator for 20 minutes, until firm, then remove from the refrigerator and unwrap. Brush with the beaten egg yolk on all sides. Cut across into 1-cm/½-inch thick slices. Place the slices on the prepared baking sheet.

MAKES 20

Bake in the preheated oven for 10 minutes, or until crisp and golden. Remove from the oven and immediately sprinkle over the Parmesan cheese. Serve the palmiers warm or transfer to a wire rack and leave to cool to room temperature.

ingredients

butter, for greasing

plain flour, for dusting

250 g/9 oz ready-made puff pastry

3 tbsp green or red pesto

1 egg yolk, beaten with 1 tbsp water

25 g/1 oz freshly grated
　Parmesan cheese

roasted garlic mashed potatoes

Preheat the oven to 180°C/350°F/Gas Mark 4.

Separate the garlic cloves, place on a large piece of foil and drizzle with the oil. Wrap the garlic in the foil and roast in the oven for about 1 hour, or until very tender. Leave to cool slightly.

Twenty minutes before the end of the cooking time, cut the potatoes into chunks, then cook in a saucepan of lightly salted boiling water for 15 minutes, or until tender.

Meanwhile, squeeze the cooled garlic cloves out of their skins and push through a sieve into a saucepan. Add the milk, butter and salt and pepper to taste and heat gently until the butter has melted.

Drain the cooked potatoes, then mash in the saucepan until smooth. Pour in the garlic mixture and heat gently, stirring, until the ingredients are combined. Serve hot.

ingredients

2 whole garlic bulbs

1 tbsp olive oil

900 g/2 lb floury potatoes, peeled

125 ml/4 fl oz milk

55 g/2 oz butter

salt and pepper

COOK'S TIP

When roasted, garlic loses its pungent acidity and acquires a delicious, full-flavoured sweetness. So although using two whole bulbs may seem excessive, you will be surprised at the uniquely mellow flavour. In addition, roasted garlic leaves very little trace of its smell on the breath.

ingredients

500 g/1 lb 2 oz lean minced beef

1 onion, grated

55 g/2 oz fresh white breadcrumbs

1 egg, beaten lightly

25 g/1 oz fresh parsley, chopped
finely

salt and pepper

olive oil

2 large onions, sliced thinly

1 quantity Tomato Sauce (see page
66, March 8)

200 g/7 oz frozen peas

meatballs with peas

Put the meat in a bowl with the grated onion, breadcrumbs, egg, parsley and salt and pepper to taste. Use your hands to squeeze all the ingredients together. Fry a small piece of the mixture and taste to see if the seasoning needs adjusting.

With wet hands, shape the mixture into 12 balls. Put on a plate and chill for at least 20 minutes.

When ready to cook, heat a small amount of the oil in 1 or 2 large frying pans: the exact amount needed will depend on how much fat there is in the beef. Arrange the meatballs in a single layer, without over-crowding, and fry, stirring, for about 5 minutes until brown on the outside; work in batches if necessary.

Set the meatballs aside and remove all but 2 tablespoons of oil from the frying pan. Add the sliced onions and fry for about 5 minutes until soft, but not brown. Return the meatballs to the frying pan.

Stir the Tomato Sauce into the frying pan and bring to the boil, gently spooning the sauce and onions over the meatballs. Reduce the heat, cover and simmer for 20 minutes. Add the peas and continue simmering for 7–10 minutes until the peas are tender and the meatballs cooked through. Serve at once.

tomato pilaf

Heat the oil in a large, heavy-based saucepan, add the onion and garlic and fry for 5 minutes, until softened. Add the rice and cook for 2–3 minutes, stirring all the time, until the rice looks transparent.

Add the tomatoes with their juice, the sugar, stock, mint, salt and pepper. Bring to the boil then cover the saucepan with a tightly fitting lid and simmer for about 15 minutes, until the rice is tender and the liquid has been absorbed. Do not stir during cooking. When cooked, gently stir in the pine kernels.

Remove the lid, cover the saucepan with a clean tea towel, replace the lid and leave in a warm place for 10 minutes to dry out. Stir with a fork to separate the grains and serve with lemon wedges to squeeze over.

ingredients

3 tbsp olive oil

1 onion, chopped finely

1 garlic clove, chopped finely

225 g/8 oz long-grain white rice

400 g/14 oz canned chopped
    tomatoes in juice

pinch of sugar

600 ml/1 pint chicken or vegetable
    stock

1 tsp dried mint

salt and pepper

2 tbsp pine kernels

lemon wedges, to serve

VARIATION

An additional scattering of toasted pine kernels would enhance this pilaf. To prepare these, heat 1 tablespoon olive oil in a frying pan, add 55 g/2 oz pine kernels and fry until golden brown shaking the pan constantly.

prawn & vegetable bisque

Melt the butter in a large saucepan over a medium heat. Add the garlic and onion and cook, stirring, for 3 minutes, until slightly softened. Add the carrot and celery and cook for a further 3 minutes, stirring. Pour in the stock and red wine, then add the tomato purée and bay leaf. Season with salt and pepper. Bring to the boil, then lower the heat and simmer for 20 minutes. Remove from the heat and leave to cool for 10 minutes, then remove and discard the bay leaf.

Transfer half of the soup into a food processor and blend until smooth (you may need to do this in batches). Return to the pan with the rest of the soup. Add the prawns and cook over a low heat for 5–6 minutes.

Stir in the cream and cook for a further 2 minutes, then remove from the heat and ladle into serving bowls. Garnish with swirls of single cream and whole cooked prawns and serve at once.

ingredients

3 tbsp butter

1 garlic clove, chopped

1 onion, sliced

1 carrot, peeled and chopped

1 celery stick, trimmed and sliced

1.2 litres/2 pints fish stock

4 tbsp red wine

1 tbsp tomato purée

1 bay leaf

salt and pepper

600 g/1 lb 5 oz prawns, peeled and deveined

100 ml/3½ fl oz double cream

TO GARNISH

swirls of single cream

whole cooked prawns

roast turkey with two stuffings

SERVES 4

Preheat the oven to 220°C/425°F/Gas Mark 7.

Wipe the turkey inside and out with kitchen paper. Season, both inside and out, with salt and pepper.

To make the celery and walnut stuffing, fry the onion in the butter in a frying pan until soft. In a bowl, mix together the breadcrumbs, celery, apple, apricots and walnuts. Add the cooked onion and season to taste with salt and pepper. Stir in the parsley.

To make the chestnut stuffing, cook the lardons and onion in the butter in a frying pan until soft. Add the mushrooms and cook for 1–2 minutes, then remove from the heat. In a bowl, mix together the chestnut purée with the parsley and lemon rind and season well with salt and pepper. Add the contents of the frying pan to the bowl and mix well. Cool before using to stuff the turkey.

Stuff the body cavity of the turkey with the celery and walnut stuffing and the neck with the chestnut stuffing. Secure the neck skin with metal skewers and the legs with string.

Cover the bird all over with the butter and squeeze some under the breast skin. Use a little to grease the roasting tin. Place the bird in the tin, season again with salt and pepper and cover the turkey breast with the bacon rashers.

Cover the bird with foil and roast in the oven for 30 minutes. Reduce the oven temperature to 180°C/350°F/Gas Mark 4 and continue to cook for 2½–3 hours, basting the turkey every 30 minutes with the pan juices.

Forty-five minutes before the end of the cooking time, remove the foil and allow the turkey to brown, basting from time to time. Remove the bacon rashers when crispy and keep warm.

ingredients
4.5 kg/10 lb turkey

salt and pepper

115 g/4 oz butter, softened

10 streaky bacon rashers

CELERY AND WALNUT STUFFING

2 onions, finely chopped

2 tbsp butter

55 g/2 oz fresh wholemeal
    breadcrumbs

4 celery sticks, chopped

2 Cox's apples, cored and roughly
    chopped

115 g/4 oz dried ready-to-eat
    apricots, chopped

115 g/4 oz walnuts, chopped

salt and pepper

2 tbsp chopped fresh parsley

CHESTNUT STUFFING

115 g/4 oz lardons or strips of
    streaky bacon

1 onion, finely chopped

2 tbsp butter

115 g/4 oz button mushrooms,
    sliced

225 g/8 oz chestnut purée

2 tbsp chopped fresh parsley

grated rind of 2 lemons

salt and pepper

GRAVY

2 tbsp plain flour

1 litre/1¾ pints stock, if possible
    made from the giblets

125 ml/4 fl oz red wine or sherry

Test that the turkey is cooked by piercing the thickest part of the leg with a sharp knife or skewer to make sure the juices run clear. Also, pull a leg slightly away from the body; it should feel loose.

Remove the turkey from the roasting tin and place on a warm serving plate, cover with foil and leave to rest whilst you complete the remainder of the meal. Don't worry, you can leave it for up to 1 hour!

To make the gravy, drain the fat from the tin and place over a low heat on top of the stove. Sprinkle in the flour, stir well using a small whisk to make a smooth paste and cook for 1 minute. Add the stock a little at a time, whisking constantly, until you have a smooth gravy. Add the wine and bubble together until the gravy is slightly reduced. Season to taste. When you carve the turkey some meat juices will escape: add these to the gravy and stir.

Carefully pour the gravy into a warmed serving jug and serve with slices of carved turkey and the spare stuffing spooned into a warm dish.

pasta with green vegetables

NOVEMBER

23

SERVES 4

Bring a large, heavy-based saucepan of lightly salted water to the boil. Add the pasta, return to the boil and cook for 8–10 minutes, or until tender but still firm to the bite. Drain the pasta in a colander, return to the saucepan, cover and keep warm.

Steam the broccoli, courgettes, asparagus spears and mangetout over a saucepan of boiling, salted water until just beginning to soften. Remove from the heat and plunge into cold water to prevent further cooking. Drain and reserve. Cook the peas in boiling, salted water for 3 minutes, then drain. Refresh in cold water and drain again.

Place the butter and vegetable stock in a saucepan over a medium heat. Add all the vegetables except for the asparagus spears and toss carefully with a wooden spoon to heat through, taking care not to break them up. Stir in the cream, allow the sauce to heat through and season to taste with salt, pepper and nutmeg.

Transfer the pasta to a warmed serving dish and stir in the chopped parsley. Spoon the sauce over, and sprinkle on the freshly grated Parmesan. Arrange the asparagus spears in a pattern on top. Serve hot.

ingredients

225 g/8 oz dried gemelli or other
   pasta shapes
2 tbsp chopped fresh parsley
2 tbsp freshly grated Parmesan
   cheese

SAUCE

1 head green broccoli, cut into
   florets
2 courgettes, sliced
225 g/8 oz asparagus spears,
   trimmed
125 g/4½ oz mangetout
125 g/4½ oz frozen peas
25 g/1 oz butter
3 tbsp vegetable stock
5 tbsp double cream
salt and pepper
large pinch of freshly grated nutmeg

thai baked fish

Reserve a few fresh basil leaves for garnish and tuck the rest inside the body cavity of the fish. Heat one tablespoon oil in a wide frying pan and fry the fish quickly to brown, turning once. Place the fish on a large piece of foil in a roasting tin and spoon over the fish sauce. Wrap the foil over the fish loosely and bake in a preheated oven, 190°C/375°F/Gas Mark 5, for about 25–30 minutes until just cooked through.

Meanwhile, heat the remaining oil and fry the garlic, galangal and chillies for 30 seconds. Add the pepper and stir-fry for a further 2–3 minutes until softened, but not browned. Stir in the sugar, rice vinegar and water, then add the tomatoes and bring to the boil over a low heat. Remove the pan from the heat.

Remove the fish from the oven and transfer to a warmed serving plate. Add the fish juices to the pan, stir in, then spoon the sauce over the fish and sprinkle with the reserved basil leaves. Serve immediately.

ingredients

handful of fresh sweet basil leaves
750 g/1 lb 10 oz whole red snapper, sea bass or John Dory, cleaned
2 tbsp groundnut oil
2 tbsp Thai fish sauce
2 garlic cloves, crushed
1 tsp finely grated fresh galangal or root ginger, finely grated
2 large fresh red chillies, sliced diagonally
1 yellow pepper, deseeded and diced
1 tbsp palm sugar
1 tbsp rice vinegar
2 tbsp water or fish stock
2 tomatoes, deseeded and sliced into thin wedges

roasted root vegetables

Preheat the oven to 220°C/425°F/Gas Mark 7.

Arrange all the vegetables in a single layer in a large roasting tin. Scatter over the garlic and the herbs. Pour over the oil and season well with salt and pepper.

Toss all the ingredients together until they are well mixed and coated with the oil (you can leave them to marinate at this stage to allow the flavours to be absorbed).

Roast the vegetables at the top of the oven for 50–60 minutes until they are cooked and nicely browned. Turn the vegetables over halfway through the cooking time.

Serve with a good handful of fresh herbs scattered on top and a final sprinkling of salt and pepper to taste.

ingredients

3 parsnips, cut into 5-cm/2-inch chunks
4 baby turnips, quartered
3 carrots, cut into 5-cm/2-inch chunks
450 g/1 lb butternut squash, peeled and cut into 5-cm/2-inch chunks
450 g/1 lb sweet potatoes, peeled and cut into 5-cm/2-inch chunks
2 garlic cloves, finely chopped
2 tbsp chopped fresh rosemary
2 tbsp chopped fresh thyme
2 tsp chopped fresh sage
3 tbsp olive oil
salt and pepper
2 tbsp chopped fresh mixed herbs, such as parsley, thyme and mint, to garnish

baked lamb and potatoes

Preheat the oven to 160°C/325°F/Gas Mark 3.

Trim the chops of any excess fat. Cut the kidneys in half, remove the core and cut into quarters. Season all the meat well with salt and pepper.

Butter a large, shallow ovenproof dish or deep roasting tin with half the butter and arrange a layer of potatoes in the bottom. Layer up the onions and meat, seasoning well with salt and pepper and sprinkling in the herbs between each layer. Finish with a neat layer of overlapping potatoes.

Pour in most of the stock so that it covers the meat.

Melt the remaining butter and brush the top of the potato with it. Reserve any remaining butter. Cover with foil and cook in the oven for 2 hours.

Uncover the hotpot and brush the potatoes again with the melted butter.

Return the hotpot to the oven and cook for a further 30 minutes, allowing the potatoes to get brown and crisp. You may need to increase the temperature if not browning sufficiently, or pop under a hot grill.

ingredients

900 g/2 lb best end lamb chops

3 lambs' kidneys

salt and pepper

55 g/2 oz butter

900 g/2 lb floury potatoes, such
    as King Edwards or Maris Piper,
    peeled and sliced

3 onions, halved and finely sliced

2 tsp fresh thyme leaves

1 tsp finely chopped fresh rosemary

600 ml/1 pint chicken stock

chicken teriyaki

Place the chicken strips in a large, shallow dish. Mix the tamari, rice wine, sherry, sugar and orange rind together in a jug, stirring until the sugar has dissolved. Pour the marinade over the chicken, stir to coat and leave to marinate for 15 minutes.

Meanwhile, place the rice in a large, heavy-based saucepan. Pour in the water, add the salt and bring to the boil. Stir once, reduce the heat, cover tightly and simmer very gently for 10 minutes. Remove the saucepan from the heat, but do not remove the lid.

Heat a wok or large, heavy-based frying pan. Add the chicken and the marinade and cook, stirring constantly, for 5 minutes, or until the chicken is cooked through and tender. Remove the lid from the rice and fork through the grains to fluff up, then serve immediately with the chicken.

ingredients

450 g/1 lb skinless, boneless
    chicken breasts, thinly sliced into
    strips
2 tbsp tamari or dark soy sauce
1 tbsp Chinese rice wine
1 tbsp dry sherry
1 tsp sugar
grated rind of 1 orange
225 g/8 oz long-grain rice
500 ml/18 fl oz water
salt

creamy rice pudding

Preheat the oven to 160°C/325°F/Gas Mark 3. Grease an 850-ml/ 1½-pint ovenproof dish with butter.

Put the sultanas, sugar and rice into a mixing bowl, then stir in the milk and vanilla essence. Transfer to the prepared dish, sprinkle over the grated lemon rind and the nutmeg, then bake in the preheated oven for 2½ hours.

Remove from the oven and transfer to individual serving bowls. Decorate with chopped pistachio nuts and serve.

ingredients

1 tbsp butter, for greasing
85 g/3 oz sultanas
5 tbsp caster sugar
90 g/3¾ oz pudding rice
1.2 litres/2 pints milk
1 tsp vanilla essence
finely grated rind of 1 large lemon
pinch of freshly grated nutmeg
chopped pistachio nuts, to decorate

potato and cheese pancake

Heat half the olive oil and half the butter in a 23–25-cm/9–10-inch frying pan.

Peel the potatoes if necessary (you don't need to peel small salad potatoes). Slice thinly using a mandolin or food processor. Rinse the slices quickly in cold water and dry thoroughly using a tea towel or kitchen paper.

Remove the oil and butter from the heat and arrange the sliced potato in the base of the pan. Build up layers of potato, onion and cheese, seasoning well with salt and pepper between each layer. Finish with a layer of potato and dot the remaining butter over the top.

SERVES 4

Return to the heat and cook over a medium heat for 15–20 minutes. The base should become brown but not burn. Place a large plate over the frying pan and invert the potato onto the plate by tilting the frying pan. Add the remaining oil to the frying pan and slip the potato back in, cooking the other side for a further 15 minutes until the bottom is crusty.

Remove from the heat and serve at once on a warm plate.

ingredients

4 tbsp olive oil

55 g/2 oz butter

450 g/1 lb firm potatoes, Desirée or
    waxy salad potatoes

225 g/8 oz onions, halved and thinly
    sliced

115 g/4 oz Cheddar cheese, grated

salt and pepper

COOK'S TIP

*If preferred, the dish can be made
in a shallow 25-cm/10-inch gratin
dish and cooked in the top of the
oven at 180°C/350°F/Gas Mark 4
for 45–50 minutes until piping hot
and golden brown.*

upside-down cake

Preheat the oven to 180°C/350°F/Gas Mark 4. Grease a
25-cm/10-inch cake tin and line the base with baking paper.

Cream 55 g/2 oz of the butter with the soft brown sugar and
spread over the base of the tin.

Place a hazelnut in each apricot half and invert onto the base.
The apricots should cover the whole surface.

Cream the demerara sugar together with the remaining butter
until pale and fluffy, then beat in the eggs gradually. Fold in
the flour and the ground hazelnuts, together with the milk, and
spread the mixture over the apricots.

Bake in the centre of the oven for about 45 minutes until the
pudding is golden brown and well risen. Run a knife around
the edge of the pudding and invert onto a warm serving plate.
Serve warm with cream.

ingredients

225 g/8 oz unsalted butter

55 g/2 oz soft brown sugar

14–16 hazelnuts

600 g/1 lb 5 oz canned apricot
    halves, drained

175 g/6 oz demerara sugar

3 eggs, beaten

175 g/6 oz self-raising flour

55 g/2 oz ground hazelnuts

2 tbsp milk

cream, to serve

VARIATIONS

*You could use slices of pineapple
and glacé cherries as the topping,
and ground almonds instead of
hazelnuts in the sponge.
Alternatively, use pear halves with
walnuts or canned cherries and add
2 tablespoons cocoa instead of the
nuts to make a chocolate sponge.
To make a ginger sponge, add
1 tablespoon ground ginger to the
mixture and use rhubarb. Add the
grated zest of I lemon to the sponge
mixture to make a lemon sponge
and pair with strawberries or
raspberries.*

December

ingredients

4 tbsp unsalted butter, plus 1 tsp
    extra for greasing

4 tbsp dark brown sugar, plus
    2 tsp extra for sprinkling

85 g/3 oz cranberries, thawed if
    frozen

1 large cooking apple

2 eggs, lightly beaten

85 g/3 oz self-raising flour

3 tbsp cocoa powder

SAUCE

175 g/6 oz dark chocolate, broken
    into pieces

400 ml/14 fl oz evaporated milk

1 tsp vanilla essence

½ tsp almond essence

chocolate cranberry sponge

Grease a 1.25 litre/2 pint pudding basin, sprinkle with brown sugar to coat the sides and tip out any excess. Put the cranberries in a bowl. Peel, core and dice the apple and mix with the cranberries. Put the fruit in the prepared pudding basin.

Place the butter, brown sugar and eggs in a large bowl. Sieve in the flour and cocoa and beat well until thoroughly mixed. Pour the mixture into the basin on top of the fruit, cover the top with foil and tie with string. Steam for about 1 hour, until risen, topping up with boiling water if necessary.

Meanwhile, to make the sauce, put the dark chocolate and milk in the top of a double boiler or a heatproof bowl set over a pan of barely simmering water. Stir until the chocolate has melted, then remove from the heat. Whisk in the vanilla and almond essences and continue to beat until the sauce is thick and smooth.

To serve, remove the pudding from the heat and discard the foil. Run a round-bladed knife around the side of the basin, place a serving plate on top of the pudding and, holding them together, invert. Serve immediately, handing round the sauce separately.

vietnamese rolls with caramelized pork & noodles

Blend the soy sauce and maple syrup together in a shallow dish. Add the pork and turn to coat in the mixture. Cover and leave to marinate in the refrigerator for at least 1 hour or preferably overnight.

Heat a griddle pan over a medium-high heat until hot, add a little oil to cover the base and cook the pork for 4–6 minutes each side, depending on the thickness of the fillets, until cooked and caramelized on the outside. Remove from the pan and slice into fine strips.

Fill a heatproof bowl with water that is just off the boil. Put 2 rice paper pancakes on top of one another (you will need 2 per roll as they are very thin and fragile) and soak in the water for 20 seconds, or until they turn pliable and opaque. Carefully remove using a spatula, drain for a second and place flat on a plate.

Spread a spoonful of hoisin sauce over the pancake and top with a small bundle of noodles and a few strips of pork, cucumber and spring onion. Fold in the ends and sides of the pancake to resemble a spring roll. Set aside while you make the remaining rolls. Slice in half on the diagonal and serve with a little more hoisin sauce, if liked.

ingredients

2 tbsp soy sauce or tamari

1½ tsp maple syrup

500 g/1 lb 2 oz lean pork fillets

vegetable oil, for frying

32 rice paper pancakes

70 g/2½ oz rice vermicelli noodles, cooked

TO SERVE

hoisin sauce

strips of cucumber

strips of spring onion

italian steak heroes

Heat the oil in a pan over medium heat, add the onion, garlic, pepper, and mushrooms and cook for 5–10 minutes until soft and beginning to brown.

Add the beef and cook, stirring and breaking up any lumps, for 5 minutes, or until brown on all sides. Add the wine, tomato paste and salt and pepper and simmer for 10 minutes, stirring occasionally. Remove from the heat.

Split the rolls and brush both halves with extra virgin olive oil. Put the bottom halves on a piece of foil and spoon the sauce on top. Arrange the cheese on the sauce, add the basil and cover with the tops of the rolls. Press down gently and wrap in the foil. Leave for at least 1 hour before serving.

ingredients
1 tbsp olive oil
1 small onion, finely chopped
1 garlic clove, finely chopped
1 small red pepper, cored, deseeded
  and finely chopped
100 g/3½ oz mushrooms,
  finely chopped
250 g/9 oz minced beef
125 ml/4 fl oz red wine
2 tbsp tomato paste
salt and pepper
4 ciabatta rolls
extra virgin olive oil, for brushing
85 g/3 oz mozzarella cheese, sliced
2 tbsp torn fresh basil leaves

stir-fried beef & mangetouts

Put the strips of beef in a bowl, add the soy sauce, hoisin sauce and sherry and stir together. Leave to marinate whilst cooking the vegetables.

Pour a little oil into a wok. Add the onion, garlic, ginger, carrot and mangetouts and stir-fry for 5 minutes, or until softened. Add the beef and marinade to the wok and stir-fry for 2–3 minutes, or until tender. Add the bamboo shoots and stir-fry for a further minute, until hot.

Transfer to a warm serving dish, garnish with coriander and serve with cooked rice or noodles, if desired.

ingredients
450 g/1 lb rump or sirloin steak,
  sliced thinly
2 tbsp soy sauce
5 tbsp hoisin sauce
2 tbsp dry sherry
vegetable oil
1 onion, sliced thinly
1 tsp chopped fresh garlic
1 tsp chopped fresh ginger
1 carrot, sliced thinly
450 g/1 lb mangetouts
225 g/8 oz canned sliced bamboo
  shoots, drained
fresh sprigs of coriander, to garnish
freshly cooked rice or noodles, to
  serve

buttered chicken parcels

Melt half of the butter in a frying pan over a medium heat. Add the shallots and cook, stirring, for 4 minutes. Remove from the heat and leave to cool for 10 minutes.

Preheat the oven to 180°C/350°F/Gas Mark 4. Using your hands, squeeze out as much moisture from the defrosted spinach as possible. Transfer the spinach into a large bowl, add the shallots, cheese, egg, herbs and seasoning. Mix together well.

Halve each chicken breast and pound lightly to flatten each piece. Spoon some cheese mixture into the centre of each piece, then roll it up. Wrap each roll in a slice of Parma ham and secure with a cocktail stick. Transfer to a roasting dish, dot with the remaining butter and bake in the preheated oven for 30 minutes until golden.

Divide the baby spinach leaves between 4 serving plates. Remove the chicken from the oven and place 2 chicken rolls on each bed of spinach. Garnish with fresh chives and serve.

ingredients

4 tbsp butter

4 shallots, finely chopped

300 g/10½ oz frozen spinach, defrosted

450 g/1 lb blue cheese, such as Stilton, crumbled

1 egg, lightly beaten

1 tbsp chopped fresh chives

1 tbsp chopped fresh oregano

pepper

4 large, skinless chicken breasts

8 slices Parma ham

fresh chives, to garnish

baby spinach leaves, to serve

6

SERVES 6

ingredients

1 piece of loin of pork, weighing
    1.6 kg/3 lb 8 oz, boned and rolled

4 garlic cloves, thinly sliced
    lengthways

1½ tsp finely chopped fennel fronds
    or ½ tsp dried fennel

4 cloves

salt and pepper

300 ml/10 fl oz dry white wine

300 ml/10 fl oz water

COOK'S TIP

*Ready-prepared boned and rolled
loin of pork is available from
supermarkets and butchers, or you
can ask your butcher to prepare one
especially for you.*

slow-roasted pork

Preheat the oven to 150°C/300°F/Gas Mark 2.

Use a small, sharp knife to make incisions all over the pork, opening them out slightly to make little pockets. Place the garlic slices in a small sieve and rinse under cold running water to moisten. Spread out the fennel on a saucer and roll the garlic slices in it to coat. Slide the garlic slices and the cloves into the pockets in the pork. Season the meat all over to taste with salt and pepper.

Place the pork in a large ovenproof dish or roasting tin. Pour in the wine and water. Cook in the oven, basting the meat occasionally, for 2½–2¾ hours, until the pork is tender but still quite moist.

If you are serving the pork hot, transfer it to a carving board, cover with foil and leave to rest before cutting it into slices. If you are serving it cold, leave it to cool completely in the cooking juices before removing and slicing.

paprika-spiced almonds

Preheat the oven to 200°C/ 400°F/Gas Mark 6. Put the salt and paprika in a mortar and grind with the pestle to a fine powder, or use a mini spice blender (the amount is too small to process in a full-size processor).

Place the almonds on a baking sheet and toast in the oven for 8–10 minutes, stirring occasionally, until golden brown and giving off a toasted aroma: watch carefully after 7 minutes because they burn quickly. Immediately pour into a heatproof bowl.

Drizzle over about 1 tablespoon of oil and stir to ensure all the nuts are lightly and evenly coated; add extra oil, if necessary. Sprinkle with the salt and paprika mixture and stir again. Transfer to a small bowl and serve at room temperature.

ingredients

1½ tbsp coarse sea salt

½ tsp smoked sweet Spanish paprika or hot paprika, to taste

500 g/1 lb 2 oz blanched almonds

extra virgin olive oil

COOK'S TIP

It is best, and more economical, to buy unblanched almonds and blanch them as and when required, because they begin to dry out as soon as the thin, brown skin is removed. Put the unblanched almonds in a heatproof bowl. Pour over boiling water and leave to stand for 1 minute. Drain well, then pat dry and slip off the skins.

mulled wine

Put the wine, sherry, cloves, cinnamon, mixed spice and honey into a saucepan and stir together well. Warm over a low heat, stirring, until just starting to simmer, but do not let it boil. Remove from the heat and strain through a sieve. Discard the cloves and cinnamon stick.

ingredients

750 ml/1⅓ pints of red wine

3 tbsp sherry

8 cloves

1 cinnamon stick

½ tsp ground mixed spice

2 tbsp clear honey

1 seedless orange, cut into wedges

1 lemon, cut into wedges

Return the wine to the pan with the orange and lemon wedges. Warm gently over a very low heat, but do not let it boil. Remove from the heat, pour into heatproof glasses and serve hot.

split pea dip

Rinse the split peas under cold running water. Put in a saucepan and add the roughly chopped onion, the garlic and plenty of cold water. Bring to the boil then simmer for about 45 minutes, until very tender.

SERVES 6

Drain the split peas, reserving a little of the cooking liquid, and put in a food processor. Add 5 tablespoons of the olive oil and blend until smooth. If the mixture seems too dry, add enough of the reserved liquid to form a smooth, thick purée. Add the oregano and season with salt and pepper.

Turn the mixture into a serving bowl and sprinkle with the finely chopped onion and extra oregano if liked. Drizzle over the remaining olive oil. Serve warm or cold with pitta bread.

ingredients

250 g/9 oz yellow split peas

2 small onions, 1 chopped roughly
    and 1 chopped very finely

1 garlic clove, chopped roughly

6 tbsp extra virgin olive oil

1 tbsp chopped fresh oregano

salt and pepper

warm pitta bread, to serve

sesame crackers

Put the flour, 2 tablespoons sesame seeds, the lemon rind, thyme, salt and pepper in a bowl. Cut the butter into small pieces and rub into the mixture until it resembles fine breadcrumbs. Gradually stir in the water until the mixture forms a firm dough.

Turn the mixture onto a lightly floured surface and roll out thinly. Using a 5.5-cm/2¼-inch plain cutter, cut the dough into rounds and place on baking trays.

Brush the crackers with the egg white and sprinkle with the remaining sesame seeds. Bake in the oven for 20–25 minutes, until lightly browned. Cool on a wire rack. Store the crackers in an airtight tin.

MAKES ABOUT 30

ingredients

150 g/5½ oz plain white flour

3 tbsp sesame seeds

finely grated rind of 1 lemon

2 tbsp chopped fresh thyme

½ tsp salt

freshly ground pepper

25 g/1 oz butter

3–4 tbsp cold water

1 small egg white

COOK'S TIP

The pastry cases can be made up to a week in advance and stored in an airtight container. Make the salsa just before serving. Once the cases are filled, serve them straight away, otherwise they will go soft.

filo tartlets with avocado salsa

Preheat the oven to 180°C/350°F/Gas Mark 4. To make the tartlet cases, working with 1 sheet of filo pastry at a time and keeping the rest covered with a cloth, brush the pastry sheets with melted butter. With a sharp knife, cut the sheets into 5-cm/2-inch squares.

Grease 20 cups in mini muffin trays and line each with 3 buttered filo pastry squares, setting each one at an angle to the others. Repeat until all the pastry is used up. Bake in the preheated oven for 6–8 minutes, or until crisp and golden. Carefully transfer to a wire rack to cool.

To make the salsa, peel the avocado and remove the stone. Cut the flesh into small dice and place in a bowl with the onion, chilli, tomatoes, lime juice and coriander, and add salt and pepper to taste. Divide the salsa between the pastry cases and serve immediately.

ingredients

TARTLET CASES

70 g/2½ oz ready-made filo pastry

3 tbsp melted butter, plus extra for greasing

AVOCADO SALSA

1 large avocado

1 small red onion, finely chopped

1 fresh chilli, deseeded and finely chopped

2 tomatoes, peeled, deseeded and finely chopped

juice of 1 lime

2 tbsp chopped fresh coriander

salt and pepper

fiery chicken vindaloo

Put the cumin, cinnamon, mustard, ground coriander and cayenne pepper into a bowl. Add the vinegar and sugar and mix well.

Heat the oil in a large frying pan. Add the garlic and onions and cook, stirring, over a medium heat for 5 minutes. Add the chicken and cook for a further 3 minutes, then add the chillies, potatoes, chopped tomatoes and tomato purée, and a few drops of red food colouring. Stir in the spice mixture, season generously with salt and pepper and bring to the boil. Lower the heat, cover the pan and simmer, stirring occasionally, for 1 hour.

Arrange the rice on a large serving platter. Remove the pan from the heat, spoon the chicken mixture over the rice and serve immediately.

ingredients

1 tsp ground cumin

1 tsp ground cinnamon

2 tsp dried mustard

1½ tsp ground coriander

1 tsp cayenne pepper

5 tbsp red wine vinegar

1 tsp brown sugar

150 ml/5 fl oz vegetable oil

8 garlic cloves, crushed

3 red onions, sliced

4 skinless chicken breasts, cut into
  bite-sized chunks

2 small red chillies, deseeded and
  chopped

450 g/1 lb potatoes, peeled and cut
  into chunks

800 g/1 lb 12 oz canned chopped
  tomatoes

1 tbsp tomato purée

a few drops of red food colouring

salt and pepper

freshly cooked rice, to serve

sticky toffee pudding

To make the pudding, put the fruits and bicarbonate of soda into a heatproof bowl. Cover with boiling water and leave to soak.

Preheat the oven to 180°C/350°F/Gas Mark 4. Grease a round cake tin, 20 cm/8 inches in diameter, with butter. Put the butter in a separate bowl, add the sugar and mix well. Beat in the eggs, then fold in the flour. Drain the soaked fruits, add to the bowl and mix. Spoon the mixture into the cake tin. Transfer to the oven and bake for 35–40 minutes. The pudding is cooked when a skewer inserted into the centre comes out clean.

About 5 minutes before the end of the cooking time, make the sauce. Melt the butter in a saucepan over a medium heat. Stir in the cream and sugar and bring to the boil, stirring constantly. Lower the heat and simmer for 5 minutes.

Turn out the pudding on to a serving plate and pour over the sauce. Decorate with zested orange rind and serve with whipped cream.

ingredients

PUDDING

75 g/2¾ oz sultanas

150 g/5½ oz stoned dates, chopped

1 tsp bicarbonate of soda

2 tbsp butter, plus extra for greasing

200 g/7 oz brown sugar

2 eggs

200 g/7 oz self-raising flour, sifted

STICKY TOFFEE SAUCE

2 tbsp butter

175 ml/6 fl oz double cream

200 g/7 oz brown sugar

zested orange rind, to decorate

freshly whipped cream, to serve

salmon tartare

Put the salmon into a shallow glass dish. Combine the sea salt, sugar and dill, then rub the mixture into the fish until well coated. Season with plenty of pepper. Cover with clingfilm and refrigerate for at least 48 hours, turning the salmon once.

When ready to serve, put the chopped tarragon into a mixing bowl with the mustard and lemon juice. Season well. Remove the salmon from the refrigerator, chop into small pieces then add to the bowl. Stir until the salmon is well coated.

SERVES 4

To make the topping, put the cream cheese, chives and paprika into a separate bowl and mix well. Place a 10-cm/4-inch steel cooking ring or round biscuit cutter on each of 4 small serving plates. Divide the salmon between the 4 steel rings so that each ring is half full. Level the surface of each one, then top with the cream cheese mixture. Smooth the surfaces, then carefully remove the steel rings. Garnish with sprigs of fresh dill and serve.

ingredients

500 g/1lb 2 oz salmon fillet, skin
   removed
2 tbsp sea salt
1 tbsp caster sugar
2 tbsp chopped fresh dill
pepper
1 tbsp chopped fresh tarragon
1 tsp Dijon mustard
juice of 1 lemon

TOPPING
400 g/14 oz cream cheese
1 tbsp chopped fresh chives
pinch of paprika
sprigs of fresh dill, to garnish

green chicken curry

Heat the oil in a wok or large frying pan and stir-fry the onion and garlic for 1–2 minutes, until starting to soften. Add the curry paste and stir-fry for 1–2 minutes.

Add the coconut milk, stock and lime leaves, bring to the boil and add the chicken. Lower the heat and simmer gently for 15–20 minutes, until the chicken is tender.

Add the fish sauce, soy sauce, lime rind and juice and sugar. Cook for 2–3 minutes, until the sugar has dissolved. Serve immediately, garnished with chopped coriander.

ingredients

1 tbsp vegetable or groundnut oil

1 onion, sliced

1 garlic clove, chopped finely

2–3 tbsp green curry paste

400 ml/14 fl oz coconut milk

150 ml/¼ pint chicken stock

4 kaffir lime leaves

4 skinned, boned chicken breasts, cut into cubes

1 tbsp fish sauce

2 tbsp Thai soy sauce

grated rind and juice of ½ lime

1 tsp palm sugar or soft, light brown sugar

4 tbsp chopped fresh coriander, to garnish

brazil nut brittle

Brush the base of a 20-cm/ 8-inch square cake tin with oil and line with non-stick baking paper. Melt half the plain chocolate in a heatproof bowl over a pan of simmering water and spread in the tin. Sprinkle with the nuts, white chocolate and fudge. Melt the remaining plain chocolate pieces and pour over the top.

Leave the nut brittle to set, then break up into jagged pieces using the tip of a strong knife.

ingredients

oil, for brushing

350 g/12 oz plain chocolate, broken into pieces

85 g/3 oz shelled Brazil nuts, chopped

175 g/6 oz white chocolate, roughly chopped

175 g/6 oz fudge, roughly chopped

COOK'S TIP

Put the brittle on a serving plate or in an airtight container and keep, covered, in a cool place. Alternatively, you can store it in the refrigerator for up to 3 days.

roasted garlic-&-rosemary lamb with potatoes

Rub the garlic cloves with a little oil in your hands so they are coated. Place them in a small roasting tin and roast in a preheated oven, 200°C/400°F/Gas Mark 6, for 20 minutes, or until very soft; cover the garlic with foil, shiny side in, if the cloves begin to brown too much.

As soon as the garlic is cool enough to handle, peel the cloves. Use the back of a fork, or a pestle and mortar, to pound the garlic into a coarse paste with ½ teaspoon of oil. Make small incisions all over the lamb, then rub in the garlic paste. Leave to marinate for at least 2 hours in a cool place.

When you are ready to cook, place the lamb in a roasting tin on a bed of rosemary sprigs, and season with salt and pepper. Rub the potatoes with oil and place around the lamb. Sprinkle with more rosemary and season with salt and pepper to taste. Roast in a preheated oven, 230°C/450°F/Gas Mark 8, for 10 minutes, then lower the heat to 180°C/350°F/Gas Mark 4 for 15 minutes per 500 g/1 lb 2 oz plus an extra 15 minutes for medium, or until the temperature reaches 70°C/160°F on an internal meat thermometer.

Transfer the lamb to a carving plate and leave to stand for 10 minutes before carving. The potatoes should be tender at this point, but if not, return them to the oven in a separate dish while you deglaze the tin.

Reserve the rosemary sprigs and skim off any fat in the tin. Pour the wine into the tin and bring to the boil, scraping up any glazed bits from the base. Continue boiling until reduced to half. Taste and adjust the seasoning if necessary.

Slice the lamb and serve with the potatoes and juices spooned round.

ingredients

15 garlic cloves, unpeeled, but separated into cloves

olive oil

1 leg of lamb, about 1.3 kg/3 lb

handful of fresh, tender rosemary sprigs

salt and pepper

24 new potatoes, scrubbed, but left whole

250 ml/9 fl oz full-bodied red wine, say one from Rioja

SERVES 6–8

ingredients

900 g/2 lb baking potatoes,
  scrubbed

2 tbsp vegetable oil

1 tsp coarse sea salt

115 g/4 oz butter

1 small onion, chopped

salt and pepper

115 g/4 oz grated Cheddar cheese
  or crumbled blue cheese

OPTIONAL

4 tbsp canned, drained sweetcorn
  kernels

4 tbsp cooked mushrooms,
  courgettes or peppers

snipped fresh chives, to garnish

stuffed baked potatoes

Preheat the oven to 190°C/375°F/Gas Mark 5. Prick the potatoes in several places with
a fork and put on a baking tray. Brush with the oil and sprinkle with the sea salt. Bake in
the preheated oven for 1 hour, or until the skins are crispy and the insides are soft when
pierced with a fork.

Meanwhile, melt 1 tablespoon of the butter in a small frying pan over a medium–low
heat. Add the onion and cook, stirring occasionally, for 8–10 minutes until soft and
golden. Set aside.

Cut the potatoes in half lengthways. Scoop the flesh into a large bowl, leaving the skins
intact. Reserve the skins. Increase the oven temperature to 200°C/400°F/Gas Mark 6.

Roughly mash the potato flesh and mix in the onion and remaining butter. Add salt and
pepper to taste and stir in any of the optional ingredients, if using. Spoon the mixture
back into the reserved potato skins. Top with the cheese.

Cook the filled potato skins in the oven for 10 minutes, or until the cheese has melted
and is beginning to brown. Garnish with chives and serve at once.

stilton & walnut tartlets

Lightly grease a 7.5-cm/3-inch, 12-hole muffin tin. Sift the flour with the celery salt into a food processor, add the butter and process until the mixture resembles breadcrumbs. Tip into a large bowl and add the walnuts and a little cold water, just enough to bring the dough together.

Turn out onto a lightly floured work surface and cut the dough in half. Roll out the first piece and cut out 6 x 9-cm/3½-inch rounds. Roll out each round to 12 cm/4½ inches in diameter and use to line the muffin holes. Repeat with the remaining dough. Line each hole with baking paper and fill with baking beans. Chill in the refrigerator for 30 minutes. Meanwhile, preheat the oven to 200°C/400°F/Gas Mark 6. Bake the tartlet cases for 10 minutes. Remove from the oven, then remove the paper and beans.

To make the filling, melt the butter in a frying pan over a medium–low heat, add the celery and leek and cook, stirring occasionally, for 15 minutes until very soft. Add the 2 tablespoons of cream, crumble in the cheese and mix well. Season to taste with salt and pepper. Put the remaining cream in a saucepan and bring to simmering point. Pour onto the egg yolks in a heatproof bowl, stirring constantly. Mix in the cheese mixture and spoon into the tartlet cases. Bake for 10 minutes, then turn the tin around in the oven and bake for a further 5 minutes. Leave the tartlets to cool in the tin for 5 minutes. Serve garnished with parsley.

ingredients

WALNUT PASTRY

225 g/8 oz plain flour, plus extra for
    dusting
pinch of celery salt
100 g/3½ oz cold butter, diced,
    plus extra for greasing
25 g/1 oz walnut halves, chopped
ice-cold water

FILLING

25 g/1 oz butter
2 celery sticks, finely chopped
1 small leek, finely chopped
200 ml/7 fl oz double cream plus
    2 tbsp
200 g/7 oz Stilton cheese
3 egg yolks
salt and pepper
fresh parsley, to garnish

candied fruit ice cream

Put the sultanas and raisins in a bowl and pour over
4 tablespoons of almond liqueur. Cover with clingfilm
and leave to soak.

Beat the egg yolks and sugar together in a large bowl until
fluffy. In a separate bowl, whisk together the cream and
remaining almond liqueur, then whisk the mixture into the
beaten egg yolks. In a separate bowl, whisk the egg whites
until stiff peaks form, then fold into the cream mixture along
with the soaked fruit, cherries, citrus peel and almonds.

Transfer the mixture into a heatproof pudding basin, cover and
freeze for 4–5 hours until set. To serve, dip the pudding basin
in hot water to loosen the ice cream, then turn it out onto a
serving plate. Decorate with strips of peel and serve.

ingredients

75 g/2¾ oz sultanas

75 g/2¾ oz raisins

6 tbsp almond liqueur, such
  as Amaretto

4 eggs, separated

100 g/3½ oz caster sugar

600 ml/1 pint double cream

100 g/3½ oz glacè cherries

50 g/1¾ oz crystallised citrus peel

70 g/2½ oz blanched almonds,
  chopped

strips of crystallised peel, to
  decorate

chorizo & quail's eggs

Preheat the grill to high. Arrange the slices of bread on a baking sheet and grill until goldon brown on both sides.

Cut or fold the chorizo slices to fit on the toasts; set aside.

Heat a thin layer of oil in a large frying pan over a medium heat until a cube of day-old bread sizzles – this takes about 40 seconds. Break the eggs into the frying pan and fry, spooning the fat over the yolks, until the whites are set and the yolks are cooked to your liking.

Remove the fried eggs from the frying pan and drain on kitchen paper. Immediately transfer to the chorizo-topped toasts and dust with paprika. Sprinkle with salt and pepper to taste, and serve at once.

ingredients

12 slices French bread, sliced on the diagonal, about 0.5 cm/¼ inch thick

about 40 g/1½ oz cured, ready-to-eat chorizo, cut into 12 thin slices

olive oil

12 quail's eggs

mild paprika

salt and pepper

MAKES 12

COOK'S TIP

Despite their delicate appearance, quail's eggs can be difficult to crack because of a relatively thick membrane under the shell. It is useful to have a pair of scissors handy to cut through the membrane as you break the eggs into the frying pan.

brussels sprouts with buttered chestnuts

Bring a large saucepan of salted water to the boil. Add the Brussels sprouts and cook for 5 minutes. Drain thoroughly.

Melt the butter in a large saucepan over a medium heat. Add the Brussels sprouts and cook, stirring, for 3 minutes, then add the chestnuts and nutmeg. Season with salt and pepper and stir well. Cook for another 2 minutes, stirring, then remove from the heat. Transfer to a serving dish, scatter over the almonds and serve.

ingredients

350 g/12 oz Brussels sprouts, trimmed

3 tbsp butter

100 g/3½ oz canned whole chestnuts

pinch of nutmeg

salt and pepper

50 g/1¾ oz flaked almonds, to garnish

SERVES 4

white chocolate truffles

Put the chocolate pieces into a heatproof glass bowl and place over a pan of hot but not simmering water. When it starts to melt, stir gently until completely melted. Do not overheat, or the chocolate will separate. Remove from the heat and gently stir in the butter, then the cream and brandy.

Leave to cool, then cover with clingfilm and refrigerate for 2–2½ hours until set.

Remove the chocolate mixture from the refrigerator. Using a teaspoon, scoop out small pieces of the mixture, then use your hands to roll them into balls. To decorate, roll the balls in grated white chocolate. To store, transfer to an airtight container and refrigerate for up to 12 days.

ingredients

120 g/4¼ oz white chocolate, broken into small, even-sized pieces

4 tbsp butter, softened to room temperature

2 tbsp double cream

½ tsp brandy

grated white chocolate, to decorate

herbed salmon with hollandaise sauce

Preheat the grill to medium. Rinse the fish fillets under cold running water and pat dry with kitchen paper. Season with salt and pepper. Combine the olive oil with the dill and chives, then brush the mixture over the fish. Transfer to the grill and cook for about 6–8 minutes, turning once and brushing with more oil and herb mixture, until cooked to your taste.

Meanwhile, to make the sauce, put the egg yolks in a heatproof bowl over a pan of boiling water (or use a double boiler). Add the water and season with salt and pepper. Lower the heat and simmer, whisking constantly, until the mixture begins to thicken. Whisk in the butter, cube by cube, until the mixture is thick and shiny. Whisk in the lemon juice, then remove from the heat.

Remove the fish from the grill and transfer to individual serving plates. Pour over the sauce and garnish with chopped fresh chives. Serve with new potatoes and mangetouts.

ingredients

4 salmon fillets, about 175 g/6 oz each, skin removed

salt and pepper

2 tbsp olive oil

1 tbsp chopped fresh dill

1 tbsp chopped fresh chives

HOLLANDAISE SAUCE

3 egg yolks

1 tbsp water

salt and pepper

225 g/8 oz butter, cut into small cubes

juice of 1 lemon

chopped fresh chives, to garnish

TO SERVE

freshly cooked new potatoes

freshly cooked mangetouts

ingredients

1 oven-ready turkey, weighing
   5 kg/11 lb
1 garlic clove, finely chopped
100 ml/3½ fl oz red wine
75 g/2½ oz butter

STUFFING

100 g/3½ oz button mushrooms
1 onion, chopped
1 garlic clove, chopped
85 g/3 oz butter
100 g/3½ oz fresh breadcrumbs
2 tbsp finely chopped fresh sage
1 tbsp lemon juice
salt and pepper

PORT AND CRANBERRY SAUCE

100 g/3½ oz sugar
250 ml/9 fl oz port
175 g/6 oz fresh cranberries

DECEMBER

25

SERVES 4

traditional roast turkey
with wine & mushrooms

Preheat the oven to 200°C/400°F/Gas Mark 6.

To make the stuffing, clean and chop the mushrooms, put them in a saucepan with the onion, garlic and butter and cook for 3 minutes. Remove from the heat and stir in the remaining stuffing ingredients. Rinse the turkey and pat dry with kitchen paper. Fill the neck end with stuffing and truss with string.

Put the turkey in a roasting tin. Rub the garlic over the bird and pour the wine over. Add the butter and roast in the oven for 30 minutes. Baste, then reduce the temperature to 180°C/350°F/Gas Mark 4 and roast for a further 40 minutes. Baste again and cover with foil. Roast for a further 2 hours, basting regularly. Check that the bird is cooked by inserting a knife between the legs and body. If the juices run clear, it is cooked. Remove from the oven, cover with foil and leave to stand for 25 minutes.

Meanwhile, put the sugar, port and cranberries in a saucepan. Heat over a medium heat until almost boiling. Reduce the heat, simmer for 15 minutes, stirring, then remove from the heat. Serve with the turkey.

roast gammon

SERVES 6

Place the joint in a large saucepan, cover with cold water and gradually bring to the boil over a low heat. Cover and simmer very gently for 1 hour. Preheat the oven to 200°C/400°F/Gas Mark 6.

Remove the gammon from the saucepan and drain. Remove the rind from the gammon and discard. Score the fat into a diamond-shaped pattern with a sharp knife.

Spread the mustard over the fat. Mix the sugar and ground spices together on a plate and roll the gammon in it, pressing down to coat evenly.

Stud the diamond shapes with cloves and place the joint in a roasting tin. Roast in the oven for 20 minutes until the glaze is a rich golden colour.

To serve hot, cover with foil and leave to stand for 20 minutes before carving. If the gammon is to be served cold, it can be cooked a day ahead.

To make the Cumberland sauce, using a citrus zester, remove the zest from the oranges and reserve. Place the redcurrant jelly, port and mustard in a small saucepan and heat gently until the jelly has melted. Squeeze the juice from the oranges into the saucepan. Add the orange zest and season to taste with salt and pepper. Serve cold with the gammon. The sauce can be kept in a screw-top jar in the refrigerator for up to 2 weeks.

ingredients

1 boneless gammon joint,
    weighing 1.3 kg/3 lb, pre-soaked
    if necessary
2 tbsp Dijon mustard
85 g/3 oz demerara sugar
½ tsp ground cinnamon
½ tsp ground ginger
18 whole cloves

CUMBERLAND SAUCE
2 Seville oranges, halved
4 tbsp redcurrant jelly
4 tbsp port
1 tsp mustard
salt and pepper

feta cheese & cranberry tarts

Preheat the oven to 350°F/180°C/Gas Mark 4. Heat 2 tablespoons of oil in a frying pan over a medium heat. Add the onion and cook, stirring, for 3 minutes, until slightly softened. Remove from the heat and stir in the olives and cranberries. Core and chop the apple and add it to the pan with the lemon juice. Stir well and set aside.

Brush the filo squares with the remaining oil and use them to line 4 small greased flan tins. Place 4 sheets in each tin, staggering them so that the overhanging corners make a decorative star shape.

Divide the cranberry filling between the 4 pastry cases. Scatter over the feta cheese and bake in the centre of the preheated oven for about 10 minutes until golden. Serve warm.

ingredients
4 tbsp olive oil
1 onion, chopped
8 black olives, stoned and chopped
85 g/3 oz cranberries
1 eating apple
1 tbsp lemon juice
8 sheets of filo pastry, cut into 16 squares measuring 13 cm/5 inches across
125 g/4½ oz feta cheese, cut into small cubes

turkey tortillas with soured cream

Heat the oil in a frying pan over a medium heat. Add the onion, garlic and courgette and cook, stirring, for 4 minutes. Add the tomatoes, chilli and red wine, cook for another 5 minutes, then remove from the heat.

Arrange the warmed tortillas on a clean work surface and spoon some tomato mixture onto each one. Add some shredded turkey and a spoonful of soured cream, then roll up the tortillas and arrange them on serving plates. Garnish with salad leaves and serve.

ingredients
1 tbsp olive oil
1 onion, chopped
1 garlic clove, chopped
1 courgette, trimmed and sliced
2 tomatoes, sliced
1 small red chilli, deseeded and finely chopped
1 tbsp red wine
8 flour tortillas, warmed
350 g/12 oz cooked turkey meat, shredded
100 g/3½ oz soured cream
fresh salad leaves, to garnish

panettone pudding

Grease an 850-ml/1½-pint shallow ovenproof dish. Butter the slices of panettone and arrange in the dish. Place the milk, cream and vanilla pod in a saucepan over a low heat until the mixture reaches boiling point. Place the eggs and sugar in a bowl and beat together, then pour in the milk mixture and beat together.

Pour the custard through a sieve over the buttered panettone. Leave for 1 hour so that the panettone soaks up the custard. Preheat the oven to 160°C/325°F/Gas Mark 3.

Bake the pudding in the preheated oven for 40 minutes, then drizzle the apricot jam over the top. If the top crusts of the pudding are not crisp and golden, heat under a preheated hot grill for 1 minute before serving.

ingredients

40 g/1½ oz butter, softened, plus extra for greasing
250 g/9 oz panettone, cut into slices
225 ml/8 fl oz milk
225 ml/8 fl oz double cream
1 vanilla pod, split
3 eggs
115 g/4 oz golden caster sugar
2 tbsp apricot jam, warmed and sieved

COOK'S TIP

The vanilla pod used in this recipe may be rinsed clean, patted dry with kitchen paper and used again in another recipe.

turkey, leek & stilton soup

Melt the butter in a saucepan over a medium heat. Add the onion and cook, stirring, for 4 minutes, until slightly softened. Add the leek and cook for another 3 minutes.

Add the turkey to the pan and pour in the stock. Bring to the boil, then reduce the heat and simmer gently, stirring occasionally, for about 15 minutes. Remove from the heat and leave to cool a little.

Transfer half of the soup into a food processor and blend until smooth. Return the mixture to the pan with the rest of the soup, stir in the Stilton, cream and tarragon and season with pepper. Reheat gently, stirring. Remove from the heat, pour into 4 warm soup bowls, garnish with tarragon and croûtons and serve.

ingredients

4 tbsp butter
1 large onion, chopped
1 leek, trimmed and sliced
325 g/11½ oz cooked turkey meat, sliced
600 ml/1 pint chicken stock
150 g/5½ oz Stilton cheese
150 ml/5 fl oz double cream
1 tbsp chopped fresh tarragon
pepper
fresh tarragon leaves and croûtons, to garnish

boned & stuffed roast duck

Wipe the duck with kitchen paper both inside and out. Lay it skin-side down on a board and season with salt and pepper.

Mix together the sausage meat, onion, apple, apricots, walnuts and parsley and season well with salt and pepper. Form into a large sausage shape.

Lay the duck breast(s) on the whole duck and cover with the stuffing. Wrap the whole duck around the filling and tuck in any leg and neck flaps.

Preheat the oven to 190°C/375°F/Gas Mark 5.

Sew the duck up the back and across both ends with fine string. Try to use one piece of string so that you can remove it in one go. Mould the duck into a good shape and place, sewn-side down, on a wire rack over a roasting tin.

Roast for 1½–2 hours, basting occasionally. Pour off some of the fat in the tin. When it is cooked, the duck should be golden brown and crispy.

Carve the duck into thick slices at the table and serve with the apricot sauce.

ingredients

1.8 kg/4 lb duck (dressed weight), ask your butcher to bone the duck and cut off the wings at the first joint

1 large or 2 smaller duck breasts, skin removed

salt and pepper

450 g/1 lb flavoured sausage meat, such as Duck & Mango or Pork & Apricot

1 small onion, finely chopped

1 Cox's apple, cored and finely chopped

85 g/3 oz ready-to-eat dried apricots, finely chopped

85 g/3 oz chopped walnuts

2 tbsp chopped fresh parsley

Apricot Sauce (see Accompaniment), to serve

ACCOMPANIMENT

To make the Apricot Sauce, *purée 400 g/14 oz canned apricot halves in syrup in a blender. Pour the purée into a saucepan and add 150 ml/5 fl oz stock, 125 ml/4 fl oz Marsala, ½ teaspoon ground cinnamon and ½ teaspoon ground ginger and season with salt and pepper. Stir over a low heat, then simmer for 2–3 minutes. Serve warm.*

index